# More Praise for *Unstoppable You*

"*Unstoppable You* cracks the code on learning more effectively in the complex and fast-moving 21st century. It provides the formula for making learning a lifelong partner in achieving your dreams."

—Walter McFarland
Founder, Windmill Human Performance

"Patricia McLagan's ability to take something apart and put it together in an exciting and understandable way brings each chapter to life. *Unstoppable You* is a must-have for anyone who wants to stay on the cutting edge. The possibilities for what you could do with these ideas are endless."

—Beverly Kaye
Founder, Career Systems International
Author, *Love 'Em or Lose 'Em* and *Help Them Grow or Watch Them Go*

"Patricia McLagan says that the way the world works is changing—it's more connected and complex—and that learning 4.0 is the upgrade for surviving and thriving in this nonstop world. She's right. This book is not old stuff redone; it is new, brilliant, helpful thinking about learning."

—Julie O'Mara
Diversity and Inclusion Author and Consultant

"As a strong advocate of lifelong learning and the reality that the world is moving at a rapid pace, Patricia McLagan helps us navigate the learning landscape with pragmatic practices and tools to guide us through the age of connectivity."

—Annette Clayton
CEO and President, Schneider Electric North America

"Patricia McLagan has done a masterful job of merging the latest in brain science and neurolearning to provide a blueprint for developing a 4.0 learning mindset. I highly recommend *Unstoppable You* to anyone interested in becoming their own career advocate and a successful lifelong learner in today's competitive and global lar

Co-Author, C

Nowack
Learning
on't Get It

D1166883

"The unstoppable Patricia McLagan offers life-changing learning advice and tools in this book for those who want to strengthen their self-managed learning muscle. She integrates research and opinions from other experts in a way that makes this book a must-have for business leaders and professionals, as well as any adult eager to redefine how learning can and does happen."

—Martha Soehren
Chief Talent Development Officer, Comcast Cable

"With *Unstoppable You*, Patricia McLagan focuses on making us all successful in the ever-more complex multidimensional world in which we live and work. It is an essential read for the novice and the professional with advancement in their future."

—James Howe
Founder and CEO, AgNovos Healthcare

"*Unstoppable You* offers research insights and valuable tools and methods for a new attitude and relationship to learning that is specifically designed for our times of constant change. What a gift to individuals who recognize this need, and to mentors and coaches who strive to support a lasting change."

—Magdalena N. Mook
CEO and Executive Director, International Coach Federation

"Patricia McLagan's new book helps us all prepare for and navigate the future workplace. The concept of adopting a learning 4.0 mindset and making learning your daily habit is critically important to staying employable."

—Jeanne C. Meister
Co-Author, *The Future Workplace Experience*

"Drawing on her wisdom and experience, Patricia McLagan synthesizes the latest insights from neuroscience, psychology, adult development, and transformative learning to help readers upgrade and retool for the next century. Her seven-practice framework is supported by advice and tried-and-true tools that will open the door to sustainable learning for you and the teams you lead!"

Victoria J. Marsick
Professor and Academic Director, Adult Learning & Leadership,
Columbia University Teachers College

"Patricia McLagan's 4.0 learning is a breakthrough concept for leadership success in the 21st century. The book is a gem, featuring solid concepts with very practical concepts and tools for becoming a 4.0 learner. This is a must-read for leaders."

—Noel Tichy
Professor, University of Michigan
Author, *Succession*

"Successful leaders continually learn, making lasting connections between the wide range of facts, figures, and ideas they encounter. *Unstoppable You* is a logical, practical, and engaging guide to enhancing learning for yourself and those you develop for the future."

—Steve Campbell
Vice President, Organizational Development, UPS

"I can think of nothing more valuable than to teach people that learning is a lifelong process, because that's how our brains are wired. *Unstoppable You* breaks down the research on how we best learn, both from our internal and external world, to apply the findings to our own lives in a user-friendly manner."

—Dan Radecki
Chief Scientific Officer, The Academy of Brain-Based Leadership

"*Unstoppable You* is a great resource that guides us in processing and deciphering information in a positive way. It will help those of us who are part of the younger generation propel our status in school, the workplace, and life."

—Lauren Cozza
Executive Assistant

"Many books overpromise and underdeliver, but this book is not one of those! *Unstoppable You* helped me understand how the brain works, how to stay motivated, and how to apply the seven learning 4.0 practices in nearly every area of my life. This book is a must-have for anyone who wants to maximize their time and increase their quality of life."

—Martin Illetschko
Business Partner, Xcel Energy

"This is a rare find: a practical and authoritative book about how to become a better thinker and learner. If you want the tools to continually reinform yourself for life, *Unstoppable You* is a must."

—Bruce A. Jacobs
Author, *Race Manners for the 21st Century*

"This important and timely book places the responsibility for adult learning where it should be, squarely on the individual. *Unstoppable You* provides the motivation and tools to become an efficient and effective learner in the 21st century. It should be given to participants in learning centers everywhere."

—Jack Phillips
Chairman, ROI Institute

# ADOPT THE NEW
# LEARNING 4.0 MINDSET
# AND CHANGE YOUR LIFE

# UNSTOPPABLE
# YOU

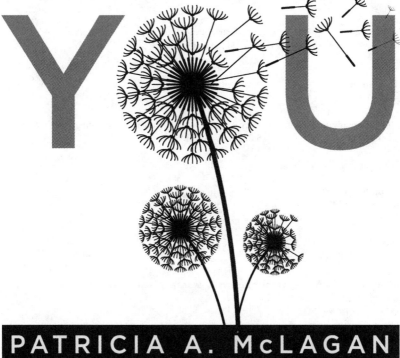

## PATRICIA A. McLAGAN

atd
PRESS

**ATD Press** is an internationally renowned source of insightful and practical information on talent development, workplace learning, and professional development.

ATD Press
1640 King Street
Alexandria, VA 22314 USA

**Ordering information:** Books published by ATD Press can be purchased by visiting ATD's website at www.td.org/books or by calling 800.628.2783 or 703.683.8100.

Library of Congress Control Number: 2017939281

ISBN-10: 1-56286-109-3
ISBN-13: 978-1-56286-109-4
e-ISBN: 978-1-56286-102-5

**ATD Press Editorial Staff**
Director: Kristine Luecker
Manager: Christian Green
Community of Practice Manager, Senior Leaders & Executives: Ann Parker
Developmental Editor: Kathryn Stafford
Senior Associate Editor: Melissa Jones
Text Design: Iris Sanchez
Illustrations: Francelyn Fernandez
Cover Design: theBookDesigners
Printed by Versa Press Inc., East Peoria, IL

*My new granddaughter will be born the month this book is released. Her learning is already unstoppable—her brain is adding 250,000 neurons per minute. What an adventure she will have as she learns, develops, and thrives into the 22nd century. I dedicate this book to her; her cousins, Colin, Kathryn, and Ryan; and all children. They will experience and help create a world of learning that is inconceivable to us today.*

# Contents

*You have a powerful force in you. It is a force that emerged, at the rate of 250,000 new brain neurons per minute, in the months before you were born. It's a force that gathers momentum throughout your life; a major part of what it means to be alive.*

*This amazing, unstoppable force within you is your ability to learn.*

Unstoppable You *is about your unstoppable learning power. It's about how you can upgrade your own learning ability to learning 4.0 by implementing seven learning practices. With learning 4.0, your development and fulfillment will be unstoppable, and you'll unleash the full power of this amazing force for changing your life and supporting others in changing theirs.*

*Welcome to your future as the unstoppable you!*

*Visit www.learning40.com/unstoppable for a two-minute audio overview of the book and to take a short self-assessment.*

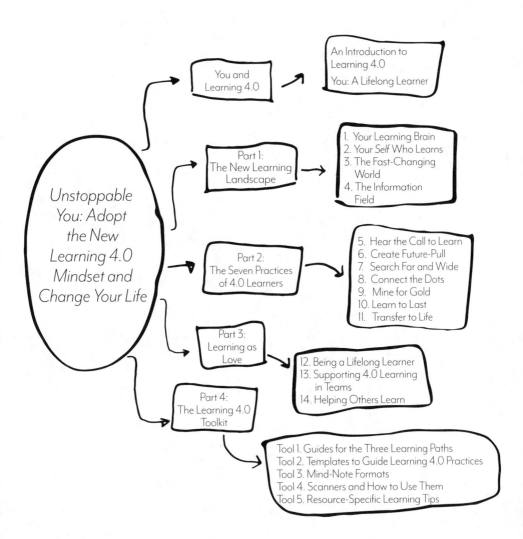

Unstoppable You: Adopt the New Learning 4.0 Mindset and Change Your Life

You and Learning 4.0

An Introduction to Learning 4.0
You: A Lifelong Learner

Part 1: The New Learning Landscape

1. Your Learning Brain
2. Your *Self* Who Learns
3. The Fast-Changing World
4. The Information Field

Part 2: The Seven Practices of 4.0 Learners

5. Hear the Call to Learn
6. Create Future-Pull
7. Search Far and Wide
8. Connect the Dots
9. Mine for Gold
10. Learn to Last
11. Transfer to Life

Part 3: Learning as Love

12. Being a Lifelong Learner
13. Supporting 4.0 Learning in Teams
14. Helping Others Learn

Part 4: The Learning 4.0 Toolkit

Tool 1. Guides for the Three Learning Paths
Tool 2. Templates to Guide Learning 4.0 Practices
Tool 3. Mind-Note Formats
Tool 4. Scanners and How to Use Them
Tool 5. Resource-Specific Learning Tips

# An Introduction to Learning 4.0

You began an amazing learning journey the day you were born and it continues to this day. However, the world and you are changing; to keep up, you need to upgrade your learning skills so that you have the capabilities to survive and thrive in today's fast-changing world. *Unstoppable You: Adopt the New Learning 4.0 Mindset and Change Your Life* invites you to adopt a new learning upgrade—learning 4.0. Learning 4.0 is your ticket to a fulfilling and successful life—a life where you not only actively shape, but keep up with, these fast-changing times. It is a survival skill for the 21st century. This book is an invitation to upgrade yourself to learning 4.0. And it shows you how to do it.

## How Is Learning Changing? A Story of Upgrades

Think of how you learn as software that you use in your daily life. Like all software, it requires upgrades to help you adapt when conditions change. With these upgrades, you can do new things, solve more complex problems, take advantage of new discoveries and technologies, and learn better and faster.

Imagine three learning software upgrades that have occurred so far in human history: Learning 1.0 is the basic program that you were born with. It supported your trial and error learning by watching and imitating others. Your earliest learning ran primarily on that software.

You upgraded to learning 2.0 during your school years. Within structures that teachers and parents provided, you developed the foundational knowledge and skills for being part of society and getting ready for work. You learned how to study and direct your learning toward goals that others set. Your 2.0 software helped you function in structured learning environments.

Then you left the structured primary and secondary school environment and entered a world where you were on your own. The capacity of learning 2.0 was not—is not—adequate for you as an adult. You need to be able to self-direct your learning, learn efficiently from both informal and unstructured situations, and make and implement learning choices on your own. As an adult, you are also in many situations where you can help others learn, whether in teams or from a parent, leader, or mentor position. The learning 3.0 upgrade supports you in these roles by including support for your self-managed learning and helping skills. It also helps you learn better from all information sources, both formal and informal. And with 3.0 you integrate information from diverse experiences, relationships, and resources so you can achieve your learning and change goals.

Many people—perhaps you—are not yet fully using or have not upgraded to learning 3.0. Are you taking advantage of its self-managed learning skills, increased capacity to learn and integrate ideas from a variety of sources, and mandate to help others? Without the upgrade to learning 3.0, most learning happens by trial and error. It's occasionally supplemented by something formal, such as a professional development class, an online learning module, or a training program at work. But if you haven't fully downloaded this important learning 3.0 software, this book will help you do it, because the 4.0 practices incorporate the best from all three previous software releases.

Learning 4.0 is the fourth major learning upgrade. It is still evolving; think of it as being in beta test form. But its implications for your learning and life are so important for thriving in today's nonstop world that it is worth launching it today and sharing it with every other adult in your network.

## Learning 4.0

Learning 4.0 builds on and sometimes transforms the capabilities in the three previous upgrades. But it is also radically different because it responds to some of the profound changes and new insights that are occurring in our world, including:

- **New knowledge about how our brains work.** We are learning more about our brains—and that knowledge opens doors to new techniques and better ways to work with our brains for great learning results. (Read more about this in chapter 1.)

- **Appreciation of the subjective.** We understand and are more willing to acknowledge the psychological and spiritual (nonrational) side of ourselves as humans—and how this affects the way we live and learn. (Read more about this in chapter 2.)

- **New dynamics of a nonstop world.** The way the world works is changing, because it is more connected and networked than ever before. This complexity affects everyone in some way, whether at home, at work, socially, or economically. (Read more about this in chapter 3.)

- **Exploding information field.** Information is increasing at accelerating rates, and it is being packaged and presented in a dizzying array of formats. This affects all areas of our lives and work. (Read more about this in chapter 4.)

## What's New in Learning 4.0?

Learning 4.0 is a necessary and exciting upgrade for surviving and thriving in this nonstop world. It is also the upgrade that will keep you in charge of, rather than becoming a servant to, increasingly intelligent technologies as they emerge. Let's look at a few of the special qualities of learning 4.0:

- **Imagination.** Learning 4.0 helps you anticipate the future and imagine yourself in it. With your learning 4.0 imaginative capability, you create and are guided into the future by your own self-generated virtual reality.

- **Whole brain and whole body.** Learning 4.0 helps you use the full capacity of your learning brain and body—your physiological, conscious, and unconscious functions.

- **Self-transformation.** Learning 4.0 draws on your deeper self-knowledge to help you more consciously transform yourself and your talents to live a meaningful and complete life.

- **Deep learning.** With learning 4.0, you see patterns in data, experiences, and even your own thoughts and actions. You use the increasingly powerful smart technologies, instead of being used by them.

- **Anywhere and anytime.** You develop the learning capacity to continually transform yourself for success in today's rapidly changing, digital world.
- **Smart use of information.** With learning 4.0, you find the best information for your needs, while recognizing and not being swayed by biases and data manipulation that are intended to influence your decisions and actions.
- **Resource versatility.** Learning 4.0 sees all learning resources as extensions of your brain, providing specific strategies for mining the gold in any resource or experience.
- **Change agency.** Learning 4.0 helps you successfully transfer your learning into your work and life environments. With learning 4.0 you make a difference in the world!
- **Co-evolution with technology.** Learning 4.0 helps you use smart technologies to achieve important and life-sustaining goals. You remain in charge of these technologies.
- **Shared experiences.** Learning 4.0 capabilities are sharable—you can bring these practices into groups and teams, and use them when you guide and support others' learning.

Learning 4.0 is just emerging, and it includes what you acquired in the first three updates (Figure P-1). But you can expect many more enhancements as we continue learning from brain research and psychology, and as we better understand the learning implications of the profound changes occurring in the world and the information field around us.

# Become a 4.0 Learner

I want to help you become a 4.0 learner. For now, this means imagining yourself as a 4.0 learner and then creating a strategy for reading and using this book. Start by engaging your imagination. Imagine yourself in five years, 10 years, even one year! What are you doing? What are you feeling? Who is around you? What impact are you having? How have you changed? What have you learned?

## Figure P-1. Understanding Learning 1.0, 2.0, 3.0, and 4.0

|  | Learning 1.0 | Learning 2.0 | Learning 3.0 | Learning 4.0 |
|---|---|---|---|---|
| Type | Search | Social | Self-managed | Smart |
| Motivation | Consequences | Social approval | Meaning | Imagination |
|  | Your basic genetic programming guides you to try things, imitate others, and learn from experience. | You learn the basic knowledge building blocks of society within the controlled school environment. | On your own, after formal schooling, you create ways to meet the challenges of adult life and roles. | You develop the learning capacity to continually transform yourself for success in today's rapidly changing, digital world. |
| Key Qualities | • curiosity<br>• trial and error<br>• imitation<br>• behavior shaped by rewards and punishments | • study skills<br>• test-taking ability<br>• learning within others' frameworks | • recognize situations requiring learning<br>• prioritize goals<br>• self-discipline to achieve longer-term goals<br>• guide and teach others | • the 10 qualities of learning 4.0 |

*Note: Each upgrade builds on or replaces capabilities from the previous versions.*

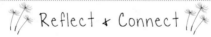

## Reflect + Connect

Learning 4.0 uses your powers of imagination. Take this opportunity to bring imagination into your learning about learning.

Imagine yourself being a 4.0 learner. See yourself using and directing your amazing brain, learning while awake and while you sleep, and keeping up with and a bit ahead of the changes in your work and life in general. In this future vision, you are confidently learning in many diverse situations. You are aware of your own biases and you recognize misinformation and when others are trying to manipulate you. You are a smart learner, curious in the moment, and aware of learning opportunities even when they are subtle and easy to miss.

When you work with others, you bring curiosity and a learning orientation—you are open to new thinking and supportive of others' development. And you are courageous in bringing learning into your day-to-day life, even if it means influencing others and the environment around you.

Picture yourself grasping and remembering new knowledge, successfully developing new skills and habits, broadening your perspectives, moving to a higher plane of being "you." Imagine what it's like to feel confident when you face a big learning challenge—a life change, a new assignment, a relationship change, a job challenge. See yourself on top of the information around you, not buried under it.

Steep yourself in this learning 4.0 vision, this self-generated virtual reality version of yourself in the future. Let it guide you as you read this book.

# Be a 4.0 Learner as You Use This Book

Like any book, *Unstoppable You* moves from the first page through to the end, but you don't have to read it that way. Tailor your approach to your needs and interests. First do a quick survey: Take a quick look at the sections and chapters, and check out the summaries, templates, and guides. Then, choose and use what you are interested in based on your needs. Read what you want, in the order you want. Use the information to help you develop a broad learning mastery, to advance in a specific learning 4.0 practice area, as a reference when you are learning, or for something else.

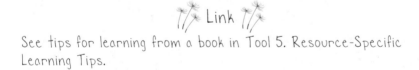

Link

See tips for learning from a book in Tool 5. Resource-Specific Learning Tips.

The mind map at the beginning of this book helps you visualize the book's sections and chapters. How do you think this book can support you as you move toward your learning 4.0 future vision? What do you want to get out of it? What looks most interesting? What will you read? What will you skip over (for now!)? What will you use later when you are in other learning situations? Will you take some notes along the way? How? Where will you start your reading?

## ⚘ Link ⚘

Consider taking some notes using one of the mind-note formats in Tool 3.

Here are some options for your interactions with this book:

- If you are eager to learn the "how tos," start in Part 2. The Seven Practices of 4.0 Learners.
  - Each of the seven practices has its own chapter. You can read any or all of them.
  - For a summary of the practices, see Tool 2. Templates to Guide Learning 4.0 Practices.
- If you are curious about the new learning landscape (your learning brain, your learning psychology, the fast-changing world, and the expanding information field), read any or all four chapters in Part 1. The New Learning Landscape.
- If you want to see how it all comes together for your lifelong learning, when you are working in teams, or when you are helping others, go to Part 3. Learning as Love.
- If you want to use this book as a toolkit and reference guide, but don't want to read anything in detail now, skim through all the pages to see what is here, and read the introduction. Make a mental note to use the templates, charts, and note-taking formats whenever they can help you learn.

Whatever approach you choose, I hope you will think about your time here as a conversation with me, the author. Ask questions, examine what's here, and link it to what you know. I'll offer my expertise and suggestions in response. We have a relationship, bound together by our interest in one of the most human of all abilities: the ability to learn, develop, and change!

Before you move into your strategy, I strongly recommend that you read the introduction, "You: A Lifelong Learner." It will help you appreciate how far along you have come on this learning journey of yours—and encourage you to continue along your learning path. In addition, visit www.learning 40.com/unstoppable to hear a two-minute book overview from the author and take a quick assessment of your learning quotient.

# You:
# A Lifelong Learner

Think of yourself on a lifelong learning journey where you periodically upgrade your learning skills and approach. Changes in you and changes in the world around you drive these upgrades. How has your learning evolved throughout your life? You are now entering a new era for learning and are on the precipice of new and exciting upgrade possibilities.

## Your Earliest Learning

You have been learning since before you were born. You learned to recognize your mother's voice. You began to develop preferences for music and city or country sounds. You learned about stress and calm from the chemistry in your mother's body. During that early development time, billions of neurons and potential capability pathways burst into being, readying you for the most complex programming that we know of in the universe.

The brain pathways that formed while you were in your mother's womb were not random. Some were organized into patterns of potential behavior drawn from eons of human evolution. You were getting ready for the growth of you, ready for a lifetime of constant wiring, rewiring, and developing your brain. In other words, you were getting ready to launch into a life of continuous learning!

Then came a massive burst of development as all your senses and that marvelous brain inside you encountered the external world, creating many more potential learning pathways than you would ever need as an adult. The connections that are not used by age three will gradually disappear. Brain scientists call this "blooming and pruning." So, your first years were very important for creating your brain infrastructure.

When you were little, most of your learning happened without your conscious awareness because you didn't have the language to help you make meaning. You watched the people around you and began shaping your behavior to be like theirs. Without your conscious direction, the part of your brain that operates "incognito" (even today, this is most of your brain) began learning all it could about love and safety, food and feelings, cause and effect, and so forth.[1] Your brain continued to wire, rewire, and develop.

Then you began to acquire language and mobility—and wow, did your body and brain development accelerate. You soon developed the ability to expand your environment and to create information in your internal world. Your environment and the people around you played a major role in this early programing: You were significantly influenced by the rewards, punishments, and role models around you. More wiring, building, and developing.

This process of wiring, rewiring, and developing of material and connections in your brain continued through your childhood, adolescence, and early adulthood. And it goes on today!

## Your Learning Through Adolescence

Most of what you know about learning as a process is based on experiences in childhood and adolescence—in and for school. Your school experiences helped you upgrade from learning 1.0 to learning 2.0. You learned to learn to make good grades, pass tests, and please someone in authority. You probably equated "learning" with "studying" and filling your head with facts. Sometimes, maybe a lot of the time, you felt joy and discovery, but it was often in the context of the school experience. You may have seen learning as something somebody else organized and you didn't often feel in control of the process.

Brain science tells us that during your school years and into early work life, hormone shifts make it difficult to consciously focus on learning. And this is all happening at a time when your conscious, executive brain functions are still under construction! Brain researchers tell us that the prefrontal cortex—the front part of our brain responsible for self-control and planning—isn't fully developed until our mid-20s.

So, through your mid-20s, learning was your main job. However, the school context and your own chemistry determined many of your learning goals, what you did to learn, and your overall attitude toward the process.

## Your Learning as an Adult: Upgrading to 3.0 and 4.0

After these early years, you are left on your own as a learner. It is time for a new perspective and methods—for a broadened sense of yourself as a magnificent learning organism. However, research tells us that although 70 percent or so of an adult's learning is self-directed and managed, most adults don't manage it very well or skillfully. (Think about how many learning projects you have dropped.) The need for competent learning is there, but few people upgrade their learning capabilities beyond the 2.0 skills they learned in school. Even when friends, family, work colleagues, or managers try to help, they often draw on the learning 2.0 assumption that learning is primarily an information absorption and sharing process. For example, they may talk when they should listen. Or they dump lots of information on you when you need space and time to experiment and absorb. Perhaps they don't support you when you are stuck and instead try to solve your problems and make your decisions for you, not realizing that part of your learning comes from tackling these issues yourself.

You have been learning all your life, yes. But imagine bringing advanced learner powers to this amazing process that you have been engaged in since before you were born. It's time to upgrade your skills to learning 4.0. Let's get started!

# PART 1

---

# The New Learning Landscape

This section shares insights from brain scientists (chapter 1) and psychologists (chapter 2) that underpin learning 4.0. Knowing what they know will help you use learning to thrive and change. You will also be exposed to changes in the world (chapter 3) and information field (chapter 4) that are fundamentally transforming the role of learning in life and requiring learning 4.0 capabilities.

# 1

## Your Learning Brain:
### What Neuroscientists Know

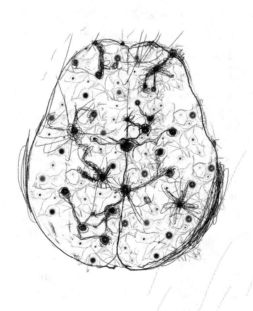

Technology now has the ability to look into our brains at work. The science is still in its infancy, but the early insights are very exciting. This chapter shares some of these insights with you so you can better use your brain's amazing powers in your life and learning. You will learn:

- about your brain as a collection of parts and as a powerful network
- what changes—in cells, chemicals, and brain waves—occur in your brain as you learn
- to see learning as a partnership between the conscious processes you direct and unconscious processes you can influence but not control
- how powerful and awesome your brain is—the most complex and mysterious phenomenon on the planet!

If you understand how your brain works, you will be a more astute user of learning 4.0 because you will know why some of the learning 4.0 practices work and be able to improvise your own methods. Thanks to your brain:

- Your eyes, ears, skin, nose, and taste buds take in and make sense out of information in your environment.
- When there are dangers or surprises, your adrenaline kicks in and you take quick action.
- You can find the information you need, even on a messy desk or through networks at work or socially.
- You can turn tasks that were hard to learn into habits that take less energy (think tying your shoes).
- You wake up in the morning with new ideas and solutions to yesterday's problems.
- You go beyond your own abilities by creating and using tools and technology to help find solutions to difficult tasks.
- You discipline yourself to follow a plan or a goal, even when tempted to do something else or just be lazy.
- Most amazing and magical of all, you are aware of yourself; you even talk to yourself while you do all of this.

You are made to learn. But how does it happen? How does your brain work? And how can you use it to learn better?

Brain science is a particularly hot topic today, thanks in part to new research and technologies (such as fMRI) that let you see what is happening inside your brain as you learn. We are just beginning to understand how the amazing brain-body-mind partnership works, and theories sometimes conflict. Learning 4.0 takes advantage of this emerging knowledge by shaping 4.0 learning practices. When you know how your brain works, you can improvise your own learning techniques. Improvisation and imagination are important qualities of a 4.0 learner.

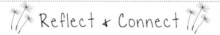

## Reflect + Connect

Stop and talk to yourself for a minute. What do you know about how your brain works? What questions would you like to answer as you read?

Use your imagination as you read this chapter. Imagine yourself on an adventure inside your brain. Prepare to go behind what you see every day in the mirror.

Start as a 4.0 learner starts: by thinking about the questions you want answered as you go inside yourself as a learner. Get ready to be curious, feel wonder at the vast capabilities inside you, and become more confident because you know you have more capacity than you ever imagined.

## Your Senses: Letting the Outside World In

First take an imaginary spin around your senses—your eyes, ears, nose, skin, mouth, and taste buds. As you quickly circle these amazing receptors, appreciate the richness and variety of their capacity to monitor and bring the world that's out there to you.

Realize that your ability to learn is grounded in your senses and your physical body—you learn with your whole body. And 4.0 learning takes advantage of this because you deliberately make learning as multisensory as possible and create multisensory visions of yourself in the future. This creates multiple paths for later remembering.

While you are thinking about how your senses keep you connected with the world around you, there is a brain quirk to be aware of. Your brain is not a neutral observer. Centuries ago, Plato said that what we see is always ourselves projected on the world—much of what we see "out there" is coming from "in here."[1] Neuroscience supports this view. As David Eagleman, science host of the television series *The Brain,* says, "We don't perceive things as they are but as we are."[2]

Because your filters are usually unconscious, you may miss or resist opportunities to acquire 4.0 learning practices that help you see beyond your own biases. This is important to understand because you don't want to get trapped in your own assumptions while the world changes around you.

## Reflect ✦ Connect

Make a mental note to be aware of your filters and more open to a wider variety of information from the world around you. Ask, "Why did I pay attention to x (person, idea, situation) and not y?"

# Your Brain Network's Parts and Particles

This is a good time to remind yourself that your daily choices (eating, sleeping, exercise, positive and negative thoughts and emotions, choice of environment, attention, and so forth) affect everything that's going on inside you. If your biological systems are not working well, they can create stress and detract attention and energy away from your ability to learn.

You are a very complex organism, and the majority of how you work is automatic, directed or supported in some way by your brain—the most complex organ on the planet. Most people take it for granted and know little about it. Even scientists who spend their lives studying the brain admit that they know very little. But take this opportunity to explore some of what we know about how your brain works so that you can use it better when you learn.

## Your Neurons: Underlying the Learning You

As your imagination travels inward past your senses and through your brain's protective layers of bone, membranes, and brain-cushioning fluid, realize that many very tiny cells are at the heart of your ability to learn. These are your nerve cells (neurons). You have about 90 billion of them. Neurons have tiny bodies that contain your DNA and do the processing that keeps them alive, and tails (some as much as a meter long) that carry messages to other neurons that may be anywhere in your brain or body.

Each neuron lives in a specific part of your brain or nervous system, receiving electrochemical signals from thousands of other neurons through thousands of little branches (dendrites) that reach across tiny spaces called synapses. When you learn, the structure of these little branches changes because of the electrochemical activity in the synapses.[3] Then the changes are communicated to other neurons along 90,000 miles or more of insulated nerve fiber channels.

On a physical level, neurons and their connections and communication routes are your ultimate learning target. But early-stage neuron changes are not very stable—something has to happen to support and strengthen them. Master learners know this and take actions like those you will learn in part 2 to help stabilize and sustain their learning.

It's a busy place inside your brain. Think about it—90 billion neurons, many with tails a meter long, making 100 trillion connections. This amazing, tightly packed, extremely complex network of neurons is the focus of a lot of brain science today, and is called the connectome.[4] And it's always changing—like right now, as you learn about your brain!

As you can imagine, your connectome uses a lot of energy. And, because a high concentration of neurons resides in the thinking, conscious—front—part of your brain, deliberate activities like learning take special effort. The practices and tools in this book recognize that your conscious learning brain consumes a lot of energy: They will help you manage the energy your learning requires.

So, if you are going to learn, your neurons and their connections must change in some way. The connections that are already in your brain are helpful here. Your brain can pull what you already know from your memory so you don't have to learn everything from scratch. Imagine what happens when people who are blind or deaf from birth are suddenly able to see or hear. The world will make no sense to them until they build up connections between the multiple, initially meaningless, sight and sound tapestries around them.

Your ready-made connections are a learning asset, but they can also be a learning liability. As you get older, it may take a bit longer to sort through your brain's existing connections to file something away or remember something. Some of those connections support very entrenched habit patterns that may not serve you well anymore. In addition, your brain naturally projects past experiences and assumptions onto your current reality. This means you may find yourself watching a movie created in your past instead of seeing what's in front of you. For example, if you meet an old high school friend, you may focus solely on what is familiar about her. When you project your past assumptions onto today, it's easy to say, "There is nothing new here." Unless you are aware of this brain distortion, you'll miss how your friend has changed since high school, when your initial view was formed.

Appreciate your brain and its billions of neurons and trillions of connections that are ready to support your learning right now! And feel confident that you have more than enough capacity inside you to shape and succeed in your learning and life.

It is utterly amazing, and it is all part of you!

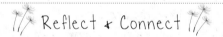

### Reflect + Connect

Reflect about what you just read. In brain language, take time to create strong and lasting connections among the neurons that you just activated. Ask yourself questions like, What are neurons and synapses? What is a neuron's role in learning? What is the connectome? How does information travel in your brain? Why do people sometimes have a different view of reality? What do you think about this brain of yours?

## The Bigger Parts and Regions of Your Brain

Each of your neurons has many thousands of connections and is part of a network vastly more complex than the Internet or even the galaxies. But your neurons also live in specific areas of the brain. If you know more about these parts you will be better able to manage your learning habits so you can choose and use the right learning techniques.

## Your Cortex

The first thing you notice on this part of your journey is your cerebral cortex—the gray matter that covers the folded and convoluted mass (the cerebrum) that you see in most pictures of the brain. Mammals have a cortex; other creatures don't. Your cortex is very thin (a 10th of an inch) and has more layers of neurons than in other mammals. Those additional layers are called your neocortex. They are thought to support a lot of your more complicated conscious brain work, which makes them important for your deliberate learning. Your cortex contains 20 percent of all your neurons, and even though your brain is only 2 percent of your total body weight, it uses 20 percent of your energy. Researchers believe your neocortex consumes half of that brain energy.

How your brain works and how its parts work together are still big mysteries. It receives, processes, and integrates information from your senses and directs a lot of your behavior. But it does most of this work without your conscious attention. (There is no way you could consciously control 90 billion neurons and 100 trillion connections, any more than an executive in any organization can control the behavior of all the people in it!)

If everything you do were run by your automatic system, you wouldn't want or need a book about learning. But your brain has mechanisms to override your automatic and habitual behavior and help you adapt to and shape the world around you. Many of these mechanisms are unique to humans (and, to a lesser extent, to apes).

## Reflect

There is a lot of scientific information in this chapter. How is your energy? Take a few deep breaths or get up and move around; take a five-minute break. It's OK to interrupt your learning and let your brain run on automatic for a few minutes.

Most important to your special abilities as a human is the front part of your brain—your prefrontal cortex. It contains the densest connections (the connectome at work!) with other parts of your brain, which makes it possible for you to manage yourself and to override your automatic behavior when hormones, excessive emotional reactions, or even habits want to take over! Electrical activity in that part of your brain sparks when you take more conscious control by planning, thinking critically, creatively solving problems, innovating, using self-control and will power, and acting for long-term benefit while sacrificing the short term.

Because it is a control center for conscious activity, your prefrontal cortex is the key to guiding learning 4.0 behavior. You use it to direct your attention and your learning process. You draw on its resources to set yourself up for success and control distractions that other parts of your brain may be drawn to. Your prefrontal cortex is a heavy energy user, though. So as a 4.0 learner you need to direct your learning knowing that you have an energy-management challenge. And you should find ways to both stimulate and minimize energy, put yourself into energy-efficient learning flows, use sleep, and strategically draw on natural brain chemicals (see chapters 9 and 10 for more).

## The Hippocampus: The Home of Your Short-Term Memory

To find additional parts of the brain that are important to your learning, you have to travel deeper into your brain. So, move your imagination to the place scientists think is your memory's first port of call: your hippocampus. This seahorse-shaped part of the brain works very closely with your neocortex when you are deliberately learning.[5] The hippocampus is like what's on your computer screen before you save it to your files. It is your working memory—the place where you first process new information before it gets stored someplace else in your brain.

### Link

In chapters 9 and 10, you will learn specific ways to assist your hippocampus in its important short- and long-term memory work!

Your hippocampus also plays an important role in storing and finding memories later. It is like an Internet search service: indexing, storing, combining, and retrieving information. Many scientists think that the hippocampus codes and indexes memory bits, helps them move to various storage places in your brain, and then finds and reconfigures the bits into meaningful memories when you call for them.

## Your Thalamus: A Busy Relay Station

This part of your brain receives electrochemical signals from your senses and sends them to the appropriate parts of your cortex, which then turn the signals into the sounds, images, and feelings you experience. During this process, the information from your senses mixes with information already in your brain. The result is that what is moving around in your brain or landing in your hippocampus is not exactly the reality outside you. Be alert to how your own stored memories are influencing your learning behaviors, even as you take the information in.

Your thalamus also regulates your sleep and wakefulness, so it plays a big role in attention, which is one of the most important success factors in learning.

## Your Amygdala: An Emotion Center

The next stop on this part of your inner-brain journey is this walnut-shaped emotional center. Your amygdala helps you recognize threatening situations, attaches emotional interpretations to events and thoughts, and helps you react fast to crises and danger. It usually gets visual, auditory, and other sense information from your thalamus. But in threat situations, it receives direct signals through a faster channel that bypasses the normal senses-to-cortex pathways.

Your amygdala is right next to your hippocampus (the place where your new memories initially land). This means that emotions will inevitably affect what you learn and how you learn and recall it. Your amygdala colors many of your memories with emotional overtones and plays a role in prioritizing your memories for storage; for example, you will be more likely to remember things that help you stay safe or that are associated with good or bad feelings. There is some evidence that your amygdala stores memories that are connected with fearful situations. This may explain why it is hard to unlearn these kinds of memories! Your amygdala is also the target of advertisers, politicians, and others who want to influence or even control your behavior. A 4.0 learner recognizes amygdala hijacking when it occurs.

## Link

An implication for you as a 4.0 learner who wants to better remember something: Add emotional overtones to your learning. Learning 4.0 practices draw on this insight; for example, imagine how you want to feel after you've learned something.

## Your Claustrum and Insula: Missing Links?

Before leaving this tour of your brain, stop to appreciate two of its more unusually mysterious parts: the claustrum and insula. They may hold the answer to the most burning question in neuroscience and psychology: How do physical parts like neurons, synapses, the cortex, and so forth translate into consciousness and self-awareness? That is, how can something physical (neurons, chemicals, brain parts) produce something intangible and subjective (your awareness). Currently nobody can answer this, and the laws of physics don't seem to apply!

One brain part that may be the link between the *what* (physical) of you and the *who* (mental, spiritual) of you is your claustrum, a thin sheet stuck under your cortex deep in your brain. It is unique because it seems to simultaneously give and receive input from everywhere in the brain. It also seems to bring various inputs together in some bigger orchestration, perhaps creating what you experience as consciousness. If this is true (and this is a controversial area in neuroscience), the claustrum may be a kind of internal missing link. Does it hold a key to understanding how biological parts create consciousness and our awareness of ourselves? Francis Crick, the co-discoverer of DNA, called the claustrum the "Neuronal Super Hub" and spent his last days trying to understand it.[6]

## Reflect + Connect

Think about the power in your brain. Imagine your senses taking in information, your thalamus routing it through your neurons and connectome, your hippocampus and amygdala processing it, and your cortex storing it. And maybe your prefrontal cortex, claustrum, and insula helping to turn all the electrochemical signals into thoughts and feelings!

Another interesting part of your brain that seems to play a big role in consciousness—especially feelings and social interactions—is your insula. This part of your cortex is folded deeply into your brain, and seems to affect your ability to empathize and to recognize, feel, and act on emotions. It is part of what makes your brain appreciate and participate in social learning. Like the claustrum, it may be the key to a larger integration, possibly of your entire emotional and social landscape.

Undoubtedly, someday we'll know more about how the claustrum and insula work and what they do. Can they turn the physical activities of your brain into thoughts and feelings? In that case, they are very important for your most difficult learning challenges. For now, it's mind-boggling just to know that your brain is designed to make all these complex associations and connections that are the physical basis of you.

# Your Chemicals and Waves

Chemicals and electrical waves also influence your learning success. When you know something about what they do and how they are triggered, you can design a learning approach that works for you, whether you are working toward a long-term goal or just trying to get something out of a 30-minute mobile course or game or conversation.

## Your Brain Chemicals

Your body contains and creates more than 100 chemicals! Let's look at a few you should be aware of in your 4.0 learner role.

**Adrenaline** helps you stay alert by releasing the brain energizing nutrient glucose. It also helps make your neurons' memory traces stronger. However, it can be addictive and depleting. (I'm sure you've heard of adrenaline junkies.)

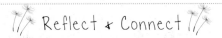

Reflect + Connect

Plan to design your learning to optimize adrenaline (urgency), endorphins (well-being), dopamine (feeling of accomplishment), and oxytocin (feeling part of a supportive community) as you advance toward your goal. And manage your stress levels to limit the damage that too much cortisol (anxiety) can cause. The tips in the rest of this book will help you optimize and minimize these chemicals.

Your system unleashes **dopamine**—a motivating "feel good" chemical—when you achieve goals, satisfy a curiosity, or are surprised in any way. That rush of dopamine helps keep you motivated so you can continue working.

**Endorphins** are also important for feeling good. When high endorphin levels are present, you feel a general sense of well-being, which creates a receptive environment for learning. Aerobic exercise is a good way to increase your endorphins.

Another chemical that increases when you are with others or learning in teams is **oxytocin**. When you are bonding with other people and feeling empathy and connection, that's oxytocin at work. It creates good feelings that you can use to help you keep learning, which is one reason to consider learning with others.

Then there is **cortisol**, the stress hormone. It keeps you on your toes in reaction to a threat, an anxiety, or a fear (including the perceived threat of a test). But it is generally damaging to your learning. While a small dose of it can help focus your attention and store memories, too much of it interferes with retrieving memories. Cortisol may help you prepare for a test, but will also make it difficult to take it! Cortisol stays in your system for hours, and too much of it over an extended period leads to chronic stress, which damages your neurons, the networks in your prefrontal cortex, and your amygdala. So, remember that this stress hormone affects your executive mental functions as well as your emotional health, both of which are important for your learning!

Is there a way to reduce the damage from stress? The answer is yes. There is a protein called brain-derived neurotrophic factor (BDNF) that works in the synapses of your neurons, where the changes that support your learning occur. BDNF strengthens your neurons' electrical charge and even helps them grow more branches to encode your learning.[7] How do you stimulate your cells to produce this amazing asset for your learning? Through physical exercise! You can do anything from two- to three-minute sprints to longer exercise periods to stimulate BDNF production. Another big reason to keep moving!

## Your Electrical Waves

When your neurons fire, they create electrical waves that operate at different frequencies. Several wave patterns are usually operating at one time, but the dominant waves change throughout your day. These waves affect your learning, but you can influence them by using specific techniques that you will learn in part 2. For now, just know that one of your jobs as a 4.0 learner is to try to match your brain waves to your current learning stage and challenge. Let's look at the main brainwaves, arranged from lowest to highest wave frequencies (number of wave cycles per second):

- Your slowest brain waves are infra-low. They are like the deepest water layer in the ocean—providing a stable base for higher brain functions. They are so slow (one wave every two seconds) that current equipment has a hard time tracking them.

- Ratchet up the energy levels and you arrive at another low-energy delta wave state (a half to three waves per second). You want to have long periods of delta when you are sleeping because that's when your body most restores itself.

- Theta waves (four to seven waves per second) use more energy. They operate in the space between awake and sleep, and seem to be important for information's transition into memory. Theta is also active when you are dreaming. (This is very important for learning because dreams are a time when there is no conscious control, but memories are consolidated.) When you are learning something and time seems to disappear, you are probably in a theta state (some say you are in flow).

- Alpha waves (eight to 12 waves per second) are active when you are relaxed but focused on what is happening right now, in the present moment. Because these waves seem to border conscious and unconscious states, they are often the target of meditation and mindfulness activities. These waves are also associated with higher creativity.

- Your beta waves are dominant as you solve problems and go about your daily work. They operate in a broad range of wave cycles (between 13 and 30 firings per second). They are slower when you are just exploring something, and faster when you are in complex thought and trying to integrate diverse information.[8] Caffeine seems to stimulate these waves.

- Gamma waves fire fastest (31 to 120 waves per second). These recently discovered waves appear when you are concentrating especially hard or doing very complicated mental and emotional tasks. They also seem to be there when you have bursts of insight, which is something that makes us special as humans.

### Reflect & Connect

Some of the practices in part 2 are designed to help you consciously influence your brain's chemicals and waves.

While we don't fully understand the role of all these waves in learning, it's clear that different wave frequencies correspond to different kinds of brain processes. For example, when you are in a flow state of high-intensity learning, your waves are at the edge of alpha and theta. Additional mystery surrounds the slowest (infra-low) and fastest (gamma) waves. Like the claustrum and insula, these extreme-end waves may relate in an important way to higher consciousness and therefore to more learning potential. Better understanding them may help us better cope with the complex and fast-changing learning environments we are in today and continue to create. Updates to learning 4.0 will undoubtedly include ways to stimulate more of these waves. So, stay tuned to more discoveries here. In the meantime, the practices in this book will help you influence your brain-wave state.

Being a 4.0 learner starts with appreciating your brain's resources. Now that you know more about some of your brain parts, chemicals, and waves, and what they're for, it's time to learn a bit more about how your brain operates when you are learning.

## Two Processing Systems for Life and Learning

How do all these parts work together? For a start, it's useful to distinguish two major modes of brain work: automatic and conscious. On one hand, a lot of the work to keep you alive and adapting moment to moment is done automatically and unconsciously (your automatic system). On the other hand, you have immense capacity to direct what you do (your conscious system)—even if it means overriding what's automatic.

## Your Automatic System

Most of what you do is automatic. Neuroscientist David Eagleman puts it this way: "The brain runs its show incognito" most of the time.[9] What you do and how you react is usually habitual, routine, and programmed with the embedded knowledge from thousands of years of evolution and your own life experience. "Automatic" is your brain's oldest, most developed, and—in many situations—preferred way to operate. Some scientists think it takes less energy to run on automatic, and that the brain's goal is to keep it that way

Your automatic system acts fast and it takes over when you face unfamiliar or threatening situations. For example, you will automatically swerve your car when a deer jumps onto the road. You may have a flash of conscious thought, but your reaction is mostly automatic! (This is a good thing, because your automatic system processes this kind of information fast enough to save your life.)

When you are learning, your automatic system will first turn to familiar interpretations and habits, for it doesn't like to spend much time in deliberate thought. Rather, it relies on previous knowledge, emotions and heuristics (rules you've developed from experience), and programming from eons of human evolution. These shape, or bias, your actions. When you learn you may want to examine and change some of this earlier programming.

Some of your automatic actions are a reward for many years of practice and learning: playing a sport, coordinating logistics, playing the guitar, running a well-designed meeting, flying an airplane, stocking a shelf for best marketing exposure, playing chess, or finding and fixing a computer problem are some examples. In cases like these, what you do may be very complex or have a hidden logic. Observers may think you are a born "genius." But, because you worked hard to earn this deeper expertise, what you do is simply routine and automatic for you. While others look on in amazement, you achieve what looks difficult with little effort of your own.

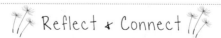 Reflect & Connect

What capabilities have you developed over the years that are automatic and seem easy today but took a lot of practice and hard work to develop?

Your automatic system is a huge ally in consolidating learning. Once you've started to learn something, your automatic system can help you process and store the new information. If you've concentrated in the first place, then while you do other things, including sleep, your automatic system continues to process and file what you've learned.

## Link

Learn more about how biases affect learning in chapter 9.

There is something else to know about your automatic system: It uses sleep to help you learn. Imagine yourself resting in a deep sleep while parts of your brain busily do a number of things in your mental underground: clearing paths; strengthening, connecting, and reconnecting neurons; sending what's in your short-term memory (hippocampus) to the neocortex for long-term filing. All this can happen in sleep because your conscious system is temporarily offline and not taking in new information.

While some of this automatic brain work happens as you go about your normal day, much of it happens while you're sleeping. To get these benefits, there must be something new in your short-term memory for your sleeping brain to process. And you need to sleep long and restfully enough to get these benefits—much of your memory storing and consolidation seems to happen your last few hours of a seven-hour sleep.[10] For this to happen, your automatic system needs the support of your conscious system to make sure you get enough sleep!

## Link

Learn more in chapters 9 and 10 about how to use sleep to support your learning.

## Your Conscious System

Your conscious system oversees your thoughts and deliberate actions. With it, you set and pursue goals that you wouldn't achieve if you stayed on automatic. You use your conscious system when you solve complex and unique problems and imagine alternate futures and ways to get there. You also use it to control and override automatic reactions, biases, and emotions that aren't appropriate for the situation or that will have negative future consequences. It is within your conscious system that you make the hard choices and judgments.

You use your conscious system for learning when you set agendas and scan for the best information and help; when you direct and focus your attention on what you want to learn; when you use deliberate learning techniques; when you replace old habits and routines with new ones; and when you make changes in your environment that support new behaviors. Use it to sustain your attention and energy for long-haul learning and difficult habit changes.

Your conscious system also helps prime, and even program, your automatic system to support and consolidate your learning while you sleep and do other things. Then, in the best learning situations, your conscious system can ensure that you draw on both!

Your conscious system uses the same physical resources as your automatic system—all your brain and body's resources. And while it relies on your automatic system, it also has the ability to override and even change what is automatic. This is something you do when you learn: You deliberately focus your senses and thought processes on your learning agenda. With extra training, you can even influence what your neurons, chemicals, and brain waves do.

## Your Learning Brain, in Brief

In this chapter, you've traveled inward to explore your learning brain. You discovered that neurons and their connections are where learning is encoded. You saw that although parts of your brain specialize in specific functions, it works as a connectome—a network filled with cross communication.

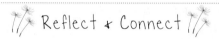

Reflect + Connect

Stop for a few minutes and use your conscious system: Talk with yourself or somebody else about three or four insights you've gained about your learning brain. Compare your knowledge now with what you knew before you read this section. This will help you remember more of what you are learning.

You briefly explored some parts of the brain that are important targets for 4.0 learning practices:

- senses (your connections with the world)
- cortex and neocortex (executive functions that drive and store learning)
- hippocampus (early memory formation, and later indexing and retrieval)
- thalamus (the information relay station)
- amygdala (an emotion processor that picks up emotional tones and colors and humanizes information)
- claustrum and insula (integrating and transforming physical impulses into consciousness).

And you saw the role that chemicals and waves play in supporting learning and moods around learning.

Finally, you learned that two information processing systems are at work inside you: Your automatic system runs most of the show, and you use your conscious system for deliberate work like overriding habits and knee-jerk reactions, mobilizing attention, and guiding behavior and learning in a purposeful way.

Being a 4.0 learner means taking charge of both your conscious and automatic systems, and supporting your entire body in the learning process. But from what perspective do you take charge? Something else is steering your conscious actions. It is your bigger you. To understand it, we leave the realm of biologists and brain scientists and enter the world of psychologists, philosophers, and mystics. They are the ones struggling to answer questions like, who is this bigger you? Who is the you who has unique aspirations and interests, the you who is on a totally unique life path, and the you who uses your amazing brain?

That's the focus of the next chapter.

# 2

## Your *Self* Who Learns:
### What Psychologists Know

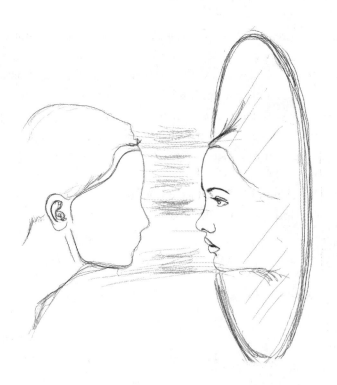

You are a complex, aware, evolving, self-creating living being, capable of thought, imagination, choice, and self-transformation. With learning 4.0 practices you will be able to access more of this vast capacity that is you. You will learn:

- what psychologists and learning experts know about the evolving you
- how your life journey is like others and how it differs
- ways to think about your needs, your life stage, and the forces in you that affect your learning
- who you are, and who is your *self* who learns.

Are you your brain? Who is the you who's using your brain? Who is the you who is doing the learning?

The answers to these questions have profound implications for you as a 4.0 learner, because who you are affects your motivation, goals, risk taking, and other important factors.

To find answers to these questions, we need to explore another dimension of you—who you are as a thinking, feeling, living, and self-aware human being. In other words, your subjective, or big self. This is the you who interests psychologists, philosophers, and spiritual guides.

You don't have to become a therapist, poet, or seer, or have any particular religious beliefs, to learn about your big self. But, this chapter does invite you to explore your inner subjective world and its implications for you as a 4.0 learner.

With that in mind and with a curious attitude about your self, read on to deepen your awareness of your big self who is learning.

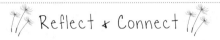

Reflect + Connect

What are three things you know about the "who" using your brain?

# Layers of You

There are many ways of thinking about the big self that can help you know yourself better. One enduring view was proposed in the last century by Carl Jung. It is very useful as a backdrop for better learning. So, think about these Jungian concepts as insights into who you are:

- **The ego.** This is your conscious self—the self you identify with and project on the world through situational adaptations or personas.
- **The personal unconscious.** These are specific personal memories, qualities, and behavior patterns that are stored inside you but that you usually don't recognize as part of you.
- **The collective unconscious.** These are psychological dynamics that operate in all humans.
- **The big self.** Your big self contains your ego with its personas and your unconscious parts, as well as your more spiritual and essential self that is not easily described by scientists, biologists, or psychologists. It is the "who" of you that encompasses everything.

Figure 2-1. The Layers of You

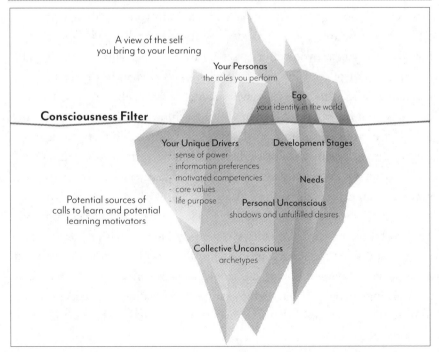

## Your Ego and Personas: The Tip of the Iceberg

Your ego is like the exposed part of an iceberg.[1] It contains the personal qualities, capabilities, accomplishments, and goals that you identify with—the person you consciously think you are and project in the world. Your ego appears as different personas in different situations; think of them as costumes that enable you to function in your various roles at work, at home, with friends, and when you give a talk. Your ego and personas may differ on the surface, but as long as they reflect similar core values and self-esteem, those differences won't cause psychological stress. When there are big disconnects (for example, when you find yourself following the crowd rather than standing up for something important to you) then your discomfort may cause personal stress and be a call to learn and change.

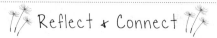

### Reflect + Connect

Stop and list your major roles (personas) in the world today. What are some core qualities that underlie them all?

Keeping your ego and personas aligned is only one challenge your big self faces. Sometimes, your ego identity itself is challenged. For example, imagine that you see yourself as a person who always wins. Admitting failure in any part of your life jeopardizes this self-image. But since failure is inevitable in life, this ego image will inevitably face a challenge. When that happens, your big self must step in with a learning agenda that helps change that part of your ego identity. Of course, it's difficult to focus on learning when your ego identity is at risk, but this is increasingly the learning challenge in today's fast-changing times. And 4.0 learners are tuned to recognize when an ego update is needed.

Sometimes the learning challenge to your ego is small; for example, you want to tweak a personal quality you already identify with or learn something that doesn't threaten your image in the world (say, learn more about a political candidate or how to use a new piece of software). But sometimes the learning challenge is large; for example, you realize you need to change some part of your visible identity or a deeper ego trait (say, become less rigid or more vulnerable).

If someone who sees herself as a self-sufficient expert moves to a job that is all teamwork, she'll need to shift her work identity to being a team member and sharing the stage with others. What happens to a person who is retiring from doing paid work but whose ego has merged completely with his work persona? He's going to have a learning challenge because his ego identity will no longer fit his life or future. Or perhaps a person realizes that a fear of speaking in groups, which originated in childhood, is holding her back. It's time for her to use that fear—buried for years—as a stepping stone to new learning and an expanded self-image.

There is an important point about your ego that you as a 4.0 learner should know: During the first part of your life, you spend a lot of time developing your ego self and defining who you are. In these early years, hormones also play a big role in directing your attention and you focus on making a place for yourself in the world, even conquering it. But in the second part of life, the challenge shifts. It's now time to develop new parts of yourself, to relate to the world on your own terms and with more personal power, and to address any unresolved issues that may be getting in the way of your living a full life. So, some of your learning as an adult will focus on bringing your ego identity more in line with your evolving big self and dealing with issues and desires you shoved under the rug years ago. This is a 4.0 learning challenge.

## Your Unconscious Self: The Sail Under the Surface

The largest part of an iceberg is under the surface. Geologists call it the "sail" because its shape determines its movement in the ocean's currents. Just as with an iceberg, there is a lot more to you and motivating you than your ego self. The less visible parts of you play a big role in your behavior and your learning.

Some of this below-the-surface self is unique because of your history (your personal unconscious), and some of it is very similar to what other adults experience (the collective unconscious). Both call you to learn as you move through your life. Your response to them can mean the difference between a fulfilling and a disappointing life.

## Your Personal Unconscious

Think of yourself being on a lifelong learning journey to become the very best, most complete, and multifaceted human you can be. Carl Jung called it a journey of individuation.[2] This life journey is your biggest adventure— it's the one where you are continually challenged and shaped. For example, when you were a child, your parents and others in authority recognized and loved you for certain behaviors, and punished or discouraged others. Your journey includes your reactions to this.

Sometimes, to create an ego identity that fits others' expectations and to keep yourself feeling loved and esteemed, you hid parts of you away in your inner shadows. For example, your parents may have punished you when you got angry. So, as a small child you sent your anger underground. Because you couldn't develop constructive ways to express it, your anger may have festered as an undeveloped and shadow part of you. Unconscious shadow parts like this want to become a constructive part of your ego identity. But unless you consciously try to understand and transform them, they stay immature and make their presence known indirectly and sometimes in damaging ways. For example, you may project your repressed anger on others, harshly judging people who have outbursts. In those moments others carry the energy of your own anger so you don't have to recognize it in yourself. Alternatively, your anger may turn on you as an ulcer.

Or perhaps you have an unfulfilled desire that you were drawn to early in life. Maybe you wanted to be a musician, an ecologist, a counselor—to be able to sing, be an expert on trees, or speak with eloquence. This unrealized desire may be a locked-up energy that lives in your inner shadows. It may peek out from time to time, but in the form of envy or excessive admiration of somebody else who has mastered it. Psychologists say you project your desires or emotion on others rather than own them yourself.

You can't directly see or touch what is hidden away in yourself. And some of what's stored there may be too sensitive to call out without help from a coach or therapist. But it is the mark of a 4.0 learner to notice when unconscious parts of you present a learning opportunity.

## ⚡ Connect ⚡

When you have an emotional reaction that is out of proportion to the situation it may be a sign that a shadow part of you is trying to come out. Next time this happens, ask yourself, "Why am I overreacting?"

The learning 4.0 mindset is alert for signals that it's time to deal with unfinished business, unexpressed dreams, problematic patterns, and opportunities to expand your big self. You don't need to be a trained therapist or coach to do this. But you can use some of these insights from psychology to recognize when your personal unconscious self is knocking at your door and asking to be let in.

## The Collective Unconscious in You

You are on a learning path—a unique path of becoming all you can be. But as a human being you have some of the same challenges and general psychological programming as everybody else. For example, we are all on a hero's journey, like Harry Potter, Luke Skywalker, or Ulysses,[3] or a heroine's journey, like Hermione Granger, Princess Leia, or Penelope.[4] You hear the call to change, and you either ignore or follow it. You find a guide or ask for help, you go through ups and downs as you learn and change, and you end up with the rewards of your work. The heroic journey resonates with everyone because we all share a collective unconscious that contains the hero archetype and other universal themes.[5]

Here are a few of the common archetypes that influence everybody's development:

- **The Shadow** represents any unacknowledged or stunted part of your personality. Integrating shadow parts is a key developmental challenge for everybody.
- **The Animus** represents the hidden masculine and "father" qualities. The learning challenge is to bring stereotypic masculine traits like assertiveness and rationality into a balance with stereotypic feminine qualities like caring and connecting. This

is an important learning area for many women who want to be more powerful influencers. Integrating the animus is part of every human's journey.

- **The Anima** represents the feminine and "mother" qualities. Effectively integrating the stereotypic feminine traits into a mostly masculine individual personality is a huge but important learning challenge for any evolving man and many women.
- **The Wise Old Man** is important when you become an elder in society, at work, or at home. Its focus is the wise use of power, and its challenge is to exercise your power with the wisdom of experience and perspective.
- **The Wise Old Woman** takes the form of an urge to connect, love, and be of service beyond yourself and for a future beyond your lifespan. It usually knocks hard on your door in the second half of life.

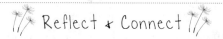

## Reflect + Connect

How are these archetypes playing out in your life right now?

These and other archetypes present learning challenges to us as we move through life. They are always there in the collective unconscious, calling on you to redefine yourself, to upgrade your ego, and to develop new capabilities. They are also there when you are learning specific skills. For example, you may think you are learning communication techniques in a course on interpersonal communication, but at a deeper level you may be expanding your ability to assert yourself (developing animus qualities) or your ability to connect with others (an anima quality). When you hitch your specific learning goal to a bigger archetype, powerful energies flow from the depths of your unconscious into your learning process. This makes you more likely to succeed.

As you learn, remember to draw on all these energies—your ego, your personal unconscious, and your collective unconscious. But there is more to the you who is using your learning brain.

## Your Big Self

Think of your big self as the timeless spirit, the ongoing and ever-changing experience that is the you who observes you, is aware of yourself and your processes, takes control of your consciousness, and disappears from the planet as we know it when you die. Your big self contains all of you: It is you, the chief designer of yourself. It starts out as a potential you, ready to become all you can be.

Developmental psychologists point out that everyone is on a natural evolutionary path to become more whole, wiser, more mature. This means there is a propulsion in you to continually expand your capabilities, self-awareness, self-control, and influence in your world.

There are two broad views of what influences your big self, which are useful for master learners to know: first, the view that what propels development is the same for everybody; and second, the view that your development is unique and different.

Both are true.

# Your Development Is Like Everybody Else's

In addition to having a similar biology to other people, you have similar needs and go through similar stages as you progress through life. As a 4.0 learner, you realize that these common needs and development stages influence your learning priorities.

## Similar Needs

Think about your basic needs. You have the same physiological needs (food, rest, a healthy body) as every other human being. Like others, you need to feel safe and secure, to be loved and feel connected to others, to feel self-respect and self-esteem, and to know that you are achieving your potential. We also seem to have a deeply planted need to believe that our lives are in harmony with something universal (God, spiritual, or scientific laws) and with values like autonomy and human dignity.[6] When any of these needs are in jeopardy, you hear an internal call to action; you have to figure out what to do to take care of things. Maybe you realize you must change or learn something.

Abraham Maslow's six needs categories present a hierarchy of human needs (Figure 2-2). You must first reasonably satisfy the lower needs before you can fully attend to the higher levels. Maslow's list is a good basis for a quick health check from time to time. How are you doing in each of these areas? What life changes or learning actions will bring you into better balance? Notice that nobody ever completely satisfies any or all of these needs, and their levels of satisfaction are not fixed because problems may occur or your standards change. Think about how your perspectives on nutrition and fitness, security, social connection, and self-management have changed over time.

## Figure 2-2. Maslow's Hierarchy of Needs

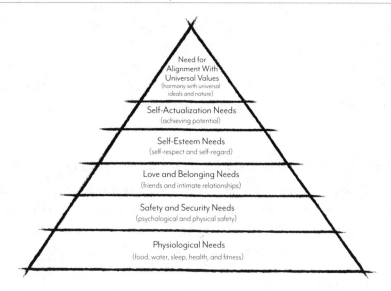

Aside from influencing your development plans, your needs may also interfere with your learning. This happens, for example, when you know you want to develop a new skill, but your need for self-esteem prevents you from going through the novice stage where you might fail. In this case, you'd need to reframe your view of self-esteem to include being someone who is courageous and agile, who learns from problems and failures.

 Reflect

Do a quick self-check. On a scale of 1 to 5 (5 = very satisfied), how satisfied are you in your needs areas right now?

## Similar Development Stages

In addition to having similar needs, there is also force at work within you, calling you to greater wisdom and integration as you age. Many psychologists have documented these as stages of human development. They roughly follow the life sequence that most people experience: early childhood, school, young adulthood, starting work and family, taking on more responsibility and influence, dealing with middle age, and the shifts in roles and self-awareness that come in later years. Two views hold gems of insight for 4.0 learners who want to be more aware of their own and others' developmental stages.

First, think about Erik Erickson's view of development stages, which is one of the more resilient views in psychology.[7] He describes eight stages, and says that development can take a positive or negative path in each stage. The learning challenge you faced or face in each stage is to adopt the positive and learn how to avoid, learn from, or move beyond the negative:

- **Trust versus mistrust.** In this stage, which occurs from 0 to 1.5 years, you learned whether the world is a safe and loving place, or a dangerous one where it is hard to satisfy your most fundamental need to trust others.
- **Independence versus shame and doubt.** In this stage (1.5 to 3 years), you learned either that you are a unique individual, separate from others and loved for your uniqueness, or you became uncertain and ashamed of yourself.
- **Initiative versus guilt.** Here (3 to 6 years) you learned to take risks and fail without damage to your self-esteem, or you learned to avoid challenge and hide failure.
- **Industry versus inferiority.** During these years (age 6 to puberty), you learned to take responsibility for your actions and delay gratification, even when you had to give up momentary pleasures, or you let yourself coast and feel like a victim.
- **Identity versus role confusion.** In this stage (adolescence), you discovered your innate talents and interests and learned how to retain your identity in groups. Or you may have taken the other path of groupthink, where others defined you and your roles.

- **Intimacy versus isolation.** Here (early adulthood) you develop your ability to connect deeply with other human beings or you fail to take the personal risks that such involvements require.
- **Generativity versus stagnation.** The task in this stage (middle adulthood) is to continue to grow and to share your increasingly broader perspective with others, or to be stuck in a rut where you do not continue to develop.
- **Integrity versus despair.** The task in life's later stage (late adulthood) is to appreciate the self you have developed and to integrate or accept all aspects of who you are. The alternative is to live with regret, dashed hopes, and sadness.

## Reflect + Connect

Think about yourself in the eight Erikson stages: What happened to you as you passed through them? Where are you now? Is there unfinished business related to earlier stages? What challenges lie ahead?

Robert Kegan has a different but compatible view that closely parallels the four learning upgrades that this book presents. He focuses on how consciousness evolves.[8] He says that you may go through as many as five major consciousness changes (he calls them orders) in your lifetime. Each one brings with it a new view of yourself and a new way of approaching the world. It's like learning to drive a car, mastering it, then moving on to fly a propeller plane, then a high-performance jet, and then the space shuttle:

- **Fantasy.** As a small child, you don't have the concepts and tools to objectively understand what is around you. The role of consciousness in this first order is to make sense out of things by making things up.
- **Instrumental mind.** In later childhood, you learn to see things in categories, distinguish your needs from others, and even compete for resources and attention. You learn that, "If I do this, then that happens." The role of consciousness in this second order is to make sense out of things through cause and effect thinking.

- **Socialized mind.** As a young adult, your focus shifts to fitting into social and other structures, often without questioning them. A crucial task in this phase is to become part of a community and accepted by others. Consciousness in this third order helps you make sense out of things by referring to community standards or defiantly rejecting them.
- **Self-authoring mind.** When you shift into this plane of consciousness, you become a fully independent and responsible owner of your thoughts and actions, whether they fit with others or not. In this fourth order, you use consciousness to craft your own life, not blaming others or the system.
- **Self-transforming mind.** This order (one that today's world needs more of) goes both broad and deep. You recognize when your beliefs, values, and mindsets don't fit what you are learning about the world—and you change them based on that knowledge. You create profoundly intimate relationships that often require you to deal with your personal unconscious. And you are also a wise integrator who can bring diverse interests together, see new solutions in conflict, and help lead others along their developmental path. The role of consciousness is to help you use your creative abilities to continually upgrade and learn.

## Reflect & Connect

What version of consciousness are you currently using? Think about your view of yourself and how you approach the world around you. Compare these consciousness frameworks with the 1.0, 2.0, 3.0, and 4.0 learning upgrades presented in the preface. How can learning 4.0 help you develop your self-transforming mind?

The world is rapidly changing, and one of your biggest learning challenges is to make sure that your big self adapts and evolves with it. What's required today are Kegan's fourth- and fifth-order responses. We all need to take full responsibility for ourselves (self-authoring), not blaming others or the system, or expecting others to take care of us. And, today's fast-changing world also calls us toward Kegan's fifth order of consciousness, the self-transforming mind. It's the vantage point for solving and inspiring others to solve some of the bigger problems of our times.

However, only about a third of all adults are in the fourth Kegan stage (which requires learning 3.0 programing), and very few ever move into the fifth (a major focus of learning 4.0). Learning 4.0, which includes updates to all previous learning programs, contains the programming and practices that will help more people move into these higher levels of consciousness.

The deeper learning challenges that your needs and stages present are always there under the surface. And they may pop up when you pursue more tactical learning goals. In fact, a seemingly innocent technical goal may not be achievable if you don't address the developmental need that underlies it. For example, you may want to learn some innovation techniques but may not use them because you fear failure and a loss of self-esteem (an Erikson stage 3 issue that you have not fully resolved).

When you focus your learning on or connect a learning task with a deeper need or life stage issue, you don't need learning to be entertaining. And you don't need the enticement of rewards somebody else offers. You learning will be inherently motivating and deeply enriching. And you will soar.

# Your Development Is Different From Others'

So, you have the same basic needs and develop through similar development stages as everyone else. You also draw on the same unconscious forces as you struggle to integrate masculine and feminine qualities, grow in wisdom, and reclaim parts of yourself hiding in the shadows. These common human qualities create rather predictable learning needs that affect everyone.

But you are also unique in many ways, including your interests and the personal values and aspirations that drive your behavior. This includes your unique skills and purpose in life, who you are today, and who you are becoming tomorrow.

Let's look at a few ways you are creating your unique self as you live your life.

## Your Sense of Personal Power

One important aspect of your big self that directly affects your learning is whether you believe you are in charge of or a victim in your life. Psychologists have long researched this important difference among people. They say you have an external locus of control or a fixed mindset if you think that you can't influence most things that happen to you, and if you judge and define yourself by what you achieve. On the other hand, with an internal locus of control and a growth mindset, you can see yourself as a powerful force in the world around you. And you see problems and failures as opportunities to learn and grow.[9]

To be a 4.0 learner, you need to believe that you can influence your life (internal locus of control). If you have a strong growth mindset, you'll be a more courageous learner, taking on the big learning challenges, shifting gears based on feedback, and managing your process through the inevitable ups and downs that occur for adults as learners.

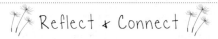

## Reflect + Connect

Are you more inclined to a fixed, external control view of yourself in the world, or a growth, internal control view?

## How You Like to Process Information

Over time you have probably developed information processing and learning preferences. You may like reading more than listening, or learning with others more than on your own. You may like to reflect before acting, or to act and then reflect. Maybe you prefer to study rules and concepts, to have a good mental grasp and a big picture of things before doing something. Or perhaps you think you learn more by trial and error and discovery, followed by learning the concepts. You may prefer knowing the big picture before plunging into the details, or you want to know the details before the big picture. If you see yourself as more intuitive and emotional, you may prioritize "feel" and "insight" over facts. Or perhaps your ego identity is more rational and logical, driving you to facts and details.

It's good to be aware of your preferences, but not be controlled by them. In today's fast-changing information world, you have to learn in any situation. If you know your preferences, you can use that knowledge when you plan your learning strategies. For example, you may want to start a learning journey by using your favorite learning resources and approach. This may launch you faster and help ramp up your motivation. But they may not be the best resources and methods for your learning task, so don't be blinded by your preferences. Plan to be a master of all resources and methods, whether they are your preferences or not.

## Link

Tool 5. Resource-Specific Learning Tips will help you learn from any resource, whether it is your preference or not.

## Your Motivated Competencies

Competencies are your knowledge and skills. You have developed many competencies through your life so far, and you probably enjoy using some more than others. These are your motivated competencies. What you are motivated to use today probably differs from years ago. The knowledge and skills you like to use are easier to develop than competencies that you aren't energized to use. Your brain chemicals are more supportive then, too.

It's possible that a knowledge or skill you are motivated to use is not currently a strength. So, don't confuse *motivated* with a *strength*.

As a 4.0 learner, know what your motivated knowledge and skills are. Use this awareness to help focus your learning and to put yourself into situations where you can further hone and develop them. When you use competencies that you enjoy or develop those you think you will enjoy, it is easier to learn and continue to grow—you tap into an available well of energy that is strongly connected to your big self. This makes it easier to put yourself into a flow state where learning accelerates.

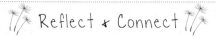

## Reflect & Connect

Stop for a minute to think about the work and activities you enjoy doing. What knowledge and skills are you using in those situations? Are they strengths? Are you continuing to develop them?

## Your Core Values

Values are deeply entrenched decision criteria you use when you make choices. They are like magnets. They draw you toward some behaviors and choices and away from others. You develop them through experience, because of the influence of culture, parenting, and education. They operate quietly and are subtle and often unnoticed. Some relate to what you want to achieve in life (such as wisdom, security, recognition, freedom, friendship, or mature love). Others relate to how you want to live your life (such as self-control, courage, politeness, logic, obedience, and helpfulness). Knowing which values are at the top of your list is important for learning. Why? Because you can use them as motivators when you are learning something (if I learn this skill, I will be more secure). Also, some of the things you learn will directly challenge your values hierarchy. For example, you may have to give up some security to be free in a situation. In this case, the learning challenge is to understand the benefits of trading off some security so you can protect your freedom.

## Your Life Purpose

Nobody can say how this happens, but each of us seems to come into the world with a disposition toward some things but not others. Even genetics don't explain it. One possible explanation is that there is some deeper purpose that you were born to achieve. That purpose is like a slight tint on your world and your learning—it's rosier when you are moving toward it and grayer when you move away. Your purpose answers the question, "Why are you here on this planet, at this time, in this place?"

Having a purpose assumes that you are an influential force in the world around you—that what you do and who you are have ripple effects. How you interact with people, the decisions and choices you make, the jobs and careers you choose, even your quiet presence changes the world in some way. Maybe that's why you have those 90 billion neurons and 100 trillion connections in your brain.

When you are aware of your purpose or pursuing a larger life purpose, it is harder for people to manipulate you with external rewards and other forms of control, because your purpose acts like the North Star or Southern Cross, guiding you through the turbulent seas and darkest storms of life.

Identify your life's purpose and connect your learning to it as often as you can.

# Your *Self* Who Learns, in Brief

This has been a rather complex chapter that asks you to think more about yourself than you might normally do. So, I hope you are still with me! The main point is that there is an amazing big self that is using that fantastic brain of yours. That self is subjective—you can't see or weigh it like you can your brain. However, there are ways to understand your self who's learning, and this chapter has invited you to explore and think about a few of them.

You learned here that there are many processes going on in your big self: Your ego and personas are the tip of the iceberg you present to the world. Your personal unconscious contains all the parts of you (positive and negative) that you have suppressed or ignored throughout your life so that you fit in or preserve your ego identity. And then there is the collective unconscious part of you that is like others—influenced by your needs (Maslow's hierarchy), life stages (Erikson's stages of development), and ways of seeing the world (Kegan's orders of consciousness).

You also learned about what else is going on in your big self, including your sense of your own power in your life, how you like to process information, your motivated competencies, your core values, and the guiding star of your life purpose.

These are all at work when you learn—sometimes motivating you, sometimes fighting or transforming you, but always ready to assist your learning. So, be willing to connect with some of these deeper parts of you and to unleash the energy they contain!

# 3

# **The Fast-Changing World:**
## A Call to Learning 4.0

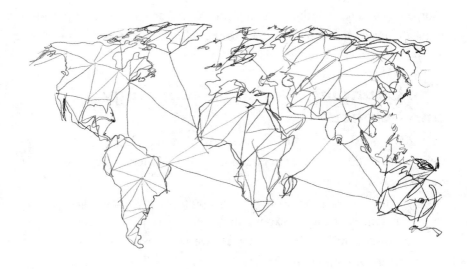

This chapter overviews some of the changes in technology, science, organizations, work, and society that are driving the need for 4.0 learning. As you read, think about:

- how technology and science are rapidly changing the world and work as we know it
- the irreversibility of these changes—we can't go back and there is no place to hide
- the importance of 4.0 learning in these times of nonstop change.

Change is on everybody's minds—how to benefit from it, stay on top of it, or resist it. One thing is clear: Change is inevitable and, unless there is a major catastrophe, it is irreversible. But how should we think about it? How can we use our amazing brains and immense powers of Self (chapters 1 and 2) to help us respond to and shape the new world we are creating? To answer this question, we must first understand what these changes are—for they are powerful forces in today's learning landscape. Then we need to equip ourselves to be influential participants and shapers in what promises to be a radically different future. Learning 4.0 and future learning updates will be important in any scenario that emerges.

## The Changing World of Technology and Science

In a 2001 essay entitled "The Law of Accelerating Returns," Ray Kurzweil discussed the fact that the rate of change is accelerating and what that means for our future:

> An analysis of the history of technology shows that technological change is exponential, contrary to the common-sense "intuitive linear" view. So, we won't experience 100 years of progress in the 21st century—it will be more like 20,000 years of progress (at today's rate). The "returns," such as chip speed and cost-effectiveness, also increase exponentially. There's even exponential growth in the rate

of exponential growth. Within a few decades, machine intelligence will surpass human intelligence, leading to The Singularity—technological change so rapid and profound it represents a rupture in the fabric of human history. The implications include the merger of biological and nonbiological intelligence, immortal software-based humans, and ultra-high levels of intelligence that expand outward in the universe at the speed of light.[1]

Whether Kurzweil's projections turn into reality or not, technology has affected how we live and work since cavemen discovered they could use stones as hammers and arrowheads. And technology will continue to change and disrupt our lives at increasingly rapid rates. Of course, today's tools and machines are more sophisticated and powerful in how they amplify and extend physical abilities. But technology today does more than perform physical tasks. Computers are also doing the brain work that used to be uniquely human: calculating, tracking and organizing information, seeing patterns and trends and abnormalities, making predictions. It's even possible for computers to sense human emotions, learn while doing, make associations between unlike things, and reprogram themselves. Computers are driving cars, doing more to manage your home, coordinating entire factories and supply chains, deciding what information to send to you. . . . You get the idea!

## Reflect

What two or three changes in the world, the workplace, or technology are going to have the most impact on your future?

## Expanding Human Abilities

On another front, biotechnology is putting the tools of creation into human hands. Genetic engineering and gene manipulation are making it possible to eradicate disease, extend lifespans, make new life, and alter our chemistry. Learning can and must play a role in ensuring we have the skills and the wisdom (Kegan's fifth stage of consciousness) to respond to and shape the new dilemmas and possibilities.

In this scenario of certain change, we have four options:

1. Fight it.
2. Ignore it until we are forced to react.
3. Incorporate it into our life and work.
4. Help develop and shape the changes.

Ultimately, the options that involve learning (3 and 4) are the only viable ones. So, being a 4.0 learner is a critical survival skill for this changing world.

## Support for Self-Management

Technology change also affects us as learners because it enables and requires more self-management, and thus more use of our executive functions. For example, you won't have to rely on a repairman for your appliances because they'll repair themselves and even teach you how to do it. You won't have to go to a doctor to find out what's happening in your body; instead, you'll simply look at the personal health monitor on your wrist, do some research, and decide your own treatments. You will become the master of your own virtual office, learning from software tutorials. With a tap on your portable communication receiver, you'll be able to publish your thoughts, and there's much more to come. Of course, specific to learning, you won't have to be in a certain place or time to learn something: You'll be able to instantly find and learn what you need in the global network of people and information.

This trend to more self-service will continue, but it comes with a cost: You need to be skilled, motivated, and wise enough to use these technologies to make your life and learning better. You need to manage yourself. Learning mastery is a survival skill.

## People and Technology Evolving Together

We are moving into an era where technology will make almost anything possible, and where very powerful tools and knowledge will be available to everybody. It's an era of self-service that will continue to expand and where the most empowered, industrious, and—we hope—ethical and moral will thrive. The dark side is that people with corrupt motives who know how to manipulate our brains will try to use technology and information for other purposes.

People have always co-evolved with technology—as you are doing right now. Technology is currently challenging you to become more transparent, more inclusive of diversity, more knowledgeable about the world, more a lert to how things and people are connected, and more self-organizing into communities.

This co-evolution challenges you to expand your impact—to see technology as a way to extend your sight, hearing, doing, thinking, creating, and relating. It is challenging you to see your life and the world as evolving, not fixed. Because knowledge is increasing and creating new possibilities, there is no final end state where all problems will be solved and all knowledge known. Rather, as the world and information evolves, you will solve some problems and create others in a continual process of learning and creating. This process is becoming more important than the end state, or at least equal to it. This is changing the nature of work and organizations.

# The Changing World of Organizations and Work

What is an organization? The answer is not as clear as it used to be. Businesses used to be defined by their location, their brick and mortar buildings. They also included all or most of the work to take a product from idea to delivery. Most of the people working to design, produce, deliver, and service customers were employees of one company, and that company "took care of them." Careers were usually well defined: You simply moved up the ladder.

## Value Streams or Brick and Mortar?

Today, the entire value stream from defining a need to delivering something to a customer is the business. Parts of the stream may be independent entities that are outsourced. Players are often global, with many companies and contractors involved. For example, the chair you are sitting on probably has parts that were made in multiple countries. Its fabric may have been made from fibers grown in one location, with processing chemicals sourced elsewhere. The workers who wove the cloth may live in a developing country, while the factory where the cloth was dyed may be in yet another region. Truckers and warehouses—who may then coordinate with ships and planes—probably have contracts to store and deliver the final product. The chair might be sold by both online and traditional retailers by a full-time or virtual sales force. And then there's the possibility that all this will be irrelevant in the future—with 3-D printing you may be able to design and produce this chair in your own home, performing the tasks of the entire supply chain!

Similar things are happening in financial, travel, hospitality, healthcare, and other service industries. Value chains containing a variety of small and large companies and independent and contract workers are increasingly the norm, with technology performing more and more tasks, and sometimes the user doing more of the process yourself. In fact, thanks to technology, you already do work that accountants, travel agents, and doctors used to do—you do your own taxes, book your own flights, and test your own blood sugar. This, of course, means you are learning about these areas as well as developing skills to use the supporting technology.

## Hierarchy, Careers, and Self-Management

As organizations give way to value streams, the role of hierarchy is also changing. Managers used to have a big coordination and information management role: distilling information, making sure people had clear roles and the resources to perform them, and keeping things as stable as possible. The traditional style was command and control, which ensured no one on the assembly line deviated from procedures.

Today's managers spend less time filtering information and keeping people from stepping out of their boxes. Technology makes information available to everybody with a simple tap on a screen. While workers begin self-organizing to meet customer needs, innovate, and refine work practices, technology can do more of the routine and dangerous work, as well as the data processing and calculating work. Top leaders create strategies, keep all the parts of the value stream aligned, and ensure that decisions are made by people with the information and skills to make them.

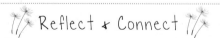

### Reflect + Connect

Take a quick break to think about the changes you've experienced recently in and around your workplace and how that has affected your learning challenges.

Some say that all these changes are flattening organizations. But a bigger change is in the works: the value stream is operating more like a network than a flatter pyramid. It's a new paradigm that blurs boundaries and requires everyone to develop skills that used to be in others' job descriptions.

In these new scenarios, jobs and careers are changing too. It's less about job security and moving upward from job to job. Today, success is more about a new kind of employability security, where you develop and continually upgrade a portfolio of skills that you can use in a variety of roles and team projects. You're evolving with technology and changes in work requirements.

The bottom line for learning is this: If you work in an organization, think about yourself as a bundle of evolving capabilities rather than a job title. In addition, your ability to manage yourself within a larger workflow picture is becoming more important if you are working virtually and on multiple teams. Your technical and specialist requirements are changing rapidly too, so these skills need continual upgrading. And, because you need to function in conditions of rapid change and multiple relationships, generic skills like communication and collaboration, decision making, thinking, innovating, self-management, and learning are key assets. These challenges apply across sectors—industrial, retail, healthcare, technology, government, consumer, and more.

This new landscape requires learning 4.0. How well prepared are you to learn and thrive in this changing world?

## A Changing Global Demographic and Society

You are part of a vast web of communication and mobility in a world where the population will reach 9 billion by 2040. Most people will be living in major metropolitan areas, and the global population centers will be in Asia and Africa. But everyone will be connected, and cultures will continually mix and clash. The learning implications are huge.

Your brain is automatically fearful of the new—of "the other." And these fears will only increase if you believe you are going to lose something, like a job or status or even your way of life, because of the other. Learning about those who are different and finding new ways of interacting during all the power shifts are increasingly important.

# You in This Changing World: Change and Stability

This book focuses on learning and change. But stability is equally important. Stability and change work together in all forms of evolution. Chinese philosophers depict this continual dance of change and stability as a yin-yang tension, where what is stable (white) gives rise to change (black), and what is changing leads to a new stability (Figure 3-1). The dots in the yin-yang symbol show that stability and change contain the seed of the other.

Figure 3-1. Yin-Yang

Your stability task in this rapidly changing world is to know and maintain your big self (see chapter 2), and to determine whether changes are worth responding to. Your change task is to anticipate, adapt to, and help shape the world around you. Sometimes this means challenging the beliefs and behaviors you hold dear.

It's tempting to idolize change and disparage stability. But without a strong counterbalancing force, change can spin out of control and cause destruction. As change accelerates, we need to invest in stability factors like values, helping people move to higher levels of consciousness, and making diversity a positive survival force. Change is happening rapidly and on a large scale, and it needs stability forces to evolve along with it. Visualize the yin-yang circle—when the black section (change) gets bigger, the white (stability) also must grow.

Learning 4.0 practices support this dynamic interaction of change and stability.

# The Changing World, in Brief

Change has always been part of life, but it is speeding up. Technology is the major driving force because it is augmenting every area of human capability, including brainpower. The implications for us as learners are profound. We need to keep learning and be willing to grow and change in important areas of our lives. We can't assume that our world or our work will be the same tomorrow as it is today. And as much as some would like, we can't go back to the old days.

## Reflect

Take a few minutes to tell yourself what you want to remember from this chapter. When learning, follow the 50/50 rule: 50 percent taking in information, 50 percent using it in some way, including associating it with what you know and care about.

While it is impossible to predict what the future will look like, it will certainly challenge our views and expectations of work and the world around us. Plan to continue developing your skills in work and life, and even to give them up when they are augmented or replaced by technology. Develop abilities that transfer across situations, such as communicating, collaborating, thinking, deciding, managing yourself, and (of course) learning.

Also, because so many of the changes that are occurring have major implications for everyone's way of life, the world needs people who can wisely guide technology, work, and social changes—those who possess a new kind of learning urgency and capability. But it also needs us all to evolve into the more advanced consciousness stages you learned about in the previous chapter. As futurist Ray Kurzweil explains:

> What does it mean to evolve? Evolution moves toward greater complexity, greater elegance, greater knowledge, greater intelligence, greater beauty, greater creativity, and more of other abstract and subtle attributes such as love.[2]

In other words, this changing world calls for learning 4.0!

# 4

## The Information Field:
### Overload or Opportunity?

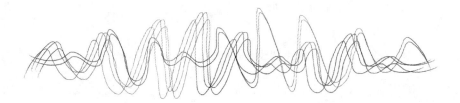

Information is the content of learning. But the information field is radically transforming; today there is more information, a greater variety of formats, and increased uncertainty about its quality or the intentions behind it. Everyone needs new approaches and a new ability to detect what's true and what's not. Read this chapter to help you appreciate that:

- Information is a unique resource that is changing in many ways.
- The information you use is always filtered by you and by others.
- Information is power: It's up to you to maintain your independence and integrity as you use it.
- Improving information management practices is an important part of the learning 4.0 upgrade.

The fourth major factor to understand about your learning landscape is the information field. As you know, information is increasing at exponential rates. By 2020, information will be doubling every 73 days! Astounding. Frightening. Exciting!

## Reflect & Connect

What are the biggest challenges you face as you deal with the information around you? On a scale of 1-10 (with 10 being very confident and 1 being not confident at all), how confident are you in your ability to keep up?

Fortunately, you are equipped to deal with this information overload. Your brain's 90 billion neurons and 100 trillion connections, the capacity of your big self, and a variety of emerging technologies and ways of packaging information are your allies. So are your learning skills if you upgrade them to 4.0 for today's reality.

Here is what you need to know about information to be a 4.0 learner today:

- Information is a unique resource.
- Information you use is always filtered and biased.

- Information is power, and others want to use it to influence and even control you.

## Information Is a Unique Resource

Most resources are finite, tangible things: Either you have them or I have them. Or they are consumed in use, like food. But information is different: It expands, spreads, and sometimes increases in value with use. As it spreads it changes and creates more information! No wonder you feel an increased urgency to be a better learner!

Information is everywhere. It may come to you as raw data (for example, as facts, opinions, observations, an experience, a tweet, a piece of feedback) or packaged in media (print, video, presentations, apps, courses, blogs, websites). These data and information packages are the resources that feed your learning. And, the same information can appear in a variety of forms. For example, imagine that you want to find information about how to care for an elderly relative or how to give feedback to a team member. The same recommendations might appear in an article, a course, a role play, a case study, or a YouTube video. Part of your learning challenge is to decide which information format is best for your purpose.

Finding the information you need is an increasingly difficult task, thanks to the expanding and complex information field. Fortunately, an increasing array of services like search engines and course aggregators (called "scanners" later in this book) is cropping up to help you find what you need in a format that you can use.

Link

For more information about scanners, see chapter 9, "Mine for Gold," and Tool 4. Scanners and How to Use Them.

## Packaged Information Is Always Biased

In its raw data form, information is neutral. But as soon as it is selected, organized, presented, packaged, or used, it takes on a point of view. In other words, it becomes biased. The content creator selects some information and ignores the rest. Then, when you use that information, you will probably focus on some aspects of an experience, an article, a speech, or a conversation and not others. Thus, your information is filtered twice—both by you and the primary source—cementing the selection bias.

However, sometimes there is more than just neutral "selection bias" at work. The question for you as a learner to always keep in mind is, "Why is some information included in a conversation (or article, course, or talk) and other information ignored?" Scientists (who claim to be more neutral) will select different information about a topic than people who are trying to push a point of view or an ulterior motive. Think of selection bias from a conservative or liberal politician, or in an article by a leadership expert who believes in participative management approaches. Or imagine an advertiser who wants you to purchase a new drug, or a teenager who wants to stay out later than usual. Now think of your own selection bias when you listen to people you agree or disagree with. For example, recall your comments to somebody who has different political beliefs or views on child-rearing. Unless you take steps to see beyond your filters, you inevitably bias your listening and comments in favor of your interests and points of view.

Remember that although the information field contains a lot of data, there is always bias and filtering at work in the information and in your own processing of it. This is OK when the motives are clear or when the information is relatively objective (for example, scientific or reliable statistical information). You can expect to see a point of view on the editorial page of the newspaper or for there to be bias toward a certain building method in a construction class. Whether you expect and seek it or not, it is important to be aware of information's more selective and subjective side. It is also vital to detect when bias goes beyond filtering to deliberate distortion, manipulation, misinformation, and propaganda. Never forget that it is up to you to recognize filters at work. It's up to you to stay a step ahead of any information you are using!

A final note related to information biases: In today's information-saturated world, it is tempting to gravitate to information sources whose points of view are like your own. It's common, for example, to listen to one news network, belong to just a few social media communities of like-minded people, and read blogs and news sources that reflect your biases. Opportunities to be part of even narrower information sharing communities are increasing as interest communities grow and then fragment into subinterests. This can be great for kinship—deepening your knowledge about special interests and helping you feel more in control of a smaller part of the information world. But it is dangerous and puts the brakes on learning when like-minded people begin to think that their views are more true than others'.

So, don't let being in your information comfort zone keep you from being curious about what's happening in the larger information arena. The more diverse information field will always contain people and views you will disagree with, but it will also help you grow and stay current. It will also help you rise above the larger biases in your work, community, and society in general, and perhaps help you understand (although not necessarily agree) where other points of view are coming from. Doing this is an important part of developing yourself through the life stages you learned about in chapter 2.

### Reflect + Connect

This may be a good time to recall the stages of adult development and other self-insights in chapter 2. There are implications for how you see your daily information world.

## Information Is Power: A Warning to 21st-Century Learners

The Internet, social media, and mass media in general are powerful instruments for spreading information. They can reach billions of people in a flash. So can formal learning programs. One online learning course or mobile app can reach anyone on the planet who has a computer or phone—and with increasingly reliable machine translation services, even language differences are not a barrier to universal access.

As despots throughout the centuries discovered, information is power (dictators always try to get control of or discredit the major information sources in their societies). But they are not the only ones trying to influence your information field; attempts to influence you are happening all the time. Businesses, advertisers, politicians, community leaders, teachers, special interest news channels—anyone with an agenda—are constantly selecting and attractively packaging information to influence the behavior they want.

People who do this use what you learned about the brain in chapter 1 to influence your thinking and behavior. They know how to appeal to your amygdala (emotion center) by playing to your fears and desires. They can present information in ways that trigger feel-good chemicals and appeal to your unconscious learning capacity.

Originally called captology, deliberate information manipulation is now called behavior design. Businesses, politicians, and others use this knowledge about your brain to create apps, marketing material, games, speeches, and propaganda that "hack (your) brain and capitalize on its instincts, quirks, and flaws."[1]

Even scientific studies can't be completely free of bias from the researcher. As a 4.0 learner, it's important to know that all information is subjective, and to keep your power and independence as you learn. It's a difficult road to walk, but it's vital to be aware of the potential for bias so you are not manipulated toward goals that are not your own and not good for you.

## Link

Chapter 9 will help you see past the various filters and biases of the information you are using for learning. It will also help you recognize your own filters and biases—because they can also limit what you learn. You may want to skip ahead to this chapter to see some of the techniques that are often used to influence you as you learn.

## The Information Field, in Brief

As a 4.0 learner, you know that there is a vast information world out there, filled with a broad array of learning resources and experiences. It is so vast and changing that you will often only be able to find what you need by working with resource scanners. But you have to do more than find the information you need in a very crowded field. It's also important to check your information for reliability and trustworthiness. Don't automatically assume objectivity.

You can expect any information you use—articles, experiences, courses, conversations, and so forth—to be selective and therefore biased in some way. This is neither good nor bad; some information is always included and some excluded. When you learn, you're also applying filters that influence what you take in and ignore. It's important to be aware of this when you choose information and learn.

People who design courses, write books, give speeches, or create simulations and apps inevitably select information and try to convince you to accept their views and methods. You expect this kind of pressure when you learn. However, because information is power, the information field is also a battleground for competing powers in the media, workplace, politics, and finance; they all want your eyeballs, attention, support, or money. And they know how to manipulate information to get it.

As a 4.0 learner, you can preserve your freedom of thought. Be aware of the vastness and the subjective nature of the information field. It is the fourth and last major part of the learning landscape to understand.

Now, it's time to upgrade your learning practices to 4.0 so that you can thrive in this new learning landscape.

# Part 2

# The Seven Practices of 4.0 Learners

It's time to upgrade to learning 4.0! This section presents seven learning 4.0 practices. Some include updates to the learning 1.0, 2.0, and 3.0 capabilities you already have in your repertoire; others will be new to you and replace the learning methods you've used in the past. You may find yourself using all the techniques, or just one or two—the situation will determine what you need. Use these 4.0 practices whenever they can help you learn.

This section contains many suggestions and explains how they can help you be a successful 4.0 learner. To get the most out of your first read-through, take advantage of the reflect and connect stops, and use the note-taking formats in Tool 3 to help you turn what you read into information you can use later. You'll also find templates to guide you through each of the seven practices in Tool 2 and online at www.learning40.com/unstoppable. Look at them now or make a mental note to use them whenever you find yourself in a learning situation.

# 5

# Hear the Call to Learn

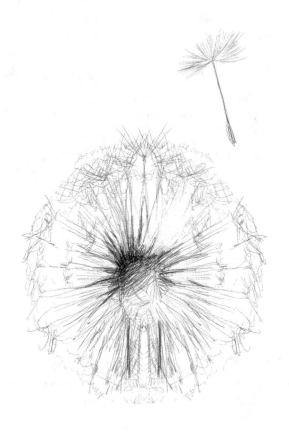

Learning 4.0 captures a broad spectrum of learning opportunities, from the most obvious to the subtlest. This chapter will help you be more alert to opportunities to learn. You'll recognize when learning calls from:

- inside
- outside
- the past
- the future
- pure wonder.

Some calls to learn are loud and clear: You face a health crisis and scour the Internet for insights. You are getting an international promotion and need to learn a new language. A project for a customer in a new industry sends you on a mission to learn about both. You are part of a team tackling a new project. Your company requires you to take a safety workshop or an online class. You are about to use some new software, so you take the tutorial. You decide to become a master gardener and begin the steps and classes to get you there. You have a new child and your pediatrician directs you to a mobile app with "everything you need to know" about how to be a good parent. You are consciously creating learning calls whenever you set goals for your work and life in general.

### Reflect

Why do you want to learn better? What's calling you to upgrade your learning practices?

For many people, learning mostly happens when calls are like those above—obvious or when there is a crisis. In fact, it is easy to go through life in a more reactive mode, simply doing what is necessary to get by. However, later in life, people who have lived this way often wish that they had lived more fully, done more with their gifts, and used more of their 90 billion brain cells.

If only they had listened to the calls that came as whispers.

As a 4.0 learner, you go beyond the obvious learning calls because you have a broader hearing range. You learn and grow by listening to the additional, subtler calls, which most of the time are barely whispers. It's easy to miss them in the midst of day-to-day activities and noise.

Signals to learn come from many places. They come from the environment around you, such as your changing world of work, personal relationships, societal shifts, and new technologies. Calls also come from inside you as your needs shift, as you move through your life stages, and as you become aware of various undeveloped parts that you need to integrate and deal with in some way. Calls to learn also happen when you look back on a success or failure and feel good or are troubled by the results.

Chances are, the voices are calling from these places right now. But the pressures of modern life and personal filters (a fear of failure, a need to look perfect, or shadow patterns) can easily drown them out.[1]

As a 4.0 learner, you can amplify these faint calls before it is too late to act or before they become crises. And you can increase your overall fitness in this important learning practice area by strengthening your ability to focus, concentrate, and reflect.[2]

To master this practice of hearing the call to learn, you need to tune to the call and speak the call. These two actions draw on brain and psychology facts described in chapters 1 and 2. For example, from psychology we know that your expectations affect what your senses take in. And neuroscientists tell us that you can consciously prime your automatic, unconscious system to notice things.

## Tune to the Call

When you tune to the call, you ask yourself the question, "What's inviting me to learn?" You calibrate your learning receptors to notice the faintest and most disguised calls to learn. Your senses, your automatic system, and your big self are finely tuned, alert, and ready to hear calls from five different channels. They are channels that tune in, tune out, tune back, tune forward, and tune wonder.

## Tune In

Your body and mind provide many indirect signals that may be calls to learn. You may feel restless, bored, or like you're going in circles. You may have an intense emotional reaction to something or somebody; a reaction that is out of proportion to the situation. Perhaps you find yourself complaining a lot, or feeling dissatisfied with a role, relationship, or job. Maybe you feel drawn to or interested in something and your juices flow, even for a moment. Or you felt an emotional high or low after finishing a difficult project, performance, or athletic event. These are potential invitations to learn something.

You know that as long as you are alive, your needs, life stages, and other forces within you will continually call you to learn; you are always evolving and changing. In fact, there is a self within you that throughout your life will call you to grow, change, and be all you can be. These deeper forces often speak in whispers, expressing themselves indirectly through feelings and body signals long before they are obvious. So, become an expert at detecting them. Keep this channel open so you can hear the calls for action when they are just beginning to appear.

## Tune Out

Keep a channel open to hear calls from the world around you. Notice signs that your habits and actions aren't working as well as they used to. Notice if you aren't getting the reactions, results, or feedback you expect or want. Be alert to changes in your relationships at work, in your family, and with friends. Are things changing? Perhaps your kids are becoming rebellious teenagers or your spouse is taking a new job. Or something may be appearing on the horizon at work that will change your role or even eliminate your job as you know it. These experiences may require new knowledge, skills, perspectives, attitudes, and capabilities. Notice when the signals first appear and act on them—before they become crises.

## Tune Back

The past is rich with potential learning lessons you can bring to the surface, or that come to the surface on their own as pride or regret. The goal of tuning back is to get a learning benefit from successes, failures, and the wisdom of hindsight. After you finish a complicated project, for example, rewind your inner movie, hit replay, and let the voice of learning come through.

Many calls to learn from the past go unheeded. The movie *Groundhog Day* is based on this idea. The hero finds himself experiencing the same day—without change, without learning—over and over until he realizes that by changing his actions he can influence a different outcome. It is only when he finally tunes back into the experience that he discovers the learning points that give him power in his future.

## Tune Forward

The future seems to occur faster than you can prepare for it, but there are always clues you can tune into today. For example, signals from the future exist in your company's strategic plan, trend data, projections about technology, and your own sensitivity to trends around you. Remember: Every major social or personal change was a very subtle, often sidelined energy before it took form. Think of major social movements (such as civil and women's rights) or your own personal changes (career and life shifts). These rarely happened overnight.

The future is calling as relationships change in and around your family and social circles. If you keep informed about what's happening in your industry, your town, the world, and your own life and relationships, your brain will start to hear the early warning signals and anticipate the future so you can prepare for, or at least not get caught off guard, when things change. This ability to detect the emerging future from very subtle clues is one of the most important powers of the 4.0 learner.

## Tune Wonder

It's a mystery to some researchers who focus more on logic than emotion, but human beings often learn for no apparent reason, for the pure wonder and joy of it all. Think about the times you just got carried away by an interest and lost your sense of time. Continue to be alert for chances to learn something for its own sake—to satisfy a curiosity or just to experience doing something new. The act of learning triggers many "joy" chemicals in your brain, such as dopamine and endorphins. So be alert for calls to learning that have no other purpose than doing it and enjoying the experience of being alive.

What channels are calling you to tune in right now? Are you listening to the whispering inside you? What's telling you to tune out, to better align yourself with the world around you? What lessons from your past are waiting to be mined, asking you to tune back? What call is the future waiting for you to answer? And, what learning is out there just for the wonder of it all?

Be on the alert for these calls. This is your first job as a 4.0 learner. One big purpose of your prefrontal cortex, the executive part of your conscious brain, is to respond to these calls. But, you have to hear a call before you can answer it!

### Reflect

Think about what is calling you to learn this week. Which of the five calls have been loudest?

## Speak the Call

So, you hear the call, but what is it saying to you? Make the call real by putting it into words that can trigger your learning. This applies to obvious calls (you are required to take a class or a company simulation) as well as to the vague signals in the other channels. Whatever the source of the call, bring it to life by speaking its message in your own words. Use self-talk to put the spotlight on what is calling and what it is asking you to do.[3] For example:

- I bought this new financial software; now how can I use it to help me save time and money?
- This international promotion means I need to learn a new language!
- I have to take this course to learn the new customer service protocols. How can I use it to help me get more comfortable when I deal with irate people?
- I've been reacting defensively when I'm in situations with Jake. I wonder what it would be like to react differently.
- I have been feeling stuck, flat, unmotivated, low energy, and restless at work lately. I think it is telling me I need to look at where I want to go next in my life.
- I have an uncomfortable feeling when this topic comes up. Is this a signal that I need to learn something?

- These recent changes in our strategy could affect my job. What more do I need to know and what do I need to do to get ahead of this?

- Some of these emerging technologies could shatter our business as we know it. Do we need to explore their implications?

- We just finished phase three of our project and people are feeling really good about the breakthroughs we made. What lessons did we learn that we can bring into future projects?

- I'm feeling good when I do this kind of work and use this set of skills. Does this mean I should set myself up to do more of this?

- As I surf this news magazine, something catches my eye. I'm really curious about this topic—I'll let my interest lead the way.

Putting your impressions into words lets you look at them more closely to see if they contain any calls to learn. Just describe what you are feeling or observing and what they might be asking you to learn.

## Hear the Call, in Brief

The first learning 4.0 practice involves recognizing when it's time to learn. Your life is full of learning opportunities—they are happening everywhere and all the time. Some are obvious, like when your employer or profession requires you to sign up for an online course or workshop, or when something radical changes in your life and you must respond.

Use the Practice 1: Hear the Call to Learn template in Tool 2 or at www.learning40.com/unstoppable to help you implement this first learning 4.0 practice.

But most calls don't initially look like opportunities for you to develop. They appear in the form of discomfort, defensiveness, curiosity, interest, and recurring desires. Or you may be experiencing boredom with the status quo, faint realizations that what always worked for you is no longer as effective, and gradual changes around you. Subtle cues like these may be saying, "It's time to learn." Don't let their whispers get lost in the noise of everyday life.

This whole brain and body awareness is a special feature that comes with the learning 4.0 upgrade. As a 4.0 learner, you'll fine-tune this ability to recognize and acknowledge calls to learn, whether they come from inside, outside, past experience, the future, or when you are just enjoying a surprise learning opportunity.

# 6

---

# Create Future-Pull

Imagination is a defining human quality and a key feature of learning 4.0. In this chapter, you'll learn how to use your imagination to program yourself for learning success. This involves:

- immersing yourself in a multisensory future that you want to create
- being clear about where you are today to create a motivational pull into the future you desire.

So, you've heard the learning call. Assuming you want to respond to it, now what? You may intend to act, but your motivation may not be strong enough to go to the next step. And you may not know enough about what you need to learn or what resources will be the best for your needs.

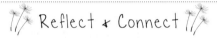

### Reflect + Connect

Imagine yourself learning better in one to two years. What does it look and feel like?

So, instead of jumping into learning activities at this point, do something to get your motivation juices going. Imagine a future that is so compelling it makes your learning success inevitable. Create a multisensory version of your future self—you in a virtual reality future. When you do this, you create a powerful psychological pull into the future you desire because you now have something tangible to guide your conscious learning decisions. This also helps to program the automatic functions in your brain to recognize learning opportunities when they appear in your day-to-day life.

There are two steps involved in creating this future-pull: Imagine a multisensory future and GPS your now.

## Imagine a Multisensory Future

"You can create your life in the same way an artist develops a work of art. When you begin to approach your life from that orientation, you transform your world."[1]

You have a natural ability to visualize lifelike movies inside you. You do this when you dream, daydream, and imagine. This ability to embody thought is an important part of being human, so much so that it is currently an important focus of artificial intelligence researchers. They recognize that human intelligence is not just an abstract process they can program with digital computers; instead, they are training robots by physically connecting them to humans and hoping they can pass on this capability to the machines!

Learning 4.0 encourages you to use your ability to imagine and dream to engage your body as well as your brain for learning success—before you actually learn. The secret is to create an immersive virtual reality that you step into and experience as though it is real.[2] This requires engaging your body, brain, mind, and emotions.

Here's how it works. Think of something that you are called to learn right now. Then, go to a quiet and spacious place, close your eyes, and take a few slow, deep breaths. Now, imagine that you have acted on your learning call and are living in your future. Ask yourself:

- Where are you?
- What is happening that is different from today?
- What are you experiencing, seeing, hearing, and smelling?
- What are you doing?
- What are you creating or achieving?
- Who else is present?
- What does it feel like to be in this scenario?

Think about this as "trying on a future." Go beyond just thinking about it—step into the skin of your future self. Experience this desirable future and see if it resonates with your important calls to learn. Bring your full physical, mental, and emotional self into your projection. If it helps, make a drawing of your experience and explore it with a friend. Keep in mind that you are mobilizing your inner resources—your self-image, motivation, brain chemicals, feelings, and the conscious thinking and imagining center in the front of your brain—to prime yourself for learning. Think about this as embodying your future—bringing it inside you.

Even if your virtual future is hazy at the start or you know it will change as you learn, put it out there to launch you on your learning path. Imagine that you have a big piece of clay in your hands and you want to make something special. You start by softening and shaping it, and eventually your process and the clay become partners in creating what emerges. (Michelangelo always had an idea about what he was sculpting, but he let the stone help determine what would ultimately emerge.)

Your future vision will help you connect the dots that create the path for your journey. What you learn on that path will then help shape and hone your future vision. Your learning journey and your future vision will influence each other, but your initial multisensory impression is an important starting point.

Don't worry about projecting a perfect virtual future; the goal is simply to create some direction and motivation. However, you do want to imagine as much as you can about the future you aspire to. Feel yourself living inside it. This is one of the most powerful things you can do as a 4.0 learner. It sets up and motivates the conscious part of your brain to notice learning opportunities and use learning practices. And it sets up a kind of automatic magnetic attraction that will unconsciously draw you toward your desired future. This virtual future will also help you keep going when the learning is difficult.

## GPS Your Now

Your learning journey will take you from the present into the future. But what is the "present" that you want to move beyond? It's a good idea to know where your virtual reality projector sits—the location of the "you are here" icon on the map of your life. Think about:

- What situations are you in now that are ready for something new?
- What are you seeing, hearing, or feeling in these situations?
- What are you doing in these situations?
- What are you creating or achieving?
- Who are the key people in your current scenario?

Step outside yourself to answer these questions from an external perspective, in addition to looking from the inside. Try to rise above your own biases and experiences. Ask for feedback from others: How do they see you now? Their views will reflect their own biases, of course, but they'll also shape how they react to you, and their feedback can give you another data point.

The difference between your virtual future and where you are now will create tension that your brain and self will want to resolve. The more real

and visceral your experience of your future and your now are, the more energized you will be to resolve the tension between them. You will be drawn,
consciously and unconsciously, toward your desired future.

# Create Future-Pull, in Brief

When you want to respond to a call to learn, take some time to set yourself up for success. Bring the power of your imagination into your learning
process. First, immerse yourself in the future you desire by creating a virtual
reality future vision that energizes and motivates you to act. Then steep yourself in where you are today. This will program your automatic self to resolve
the tension between the two visions, and it will energize your learning.

Here is how it might look if you were a first-time team leader who wants
to successfully step into a team leadership role (Figure 6-1).

Figure 6-1. The Creative Tension Between Your Now and Your
Future Vision

| You Now | Creative Tension | You in the Future |
|---|---|---|
| I get nervous when I'm with executives, so I think I appear timid. | | I feel confident and present my ideas with passion. I am able to deal with my nervousness. |
| Other technicians I interact with like me, but don't think I share or consult enough. | | I ask other technicians for their ideas and create more opportunities for team planning. |
| I don't have a lot of exposure beyond my work group. | → → | I have several important relationships with people in other departments. |
| I get most of my satisfaction from solving problems myself. | | I celebrate team results and feel a sense of accomplishment when the team succeeds. |
| I'm known as a bright technologist who works independently. | | I'm known as a coach and mentor to others as well as a thought leader. |

Even if you do nothing more than create this present-to-future view of
yourself in your imagination, you will still increase your chances of learning
success. Some people call this future-pull the law of attraction; others call it
the path of least resistance.[3] Stephen R. Covey calls it beginning with the
end in mind.[4] For spiritual leaders, prayer is a kind of future-pull. Others

are more scientific, equating it with magnetism, where the goal is to create a psychological magnetic field. The power of positive thinking and the notion that thoughts become things also relate to this idea of a future-pull. Synchronicity—when you set up conditions where more coincidences occur in your life—is another by-product of creating future-pull. You might say, "Isn't it fortunate that this opportunity related to my learning goal is arising now?" when in reality, you programmed yourself to notice the opportunity and even to put yourself in a situation where it would occur.[5]

## Link

Use the Practice 2: Create Future-Pull template in Tool 2 or at www.learning40.com/unstoppable to help you implement this second learning 4.0 practice.

Brain research supports all the ideas we've discussed in this chapter. You can program your automatic system to support your learning quest, while also setting up a framework for more conscious learning actions.[6] Don't miss out on the benefits of this simple but powerful practice.

# 7

## Search Far and Wide

As a 4.0 learner, you use the best resources and experiences for learning. And you find them using an increasing array of search services and support. This chapter advises you to:

- Be guided by questions and curiosity.
- Step back and scan the information field before landing on specific learning resources.
- Remember that your everyday environment is filled with opportunities to move toward your future vision.
- Use all resources, not just those in your comfort zone.
- Be open to surprises and new information in all stages of your learning journey.

Help! There is too much information out there and it's growing every day. How do you find the best resources and experiences for learning? How do you even know what to look for?

It's tempting to use the first resources, people, and experiences that cross your path because that's often the easiest option. You use the class, app, or coach your friend recommends. You jump right into a project you're told you can "learn something" from without thinking about the value. You always take a class, get a book, experiment on your own, or click on the first or second result in an Internet search when you want to learn. "That's my style," you say.

## Reflect + Connect

Pick something you would like to learn and then keep it in mind throughout this chapter. How would you normally find the best resources to help you learn it? Where would you look for learning help? The quality of your search will affect what and how—and even whether—you learn. Maybe this chapter will change how you think about your search habits!

It's tempting to take the first resource or experience option that comes your way when you want to learn something. But unless you are sure it will be the best use of your time, resist the urge. Step back and use learning 4.0 methods to lead with questions, use scanners, be resource-versatile, and be open to the new.

# Lead With Questions

Before you decide exactly what and how you will learn, ask yourself two important guiding questions:

- What knowledge, skills, and other qualities will help me reach my future vision?
- What resources—experiences, tools, information, media, and support—can I use to help me learn?

Unless you are an expert in your learning area—meaning you know what's going on and where to go to stay current—plan to go broad before you go deep. This means being curious and open: leading with questions.

Curiosity and questions dominated your world as a child. Somehow, many adults replace this quality with a need to look good, be perfect, and be certain. (Remember the fixed mindset we discussed in chapter 2?) The rapidly changing world begs you to rekindle your curiosity and nurture your growth mindset.[1] Curiosity is also important for your health and vitality. It may be one of your most important defenses against brain atrophy and dementia.

Be curious about what you need to learn and what's available to help you learn. Ask:

- I wonder what skills and knowledge I should focus on?
- I wonder if I need to modify any attitudes or beliefs?
- I wonder what experiences I can put myself into?
- I wonder what other learning resources and support are out there, and what will work best for me?"

When you are curious, you become an exploratory learner. You position yourself to stretch beyond your current self and world view. You tell your conscious self and your automatic system that you are willing to step out of your comfort zone and into an expanded zone of possibilities. This revives the energy that stimulated all that brain development you experienced as a child.

Leading with questions means looking for and following clues, much like a detective. You may start out thinking you need to learn one type of skill or knowledge, only to discover that there are different ways of thinking than you imagined. You will probably discover resources for learning that were not obvious at the start, which may even lead you to change your future vision as you learn more. Let this exploratory perspective lead you into the next phase of your search.

# Use Scanners

The goals of your search are greater clarity about what to learn and a list of the best resources for learning it. There is a vast array of resources at your disposal when you want to learn something: books, articles, online material, coaches, mobile apps, games, videos, podcasts, lectures, workshops, retreats, meetings, developmental job assignments, and more.

How do you find what you need in this information overload? Fortunately, you can turn to scanners—people and services that help you sort through the sea of information. Scanners don't take over your learning; instead, they help point you toward what you need while you orchestrate the search. Your job is to stay curious, opening your attention and brain to new perspectives and information. Figure 7-1 lists some scanners that can help you find resources for learning and refine your future vision. Go to one or more of these scanners before you jump onto your learning path.

## Figure 7-1. Scanners

| | |
|---|---|
| · Search engines | · Course aggregators |
| · Crowdsourcing on social media | · Human resources, training, and career |
| · Curators |   development professionals |
| · Librarians and search experts | · Professional associations and conferences |
| · Subject matter experts | · Periodical databases |
| · Citation indexes | · Mass media channels |
| · Leaders in your company or agency | |

One amazing scanner that is always working for you if it's primed with a meaningful future vision is your own brain. Remember that your brain doesn't like unfinished business (see chapter 6). When you have a future vision that is different from where you are today, your brain works to resolve that gap. When you are looking for something or wanting to be better at something, your automatic system will keep looking for help and answers. If your brain is primed, you will notice opportunities at work and in life related to your future vision that you would otherwise ignore. Set your brain up as a scanner.

## Connect

Check out Tool 4. Scanners and How to Use Them. Pick a scanner you could use to learn more about the interest you identified at the beginning of this chapter. If you have time, do a short search.

Keep track of the learning activities and resource ideas that scanners help you discover. Refine your future vision to reflect any relevant insights you gather along the way.

# Be Resource-Versatile

Learning 4.0 is highly versatile learning. This has implications for how you think about, select, and use resources for learning.

## Expand Your Range

Information is increasing at accelerating rates, and so are the ways of packaging it. You can get the same learning content in many formats. Be open to the broad array of learning resources, and be ready to embrace more as they are invented. Figure 7-2 shows some of the kinds of resources you will find in your search.

## Figure 7-2. Learning Resources

| | | | |
|---|---|---|---|
| • Apps | • Articles | • Periodicals and | • Lectures and |
| • Coaches and | • Conversations | newspapers | presentations |
| mentors | and meetings | • Social media | • Case studies |
| • Discussions | • Experts | • Books | • Online and real- |
| • Blogs and | • Past on-the- | • Online and self- | time courses and |
| websites | job and life | paced courses | workshops |
| • Search engines | experiences | and workshops | • Mobile learning |
| • Games | • Face-to-face | • Team learning | • Role play |
| • Video and | courses and | and collaborative | • Simulations |
| YouTube | workshops | work spaces | • Podcasts |

## Reflect

What kinds of learning resources are you most likely to use? How would you describe your learning preferences and style? What learning resources would take you out of your comfort zone?

## Versatility Over Learning Style

Learning 4.0 is agile across the full range of resources. Be ready to select the best resources for your learning—don't limit your search to the resources in your comfort zone. This is a challenge because, like most people, you probably prefer some learning resources over others and have developed favorite ways to learn. For example, you may prefer reading, conversations, courses, games, or learning through experience. You may like to think about ideas before you try something new. You may prefer to learn on your own instead of in conversations and team learning activities. You may think of yourself as a visual or auditory or tactile learner. These preferences are part of your learning style.

It's useful to know how you like to learn and the media you prefer to use. But learning today requires high versatility across many different types of resources and learning styles. If you limit yourself to what you are comfortable doing, you will fall behind.

As a 4.0 learner, you can't be tied down to specific resources, media, or approaches. Stretch your capabilities to learn in any situation, whether it's with and without others, conceptually through reading and listening, or reflectively by analyzing what's happening. Put aside any preconceived ideas about workshops or online learning and explore new learning formats. Be ready to use anything you encounter in the information field so that you can broaden your horizons beyond your resource comfort zone.

## Don't Forget Opportunities in Daily Life

Don't overlook the embedded learning value in your everyday life and work experience! Your daily life is filled with learning opportunities. This is especially true for physical, interpersonal, personal, and intellectual skills. If you want to develop your physical stamina, you can walk up the stairs instead of taking the elevator. Develop your listening skills by spending three times as much time listening as you do speaking. Strengthen your budget and finance knowledge by participating in the first stage of budget planning. Any situation with boisterous children or an annoying colleague will help you develop your patience. If your goal is to improve your decision making, you'll have many opportunities to do that on the job.

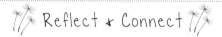

## Reflect & Connect

What natural opportunities to learn related to the goal you set at the beginning of this chapter will exist in your day-to-day life during the next month?

When you are searching for learning resources, think about options you have in your daily life or that you could access with a bit of stretch. Ask people who know your work and life situation to help you identify natural learning opportunities that are available to you now.

Experiment with the full array of learning resources around you and be on the lookout for more to appear every day. See yourself as a self-service learner and move around the information field—with or without help—in formal or informal learning situations. If you need to know something, Google it. If you find a great article, read it, even if you don't see yourself as a reader. Try out a new skill in a role-play exercise, even if it pulls you out of your comfort zone. If your company requires an online course, take the opportunity even if you stopped thinking about yourself as a student long ago. Make every life and work experience into an opportunity to learn.

## Be Open to the New

It's tempting to see this search phase as a chore or a sideways move. It may bring back memories of spending hours in the school library. But you are out of school now, an adult facing learning challenges, time pressures, and trade-offs in the many roles you play. It makes sense to search before you invest your learning time and energy.

So, approach this search phase as a 4.0 learner. Make it a time of discovery; a time in your learning process when you let your curiosity and questions roam, when you follow your needs and interests as you buzz across the information field. It can be a time of real flow—of getting lost in your curiosity and enjoying what you find. Your neurochemicals will surge as you find answers to your search questions (dopamine), explore ideas with others (oxytocin), and enjoy being exposed to something new (endorphins).

Maybe you experienced some of these feelings the last time you did an online search. You had a question, launched an Internet search, roamed around the search results, checked out some of the more relevant items, and hopefully got what you needed. Maybe your search even changed your view of what you wanted to find.

The discovery experience is one of the most important benefits of your search activities.

## Search, in Brief

As a 4.0 learner, you know that the learning resource field is far too vast for you to navigate alone. So take some time to search for the best resources and experiences before you commit major time and effort to your learning. Lead with questions, step back to see what resources are out there, and turn to scanners who can help you decide what to learn and direct you to the best resources for your needs. And don't forget to turn the spotlight on learning opportunities in your daily life. Think of these as the low-hanging fruit that is ready for you to pick and turn into new capabilities. You are resource-versatile; don't be limited by resource preferences or the learning style you've developed over the years. Instead, choose your learning material based on what's relevant for your needs.

Searching in this way helps you deal with the information overload around you. It allows you to start creating a mental framework for organizing your learning and setting up support networks that you can access as your learning unfolds. You continue to shape your future-vision.

And, you get a bonus. The search phase is often a fascinating time of exploration—a learning journey in its own right. Because you are taking a broader, search-oriented view, you'll discover ways of thinking that stretch you, and you might even change your view of what the learning project is all about.

 Link

Use the Practice 3: Search template in Tool 2 or at www.learning40.com/unstoppable to help you implement this third learning 4.0 practice.

# 8

## Connect the Dots

Learning 4.0 builds on and upgrades some of the learning 2.0 organizing skills you learned in school and the learning 3.0 methods you developed after leaving formal education. Use this chapter to fine-tune and expand your ability to assemble learning resources and actions to achieve your future vision. This involves:

- matching your effort to the difficulty of the learning challenge
- recognizing your general learning path.

You have heard the call to learn, you have a future vision, and you've found the learning resources and experiences you can use. Now it's time to decide what else you need to support your learning, and how you'll connect the dots to create a learning path. At this stage, you need to rate the learning challenge, name your path, mark waypoints, and equip yourself for the journey.

## Rate the Learning Challenge

Sometimes learning is easy (you want to learn the new features that come with a software program upgrade), but it can also be very difficult (you are a novice team leader who wants to learn how to build and coordinate a diverse team). Difficult learning will take more time, resources, and grit than easy learning, so gauge the challenge ahead. Think about what it will take to reach your future vision, and start connecting the dots by rating the level of difficulty on the learning challenge continuum (Figure 8-1).

This doesn't imply that difficult situations are drudgery, and it doesn't mean that less challenging ones are more enjoyable. Difficult learning can unleash amazing energy and flow, where you become so absorbed in your learning that you lose track of time. Conversely, something that is too easy may not be challenging enough to entice your brain waves and neurochemicals (endorphins and adrenalin) into a learning state. You need to be prepared to learn no matter where you fall on the continuum.

## Figure 8-1. Learning Challenge Continuum

| 1 | 10 |
|---|---|

◀─────────────────────────────────────────▶

| Easier | More Difficult |
|---|---|

| | |
|---|---|
| • Support an existing habit | • Change or replace a habit or pattern of behavior |
| • No emotional baggage | |
| • You have background and basic understanding | • Involves intense emotions or defenses |
| | • This is new and complex territory |
| • Your environment and the people around you are supportive | • Your environment is hostile or resisting |
| • Relates to your current role and view of yourself | • Relates to a new role or view of yourself |
| • Relates to your current values, attitudes, and mindset | • Requires you to rethink your values, attitudes, and mindsets |
| • There are right, simple, or better solutions | • Problems and solutions are complex, have many causes, and have no perfect answers |
| • Learning partners are similar in views and processes | • Learning partners are very diverse in view and process |

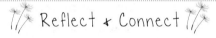

### Reflect & Connect

Think about something you want to learn. Rate it on the learning challenge continuum.

# Name Your Path

Your learning journey can take three different paths: learning in the moment, learning forward to a goal, and learning retroactively from experience. You may be on one or all paths, with different agendas, at the same time!

## Path 1: Learn in the Moment

Day-to-day life is filled with in-the-moment learning opportunities. While 4.0 learners have a broad bandwidth for recognizing these chances to learn, most people miss them.

When you learn in the moment, you notice the opportunity to learn something and then follow your curiosity, getting the information you need, and perhaps doing something to be sure you remember a point or two. For example, you may be reading a blog and find yourself wanting to know a bit more about a specific topic. Or, perhaps something sparks your interest as you talk with others, watch a video, or face a challenge on the job.

Imagine you are a new team leader having a casual conversation with a colleague when you realize that she has successfully dealt with some recent conflicts between people in her team. You are working to become a stronger team facilitator, so your interest is piqued. You ask her how she handled those difficult situations, listening and making mental notes about how you can use some of her methods. It's a short, in-the-moment conversation. But you learn something important to you that you hadn't planned.

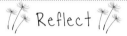

### Reflect

There are many opportunities for learning, but in the overloaded information environment, it's hard to recognize them. Learning in the moment is an unplanned learning opportunity that manages to catch your interest.

Note that behind these in-the-moment learning opportunities will always be one of the five calls to learn. That is, you will notice the opportunity because of some need in you, in your world, back from experience, forward because of a possible future challenge or vision, or pure joy and general interest in the topic. Every in-the-moment learning opportunity presents a sign that there you are being called to learn. Whenever you think, "Aha! Something interesting is happening here!" use the relevant mine for gold, learn to last, and transfer to life practices (which you will read about in the next chapters) to capture, retain, and use what you learn.

Learning opportunities lurk everywhere. Pretty exciting! It's just further proof that you are made for learning; that the 90 billion neurons and 100 trillion connections in your brain are calling out to be stimulated and used.

## Path 2: Learn Forward to a Goal

The second path is what most people associate with deliberate, conscious learning. It happens when you direct your learning toward a new future vision. This can be a complex path with many moving parts, but it can also be simple, such as becoming adept at a new version of software you already use. More complex learning toward a goal usually requires you to plan and re-plan as you progress. You plan what resources you will use and when, where to learn, what tools you will use, how you will fund some aspects (pay for a course), how you will make time, and where it will fit into your schedule. You'll also have to anticipate distractions and decide how much support you will need from others, and how to get it.

For example, you may want to prepare for a role, develop a capability, or improve your overall skill and perspective in an area. Maybe you received feedback about a personality trait or want to get ready for a new role (you heard the call to learn). When you're on this path, you will create a future vision, search for the best resources, and launch a learning plan with a time-line and a list of resources and actions you'll take along the way.

When you learn forward to a goal, you create a learning plan and then take deliberate steps to reach your future vision.

## Path 3: Learn Retroactively

Ah, the unmined riches of experience. People often look back on the past with regret or nostalgia, but another, often better, option is to learn from it. As a 4.0 learner, you can use your imagination to go back inside the experi-ence to extract the lessons and the learning.

Tool 5. Resource-Specific Learning Tips includes thoughts on how to mine lessons and learning from experience.

As you look retroactively into experience, you may uncover additional calls to learn. For example, you realize that your team misdiagnosed several problems because you didn't have an agreed upon method for problem anal-ysis or ways of bringing diverse views together. So you project a future vision of better teamwork and problem solving. Thus, what started as retroactive learning (path 3) becomes learning forward to a goal (path 2).

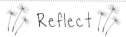

## Reflect

When you look back on an experience you can often pull a learning opportunity out of it.

Military leaders require retroactive learning as part of all important actions and engagements. They call it an after-action review. But this very rich type of learning is available to everybody; there are vast veins of unmined gold lying in your past experiences. But it will take time and conscious effort to locate and extract it!

## Reflect & Connect

What in-the-moment learning occurred for you today? What forward-to-a-goal projects are you working on? Do you have any recent experiences that are candidates for retroactive learning?

As a 4.0 learner, be ready to jump onto these three learning paths. There is potential learning all around you; you just need to become more conscious of it.

The seven learning 4.0 practices apply to all three paths, but in different intensities. Sometimes they are mere touchpoints that draw on one or two practices; for example, an in-the-moment call to learn may trigger a fleeting but conscious future vision that creates some future-pull. Other paths, such as learning forward to a goal or retroactively, take more conscious attention and draw on most or all seven practices.

Remember, learning is a process of discovery. On any path and at any time, you may discover something that will change your future vision, your decisions about resources and experiences, and the plans you will intend to follow. Learning is always dynamic, growth oriented, and about change.

## Mark Waypoints

Learning is an exploration. So, imagine being an explorer. At this point, you should have a good idea about where you want to head (future vision), where you are, and the general path you are starting on (in the moment, toward a goal, or retroactive). You've learned what you can about the territory by scanning for resources and noting where your learning journey fits on the challenge continuum. You may even have a useful map and specific path to follow (such as if you are going for a credential or following a step-by-step learning program). However, it's more likely that there is no clear route. So, how do you proceed?

You don't have to create a detailed plan (step-by-step learning plans in today's nonstop world frequently change), so waypoints on a potential path may be enough. Waypoints are important points (dots) you move toward on your learning journey; when you reach them, you take stock and confirm or revise your course. They include:

- specific learning experiences and resources, and when you plan to engage with them
- support from others, and when you will involve them
- major learning checkpoints
- steps you need to take to shape your environment or ensure you have the learning materials you need.

If you can, plot these waypoints as a visual flow, showing how you want to move along your learning path.

If you are on a retroactive learning path, your waypoints will include actions that pull learning from past experiences, as well as responses to new calls to learn that arise during your review.

## Equip Yourself for the Journey

Explorers prepare by equipping themselves to meet the challenges of their unique quest and circumstances. This also applies to 4.0 learners. If your journey is going to take you into difficult or unfamiliar terrain, consider getting a Sherpa or coach. If the environment is going to make it difficult to stay on course, set up a safe harbor where you can do some of the offline learning work, or incorporate it by using real-life experiences as part of your learning process. If your learning goal requires you to master some difficult knowledge areas, note-taking approaches will help you see deeper patterns and organize and internalize what you want to learn. You may even want to create a special file on your desktop to store everything related to your learning goal.

Create a learning-friendly environment around you, too. If you are worried you will lose energy and motivation, set up some incentives or put your future vision somewhere where you can see it, like on your desk, computer, screensaver, or bathroom mirror. Schedule weekly reminders that pop up on your calendar and cheer you on. And make sure your learning materials are ready for you to use when you need them.

The atmosphere around you matters, too. Learning is a whole brain– whole body experience: Your brain and body are in constant interaction with the environment in and around you, sensing many subtleties that you are not consciously monitoring. If you can, avoid anything that is harsh, stressful, or distracting to your senses. For example, the colors around you affect your ability to concentrate: Blue and green are more supportive and calming than red and orange.[1] A certain amount of white noise can be a great asset for learning because it increases the levels your neurons are firing, without overstressing them. Imagine your neurons resonating with low-frequency sounds—such as river and ocean sounds or soothing music—in a way that helps keep you alert, yet relaxed enough to learn. An emerging field of research called stochastic resonance is exploring how to use sound-waves to supercharge learning in this way, so look for more insights about this in the future.[2]

# A Word About the Social Aspect of Learning

When you select, organize, and connect your dots, think about getting others involved as co-learners and supporters. Learning always has a social element. Even when you learn on your own, you're drawing on humanity's entire evolutionary history as you use the language, symbols, and knowledge acquired through generations. Your learning sits within the cultural assumptions and worldviews you were born into. You use resources designed by others, and you interact with and rely on others at various stages of the process.

Link

There is more on social learning in chapter 13.

Sometimes this social aspect will be more, well, social. For example, you may have a shared learning agenda with a team, your family, or a partner. Or you may get help and guidance from others or provide that kind of support yourself. These are terrific opportunities to help everyone in your circle to upgrade to learning 4.0.

The social aspect adds color, energy, and motivation to learning. It's also vital to your success if your learning goal is at the high end of the challenge continuum. Adding social waypoints can help you share, and thus minimize, some of the struggle. It also adds rewarding benefits of comradeship and good feelings from oxytocin bursts.

## Connect the Dots, in Brief

Learning is a journey that may involve many resources and personal action steps. So you may have to select, connect, and reconnect many dots. Sometimes you have a good map with clear and obvious connections, like when your learning goal is part of a certificate or degree program, or when the path is designed by somebody else. For these journeys, you don't have to spend much time finding resources or planning.

 Link

Use the Practice 4: Connect the Dots template in Tool 2 or at www.learning40.com/unstoppable to help you implement this fourth learning 4.0 practice.

Unfortunately, there isn't a nice, paved road for most of your learning journeys. You are on an adventure of your own in uncharted or poorly mapped terrain, where you have to select waypoints and connect the dots based on imperfect and incomplete information. While planning waypoints gives your learning journey some structure, you know that your path will continue evolving as you learn.

Whether the path is immediately clear or not, and whether you are in the moment, learning toward a goal, or learning retroactively, take some time to select and connect the dots that represent what you plan to do as you learn. And don't forget that your path may change as you reconnect the dots on your journey.

# 9

## Mine for Gold

In this chapter, you learn about bringing new information into your brain so you can turn it into knowledge, skills, attitudes, and creative ideas you can use. This mine for gold practice involves several challenging but important learning 4.0 methods, including:

- being able to pull useful information from a variety of resources and experiences in the information field
- managing your attention
- distinguishing good from bad information
- looking beneath the surface to find deeper patterns and insights.

## Reflect ⁎ Connect

This is the part of the learning journey that most people equate with learning—it's the part where you process new information. What would you like to learn to do better in this phase of your own learning journey?

Welcome to one of the most challenging and engaging parts of your learning journey. This is the time when the information and insights that are "out there" move into your brain's short-term memory centers, ready to become lasting memories, skills, values, and mental models that stimulate your creative ideas. This is the point where you begin rewiring your brain and making yourself ready for change. You select what you will use in the future and begin incorporating it into your view of who you are.

If you're like many people, you don't manage this part of the process very well. You may let the learning resource take charge or have a hard time concentrating. You may feel compelled to read a book cover to cover and guilty when you don't. Or, you may drift through a course or workshop, following somebody else's plan without linking it to your own, and then evaluating the quality of the teaching but not the learning. Or, you may have lots of fun playing a learning game, but miss out on the deeper lessons for your life.

You need to learn the learning 4.0 mine for gold methods so that you don't fall into this scenario! The goal of this practice is to bring new information into your short-term memory and set yourself up for automatic and deliberate learning that creates lasting memories and skills, new mindsets, and other permanent learning results. For this you need both attention and technique to tailor for resources, be present to learn, look for real gold, detect fool's gold, and equip yourself for deep learning.

# Tailor for Resources

The resources you use (including work-life experiences) present information in unique ways. They also differ in how well designed they are to help you learn. For example, some videos are set up to help you reflect and draw out key lessons, while others just flow along, requiring you to figure out what learning value is hidden behind the dialogue and images. This is also true for books, articles, and subject matter experts. Some experts, for example, are clear about what their key concepts and skills are and can easily share them with you. Others do expert work, but can't explain how they do it. This makes learning their secrets more difficult. When you decide to turn to a book or expert to help you learn something, you need to be prepared to dig for what you need—to adjust your learning conversation to find the gold in what's in front of you.

It's your job as a 4.0 learner to extract what you need regardless of how deeply it is buried or how obscure the lesson. But how do you do this? Some practices apply to many situations, while others are specific to the type of resource, but they all require you to turn on your conscious system while priming your automatic system to help you consolidate your learning along the way.

## Survey the Terrain

The first step in tailoring your learning journey to any resource is to take a 5,000-foot view. Ask: "What can I learn from this resource and why should I trust it?" Then step back and survey the terrain.

Surveying is a 4.0 learning technique for finding what you need from any resource. But it is also important for your overall memory and learning because it helps set up the mental associations that prime your curiosity.

It also leads to questions that help motivate and focus your automatic and conscious learning systems.

How do you do a survey? If the resource is a thing (such as a book, course, app, or video), you need to get a sense of it:

- Where's the gold hidden?
- How does the creator want you to learn from or use it?
- What are the main parts and how can you get in and out of them?
- How long will it take to mine what's there?
- What other costs might be involved?

If the resource is a person (such as a coach, mentor, or subject matter expert), identify the boundaries. Ask or find out:

- What is your expertise and background?
- What are your main beliefs about the topics?
- What is the best way to work with you?
- How do you think you can help me learn what I want to learn?
- How long will it take to get to the next level?
- What will be involved in my work and cost, including time with you?

What about an experiential learning resource, like an assignment, a new project, or using a new process or technology? In that case, you'll need to know:

- What capabilities will you be able to develop?
- Who will help and how?
- What support is available to ensure this is an opportunity to learn and not just another job to do?

This also applies to experiences you have already had. Just make the questions past tense. For all types of resources, you can add questions like:

- Where is the gold I want to mine?
- Why should I trust this source?
- Who and what's behind it?
- What will it be possible for me to learn?

## Fit Your Strategy to the Resource

Books, articles, games, simulations, life experiences, workshops, e-learning programs, and work with subject matter experts all have their own logics and structures. Those who practice learning 4.0 have a smart x-ray vision that enables them to see through the surface to the inner structures—the places where the gold is likely to be buried. So, plan to approach any resource knowing what to expect: how it is structured, where to look for what you need, and how to have the best learning experience tailored to the resource at hand.

 Link

Before you go on, take a few minutes to check out Tool 5. Resource-Specific Learning Tips. Use those ideas to help you tailor your techniques to the specific resources you're using. Remember, one size does not fit all.

## Be Present to Learn

One of the most important facts about deliberate learning is that you have to be present to learn! Even your amazing automatic system can't process what you don't bring into your brain. This means that once you are in the learning process itself, a key task is to manage your attention.

Directing, focusing, and sustaining attention is a real challenge for many people today. The natural human tendency is to avoid deliberately focusing on something for a long time, so it takes energy and willpower to deliberately learn. Research shows that interspersed naps, breaks, and aerobic exercise make it easier to pay attention for longer spans of time.

Fortunately, you are more likely to focus on something that you care about, are motivated toward, or that satisfies a question or curiosity. Things that are new also grab your attention because they stand out and engage multiple senses. You are also more likely to pay attention when you believe you are making progress and achieving your goals (remember those dopamine rewards), when you are meeting a need, or when you are working with others on something challenging (think about that oxytocin at work).

Surrounding yourself with white noise also helps attention. It creates stochastic resonance in your brain waves, amplifying the signals between neurons. As mentioned in the previous chapter, this can improve the quality of your learning and memory.[1] However, attempting to multitask splits your attention and reduces your effectiveness; plus, it adds the stress of switching back and forth between tasks. Stress and anxiety, while helpful in very small doses, are distracting, release neuron-damaging cortisol, and even permanently damage the learning parts of your brain.

If you prime your attention to be ready for something new or related to your goals, you are more likely to take in all the important information you need to succeed in your learning journey. Under the right conditions, you can move into a highly efficient and attentive flow state, where you can get lost in a 100 percent attentive interaction with your learning resource.

Attention and concentration are critical for learning. Here is a closer look at the conditions that help you be present to learn.

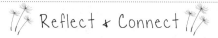

## Reflect + Connect

You must bring information into your brain in order to learn it. Failures in learning are often failures of attention! For example, you won't remember a name you didn't listen to it in the first place. How do you currently support yourself when you want to concentrate?

## Manage Your Physical Energy

Attention is a physiological as well as a mental process. It takes energy, and a lot of it! (Your brain is only 2 percent of your body weight but it uses 20 percent of your energy.) To optimize and focus your energy when you are taking in information, try these simple tips: First, remember to breathe. (How is your breathing right now?) Keep your breathing relaxed; your breaths should move deep into your stomach area. If you feel anxious or stressed, take five breaths in and out very slowly to settle yourself into a centered state. This has positive effects on your heart rate and helps you move into brain wave states that are good for learning.

Define your learning timeframes—from 10 minutes to an hour at a time—and intersperse them with a few minutes of walking around or resting your eyes. Set a timer, starting with five to 10 minute blocks, and take a short break immediately after it goes off. Then as you become accustomed to the practice, lengthen your learning periods. Don't be afraid to stop in the middle of things. Your brain will want to complete its task, so when you come back to learn, you will have a motivation advantage.

If you're tired, take a break or a short nap. Schedule your mining activities for times of day when you are fresh. Alternately, if you can, walk while you are learning or thinking about a problem you need to solve. Have walking meetings if you are talking with an expert or members of a project team. Gentle movement keeps oxygen flowing; the variety of surroundings also helps your brain make more mental associations (so, later if you forget something, think about where you were when you learned it!).

Another technique is to take short but very high-energy exercise breaks. This produces a powerful protein (BDNF; brain-derived neurotrophic factor) that stimulates your neurons to learn while also protecting them from damage.[2]

## Manage Your Motivation

Learning is motivated by questions and curiosity, so keep your questions coming as you learn. In your self-talk, say things like "I wonder what . . . ?" "How would it work if . . . ?" "What does this resource have to say about . . . ," "Why is this method better than . . . ?" Keep your self-talk positive and focused on what you are learning and why.

You should also follow your interests. If you feel your energy waning, find something that is interesting to you even if it is not the most logical area or you don't have the prerequisite knowledge to understand it. When you follow your interests and discover you need more basic knowledge, you will be more motivated to get that knowledge. For example, many years ago when I taught piano lessons, I let my students purchase any music they wanted to play. If they picked out music that was too difficult for them it motivated them to get something easier, work on basics, or practice harder and longer than they would have done otherwise. My students always loved their music, and they outperformed others who had taken lessons for the same amount of time.

Setting little interim goals and rewarding yourself in some way when you reach them is another great way to stay motivated. You'll even get a little burst of dopamine from your reward center when you check something off your to-do list.

An interesting and very powerful technique is to stop your work at a high point of interest and curiosity. It's called the Ziegarnik effect, but you can also call it "save the surprise" learning.[3] Stopping in the middle of a high-interest point primes your brain to want to finish the task. Think about what happens when you put down a mystery novel right before you find out "who dunnit?" You can't wait to start reading again! So, stop, take a break, get some exercise, and come back later. You'll be refreshed, and because your brain has been working undercover to complete the story, you'll enter with a high level of curiosity, motivation, and attention.

## ✲ Reflect ✦ Connect ✲

This may be a good time to stop and take a short break to get the benefit of the Ziegarnik effect.

## Manage and Use Distractions

Some distractions are diversions that you want to eliminate, control, or sideline. But distractions can also be helpful if they draw you further into your learning process or help make it more effective.

Any distraction that requires intense focus and mental processing will disrupt your learning—these are the kinds you need to avoid. Multitasking like texting and trying to do other complicated mental work, high-energy aerobic activity, loud and disturbing sounds, and distracting visual environments can take you off your learning track. These competing tasks take away precious mental energy from the work you want to do. Switching back and forth between tasks also takes energy a lot of energy. Research on multitasking and divided attention is very conclusive about its negative effects. According to one study, people who multitask make 50 percent more mistakes and spend 50 percent more time when learning.[4] This is a very high price to pay!

Some distractions—those that give your brain time to consolidate or that stimulate creative connections—deepen learning. You learned in chapter 1 that a big part of your learning process happens automatically in your brain's automatic system. Distractions can assist these undercover learning activities by giving your conscious brain a rest, as well as opening opportunities for creative thinking and learning you didn't plan.

Distractions can also take the form of new calls to learn. For example, in a project management course you may be learning some methods that challenge your preferred leadership style when an emotional reaction suddenly distracts you. You feel your stomach tighten up and your breathing changes. You feel tired and you begin to think about this evening's dinner rather than the new project management method. It's possible that you're just tired and need a break. But these distractions may also be a sign of a deeper learning opportunity. They may be a new call to learn, challenging you to look at your leadership style and calling you to make a deeper identity and behavior shift than you planned.

Deliberately inserting distractions into your learning process is another tool. For example, use daydreaming to imagine yourself using new skills in real life. You can also let yourself daydream without a purpose for a few minutes. Because your brain is already primed for your learning task, thoughts that appear may contain relevant, although surprising, insights and solutions. Or you can switch to an entirely different task. Go for a walk or a run to give your unconscious system some time to process what you have taken in or interrupt your learning at a high point to activate the Ziegarnik effect.

Of course, pulling yourself out of the learning situation will only help you if the new information has made it through your senses, past your thalamus and amygdala, and into your hippocampus and other parts of your brain. Distractions only add value if they are part of your mine for gold process, not its replacement. If the seeds for new learning have been planted in your brain, then distractions can provide a kind of consciousness air cover while your automatic system prepares your neurons (where the physical changes for learning happen) for longer-term change.

 Link

If you haven't already read chapter 1 and this information about the brain sounds interesting, consider circling back to read or scan it!

Using distractions to support subconscious information processing is an important step that we will return to in the next chapter. Distractions are an inevitable part of learning—what's out there always mixes with what's in here. And this always happens in the present moment, which has features of its own (your momentary feelings, the environment around you, the people you are with) that become part of your process.

## Go for Flow

Have you ever experienced flow? This is a state where you get so absorbed in what you are doing, where you feel so energized and even "high," that you lose track of time. You're usually doing something you enjoy or are curious about. Flow happens when you are challenged but not overwhelmed: It's the intersection of high interest and just enough capability.

Flow is a state of fascination where your brain is highly efficient, operating with very little oversight from your conscious system, except to begin the process with questions and curiosity. Neuroscientists have discovered that when you are in flow, the part of your brain that normally expends a lot of energy monitoring, planning, and evaluating your behavior slows down. Your brain focuses most of its energy on the learning task itself, with faster beta waves giving way to borderline alpha waves of daydreaming and theta waves of creativity. The release of performance enhancing neurochemicals also increases.[5] All your mental energy goes to pure attention; your ability to recognize deeper patterns and think creatively increases, and your information processing speeds up.

So, how do you get into flow?[6] You need to make sure that what you are learning is challenging, but not so challenging that your skill level isn't up to it. Immerse yourself in your curiosity about the subject, pursuing answers to questions beginning with who, what, when, where, why, and how. Try beginning your learning in a place of high interest, even if it is not a logical place to start. Your chances of flow also increase when you work with others to answer fascinating and challenging questions that relate to results, situations, and goals that you all care about.

## Set Up Mind-Mirroring Notes

In this mine for gold phase, start connecting new information to what you already know to help reorganize some of the neuron associations in the vast connectome network that is your brain. You can support this process by taking notes. Think of notes as mirrors of the connections you want to make in your brain to help store and ultimately retrieve what you want to remember. Creating mind-mirroring notes also engages you physically, and creates additional neural pathways to support your learning process.

---

### ✿ Link ✿

There are several formats for taking notes in Tool 3. Mind-Note Formats.

---

However, to get these benefits, be sure that you go beyond rote recording what's coming to you. Create pictures that show how the new information is connected to itself and to what you already know. Include information from other sources and your own experiences, and translate what you are learning into more meaningful terms. You can also add future-oriented action ideas, including thoughts about how and when you will use what you are learning. Draw on both the emotional/creative and rational/intellectual part of your brain to bring your imagination and future vision into the process. Note-taking will come up again in the next chapter because it helps you create "learn to last" memories.

## Look for Real Gold

Learning is a conversation with your resources where you continually ask, "What's important for me to learn, and how will I recognize and mine it?" The things you plan to learn—knowledge, skills, and insights that relate to your future vision—are important. But you may also find treasure troves you were not looking for. Be on the lookout for those surprise veins of gold, too.

---

### ✿ Reflect + Connect ✿

Stop for a minute and think about this as deep learning 4.0— where you bring your most intelligent and creative self into your learning process.

---

Here are some gold deposits you might find as you work with your learning resources:

- knowledge, skills, and insights that you are specifically looking for, that broaden your perspective, or that take you on a new path that may be more valuable than the one you are on
- ways of thinking, such as values, perspectives, and world views, that challenge your assumptions and beliefs
- information that triggers creative ideas and solutions for problems that are part of your current learning plan
- material you want to share because it is important to others.

Learning is a beautiful process because it helps satisfy needs and allows you to discover new things. It is important to be clear about what you want, but also open to and curious about surprises.

## Detect Fool's Gold

Not all gold is the real thing. This is true of the information you process.

As you learned in chapter 4, you are constantly being manipulated by information that is intentionally and unintentionally selective, and sometimes even deliberately distorted. And your brain is not an innocent bystander. As you learned in chapter 1, your brain automatically selects and skews information to fit your own worldview. This means that a lot of "fool's gold"—what looks accurate and relevant but isn't—gets through to your short-term memory and then gets filed in your long-term memory. Once there, this fool's gold can affect your intentions, actions, and further learning.

So, there are two challenges here for you as a 4.0 learner: The first is to see through the distortions and biases in the information you process. The second is to be mindful of your own biases and distortions.

This is especially difficult because it requires vigilance and self-awareness, two conditions that take a lot of energy. It is also difficult because of the shear amount of information available to you today: Anyone with a computer and access to the Internet can publish anything they want, for all the world to see. And another consideration: Detecting bias is getting more difficult because big money is being invested in sophisticated methods of information packaging. Powerful people and institutions are now focusing on information selection and packaging because the old methods of social control, such as rewards, punishments, and information secrecy and control, are less effective in today's open information world.

You know it's important to notice bias and distortion in the information you use, but how do you do it? And, how can you detect and manage bias and distortions inside yourself? The answer is, "with difficulty!" But you can't be a transformative 4.0 learner if you don't recognize when you are being manipulated or are distorting the truth yourself.

## Expect Bias

It's difficult not to embed information in a point of view. Some scientific and mathematical information are exceptions: $1 + 1 = 2$, $10 \times 10 = 100$. Two atoms of hydrogen and one atom of oxygen make up a molecule of water. Statements of observable and immediate cause and effect are also exceptions: "I knock over a full cup of coffee and it spills on the floor." But most of the knowledge, skill, and perspectives you learn are not so cut and dry. For example, did the executive's downsizing decision cause the performance improvement or was it caused by the new product that launched in the same timeframe? Or did both play a role? The world is infinitely complex and events often have many causes that may not be closely connected in space and time. Because you're only dealing with a part of reality, what you see and hear and learn is always selective and incomplete.

This means that the issue is not whether information is biased and selective. It always will be. The issue is whether you have the wherewithal to recognize that bias. As a 4.0 learner, you need to be ready with questions like, what is the point of view or bias here? What's behind this point of view? How is it expressed? What biases are affecting my learning now? How can I remain free to choose, to change, and to act?

## Bring Bias Into the Open

There are many ways to tackle bias as you mine for gold. The following sections take a look at a few different methods.

### Say the Perspectives

Get an early fix on points of view, both yours and theirs. Find out what you can about the people who packaged the information and are presenting it. What is their background? What are their affiliations? What makes them credible in this area? What do they want to gain or achieve by providing this information? Who might have points of view that differ or conflict with what you will get in this resource? What is your current view of this topic? What might other people see as your biases and values? When you think of this topic, what might "push your emotional buttons?"

## Imagine the Learning Resource on a Credibility Continuum

At one end of the continuum is information that is as complete and free of bias as possible. Then there is partial information, which is selected to support a point of view or way of acting. Farther along the continuum is misinformation, which is information that is unintentionally misleading and distorted. Next is deliberate disinformation, selected to intentionally manipulate your thinking and behavior in a way that supports a personal agenda. At the far end of the scale is propaganda—information that intends to influence large groups to support a political agenda or cause (Figure 9-1). Be aware of the resource's likely position on the continuum before you decide what you want to learn from it.[7]

### Figure 9-1. The Credibility Continuum

| Information | Partial Information | Misinformation | Disinformation | Propaganda |
|---|---|---|---|---|
| Includes all relevant info; biases acknowledged | Supports a point of view; biases acknowledged | Unintentionally misleading; biases denied | Intentionally misleading; biases denied | Information is manipulated to influence groups to support a cause or belief; biases denied |

# Watch Out for Fool's Gold Techniques

You frequently deal with selective information, viewpoints, and bias when you learn. These are inevitable in an information overloaded world. Writers, course developers, game designers, and coaches have points of view, and they use influence techniques to share them. That's OK, and you may even choose the resources because of their perspectives and biases. However, viewpoints, biases, and distortions can also take you places you would not deliberately choose to go. So, be on the lookout for attempts to sway your thinking. Take on your full learning power to decide whether you are being influenced by the selective information you encounter.

Be prepared for the following common influence techniques as you mine for gold. Notice how they take advantage of your brain's tendencies to draw quick conclusions, simplify information, and filter what's out there through your emotions and current mental models and mindsets.

## Just Like Me

When somebody just like you endorses an idea or behavior, it will be more appealing to you. For example, if you see yourself as a leader, your company could try to influence your opinion about a new initiative by having a leader you identify with talk about the importance of the change.

## Pairing

Sometimes new information is connected to something that stimulates your positive or negative emotions. Think of the fierce, sleek tiger that sits next to a sports car. Or the new management technique that has a ninja symbol, compared with the defeated warrior symbol on the technique it is replacing.

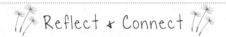

### Reflect + Connect

Think of an example of each fool's gold technique to embed your understanding so you will recognize them when they happen.

## Simple Cause and Effect

When two things happen close together, it's tempting to think that one caused the other. This tendency to jump to conclusions about causes is hard wired by many eons of evolution. But, remember, the world is dynamic and complex. When somebody says "this caused that" step back and ask whether other factors are at work. Would the statement would be true if you looked at more examples (in other words, if you did a statistical study)? For example, say an economic downturn happens at the same time as you lose a client. It is easy to blame the downturn. But could your client have left because of a problem it had with one of your products or your relationship?

## Priming

Priming, often called *framing*, occurs when an initial suggestion or statement influences how you interpret what follows. For example, you're choosing a place to go on vacation and pick up a travel brochure with a cover photo of a beautiful white sand beach. You sign up for one of the vacation packages listed in the brochure, expecting that the beach you choose will be like the one in the photo.

## Exposure

The more you are exposed to an idea or practice, the more palatable and acceptable it may become, even if it is initially unpleasant. This is the bias behind the idea that "all publicity is good publicity."

## Loss Aversion

Potential losses carry more emotional weight than potential gains. For example, a statement that you will lose your bonus if you don't change a behavior will be more inherently motivating than a statement that you can gain the same amount by changing your behavior.

## Appeal to Fear

Your brain is set up to mainline negative information because negatives are equated with threats. This also applies to negative words. So, when you hear words like job loss, evaluation, autocratic, and failure, your attention increases. Politicians know the power of fear and anger, and often use that to rally people to their beliefs and solutions. It's a powerful motivator that trustworthy sources as well as those with hidden agendas use. Just make sure you see through it when it is being used on you.

## Stories Over Statistics

Personal and individual stories, even if the example is an outlier and exception, will sway your opinion and actions more than statistics that may be far more valid. For example, a story about a single family who has lost everything in a storm will have more impact than a dry statistic about the number of families affected. This is why people focus more on the stories than on the data when they want to influence your attitudes and behavior. What you should be asking is, "How typical is this one instance?"

## Hindsight

Watch out for statements that blame or praise people after the fact using 20/20 hindsight about what worked and didn't work. It is easier to see what led to an outcome once it's already happened and to judge the participants from that perspective, rather than looking at the situation as it was when the actions occurred. Better to use hindsight to learn lessons than to pronounce judgments.

The movie *Sully*, about the commercial airline pilot who landed his plane in the Hudson River after a flock of birds flew into the engine, shows this in action. In hindsight, it looked as though this pilot had time to revert to a nearby airport and avoid landing in the Hudson River. However, when the real-time conditions were examined, it became clear that his decision to land in the water saved lives and was the only viable option.[8]

## Simplification

Your brain prefers simpler solutions to complex ones because the simpler ones require less attention and deliberate energy. This makes it is easy to be conned by straightforward answers to complex problems. Many problems and goals require longer-term commitment and multiple changes (small and large) to achieve. Watch for statements that make something complex seem too easy.

For example, think about all the ways you learn to give feedback when you take a communication skills program. When you're back in the real world, which is more complex, you have to deal with power differences and your own fears of rejection. You're likely to fall back on the simpler techniques you've been using forever because that's easier than trying to remember the new information you learned in the workshop.

## Narrow Framing

Parents use narrow framing when they offer their children a choice between peanut butter or jelly, even if there are many other snack-time possibilities. What you read or hear may make it seem like there are only one or two solutions to a problem. That is rarely the case. If you are presented with "either/or" choices but aren't satisfied with your options, don't be afraid to step outside the box to see if there are other ways to go. For example, someone tells you that you either have to take a course on Internet security or work with the security consultant. (Think: Is this really an either/or situation?)

## Ego Bias

It's a human tendency to see ourselves as rational and others as biased. This happens because we evaluate our own behavior based on our intentions (which make sense to us), but we evaluate others based on their actual behavior.[9] This self, or ego, bias reduces the accuracy of your self-perception. It also affects your ability to accept feedback in a learning situation.

These are all biasing methods that can affect your learning goal. Sometimes the effects are positive because they steer you toward positive learning results. But others may serve someone else's ulterior motives rather than your best learning interests. And don't forget that your own biases may keep you from stretching beyond what you already know and believe. Both are dangerous in today's rapidly changing world.

It's up to you to recognize when biasing effects are at work and to choose whether it is in your best interest to go along with them. Do the biases reflect viewpoints that you want to adopt? Will they be helpful in your learning and change process? Or will you reject the distortions and think in another way?

## Equip Yourself for Deep Learning

It's impossible for the information in any learning resource to be pure and objective. Even scientists admit that they cannot conduct bias-free experiments because experimenters and observers are always part of the story. This is why it's so important to look below the surface. But there are other reasons to dive beneath the surface of your learning material.

Important deep and subtle learning lessons are often buried under the information, stories, games, and other experiences that make up your learning situation. So look for recurring themes and patterns that can help you understand the material at a deeper level. Think of these themes and patterns as deeply buried veins of real gold.

Humans have a natural ability for deep learning—for seeing patterns in chaos. Think of when you first discovered the concept of a "truck" when you were a kid. You internalized a pattern that let you recognize many kinds of trucks, whether in books, in your toy box, or on the street. "Truck" is a pattern. As an adult, you recognize more subtle patterns that lead you to say things like, "This reporter's remarks usually favor conservatives" or "Sometimes you win big when you let others win" or "In all these stories of personal change, failure has stimulated learning and later success." By seeing patterns, you also help your brain's associative process, which is something that helps you store and retrieve memories.

## Deep Learning as X-Ray Vision

When you do deep learning, you use a kind of x-ray vision to see through the information you are processing. You look for what seems to be true across many situations. Statisticians and big data scientists have ways of doing this for some information. They crunch the numbers to determine whether a hurricane will pass over cities. And experts are experts because they can immediately distinguish what is important in a situation from what is not by detecting deeper patterns and rules.

When you do deeper learning, look for rules that seem to apply across many situations. These rules may take the form of "if X is happening, then Y will likely happen." They may also take the form of a mental model: "In these kinds of situations, it is important to pay attention to these factors."

Another aspect of deep learning is the ability to detect underlying values and paradigms of thought. A paradigm is a thinking framework. For example, scientists have believed since the 1700s that people are fundamentally rational. They ignored the influence of people's inner world and the fact that our behavior can't be manipulated rationally as though we are machines. Today, thanks to neuroscience and developments in psychology, we know that human behavior is influenced by more than rational arguments. This new science view underlies the thinking in this book.

## Deep Learning as Uber-Mastery

Deep learning is a big theme in artificial intelligence today. Big data experts are using new technologies to find trends and patterns that distinguish spam and fraud from legitimate information on the Internet. To do this, they crunch massive amounts of data and program computers to detect deeper patterns of cause and effect, including patterns they weren't looking for. You have this same ability to crunch massive amounts of data and see patterns. But how?

The answer explains the difference between experts and novices. Experts recognize the deeper patterns at work in their expertise area. Think of a chess champion. She looks at a chess board and sees patterns of moves that others don't see. A hotel expert can look at performance data across hotels and zero in on problem areas that are totally invisible to others. A cook tastes an appetizer and knows immediately which herbs are out of proportion.

Sometimes the experts aren't totally aware of what they know because they have tacit knowledge that is not explicit. Your role as a 4.0 learner is to discover the deeper patterns that make them experts. Watch them work, ask them to describe what they are thinking as they solve problems, or ask them directly—"What are the key things you look for when you are making a decision or solving a problem?" "What is the mental model that tells you what to look for?" "What were you thinking when you did this?"

Look below the surface of the information you take in and the exercises you do. What are the most important features of the situation? Are there any patterns that occur in similar situations? What should you look for in the future when you're in a situation to use what you've learned? How can you can be like the chess master looking at her chess board—seeing patterns and options rather than pawns and knights?

This deep learning calls for a more sophisticated type of learning journey than just looking at the surface. When you discover patterns and general decision and action rules, you'll set up a powerful associative structure for remembering what you are learning, which will help you set up your learning to last.

You don't need a PhD to be able to go under the surface to see values and patterns in the learning resources you are using. You already have this capability; remember the truck? You've been detecting patterns for most of your life.

## Mine for Gold, in Brief

The mine for gold part of your learning journey is where your brain meets the learning material. The challenge is to internalize this new information so you can turn it into enduring knowledge, skills, values, and creative ideas for the future.

## Link

Use the Practice 5: Mine for Gold template in Tool 2 or at www. learning40.com/unstoppable to help you implement this fifth learning 4.0 practice.

However, before you can start you have to pull what you need out of the information resources you are using. Resources, like people, have different personalities and ways they are wired, so tailor your approach to your resource. Tool 5. Resource-Specific Strategy Tips will help you do this.

As you mine for gold, be aware of how the information is organized and packaged to influence you. Make sure that what you're learning is real gold, which is reliable and trustworthy, rather than fool's gold, which is either intended to manipulate you based on hidden agendas or not defensible and trustworthy.

There are huge rewards for discovering the deeper patterns, models, frameworks, values, and lessons that are often buried inside the learning experience. Your goal should be to discover the deeper secrets that experts know—the ones that enable them to see through to the heart of issues, and to know when and where to use any new knowledge or skills you are learning.

By mining for real gold, both at the surface and deeper down, you can bring the best and most useful information into your brain's short-term memory.

Now that you have these new ideas and information, what do you do with them? The next step in your learning journey is making sure that the information in your short-term memory is available when you need it in the future. You need to learn to last. That's the focus of the next chapter.

# 10

## Learn to Last

This chapter will help you master the four targets of any learning path: Remember, develop skills, update your beliefs and attitudes, and stimulate your creativity. You can use learning 4.0 techniques to achieve all of them, but there are also special steps to take for each. These key practices will help you get where you want to go. You'll learn how to:

- Improve your memory.
- Develop a skill or habit.
- Upgrade your attitudes and beliefs based on new information.
- Use your learning activities to stimulate creative ideas and solutions.

In chapter 9, you learned how to process different kinds of information. But simply bringing new information into your brain doesn't mean that you're learning. The initial traces in your brain are very weak; you can't yet count on finding your new knowledge, skills, attitudes, or creative ideas when you need them. From a brain perspective, this new information is residing in your short-term memory (a critical first step), but your neurons' new structures are unstable and the changes to your brain's vast network of linked memories have only just begun.

By this point in your learning journey, you've mined the gold, but it is still in its raw form. Now you need to turn it into jewelry you can wear. So, how do you turn information into learning that lasts? The answer requires another partnership between your conscious and automatic systems. What they do together depends on the types of learning outcomes you want and how difficult your learning challenge is. There are four possible learning outcomes you can have:

- Knowledge is information you can recall when you need it.
- Skills and habits are things you can do when a situation calls for it. They might be mental, physical, interpersonal, or internal to your own way of dealing with life events and needs.

- Attitudes and beliefs are the value-laden lenses you use when you interpret things and decide what is important.
- Creative ideas are new connections you invent because you are in a learning mode.

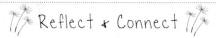

## Reflect + Connect

This chapter contains many tips and insights. Before you go on, prime your attention with a little self-test: What learning techniques do you think you will find in this chapter? Make a list of these. Then, at the end of the chapter compare your list with what you find here.

# General Ways to Learn to Last

You've learned how to bring new information into your hippocampus to launch changes in your neurons. But if you want to make sure your learning lasts, there's still more to do. Some learning techniques apply to any of the four learning results, while others are specific to developing knowledge, skills, attitudes, or creative outcomes. Let's look first at learning techniques that apply to all four learning outcomes: refine your future-pull, delegate to your automatic system, interleave different learning activities, link to real-life situations, and learn with others.

## Refine Your Future-Pull

Before you begin to consolidate your learning, take a few minutes to think about the outcomes you want. Breathe deeply and reimagine the future you want to create for yourself. Think about the benefits of success and what you will lose if you don't learn. Create a sense of the future that is motivating enough to pull you toward it.

Now, immerse yourself in that future. See yourself using your learning and reaping the benefits in accomplishments, enjoyment, greater impact, sense of personal power, and ability to do what you value. This will tell your automatic system to keep this learning goal working for you unconsciously, even while you are sleeping. A vision you can feel will also help motivate you for the learning adventure that lies ahead.

# Delegate to Your Automatic System

Most of your learning-related activity goes incognito when you daydream, take breaks, and sleep.[1] Try taking some of the following actions to increase your benefit from this activity:

- Right before you go to bed, think about what you want to remember or mentally replay the skill you are learning. While you sleep, your brain closes off the outside world and clears out the day's unneeded and unprocessed information. It also continues to consolidate new neuron structures and connections, indexing them and shifting the new information from the short-term processing center in your hippocampus to more permanent storage in your cortex. One theory is that while you sleep your brain will give priority to information that you have tagged as important.[2] So be sure to tell yourself what you want to remember before you turn off the lights.

- If you want to learn something difficult, do it right after a good sleep or after a period of aerobic exercise. In the first case, your brain will be rested and open for more processing. In the second, you will have more oxygen and endorphins to fuel your energy for learning.

- Use the Ziegarnik effect.[3] This happens when you interrupt your learning at a high point of curiosity and interest, then come back later with high motivation to find out what happens next. Stopping at a high point creates tension in your subconscious that keeps what you are learning at the top of your automatic system's to-do list.

- Space your learning instead of trying to do everything at once. Spend some time in active, conscious learning (mining for gold and doing things to learn to last) but give your automatic system time to do its undercover work. If you are working on a complex learning goal, consider actively learning something, putting it into your own words as notes or self-talk, doing a quick review before bed, and then giving yourself a day or two before you think about it again. In your next session, review some of the older information as well as new material. Then repeat! The secret is to learn a little, give yourself some space, and then think about it again in increasingly distant time periods.[4] Give it a try!

## Interleave Different Activities

*Interleaving* is a new term from cognitive science that has important implications for your learning. It means sequencing diverse but related activities in an irregular way to increase efficiency and create multiple memory pathways.[5] For example, imagine that you are learning a new sales approach. You read a manual or engage in an online learning task for 15 or 20 minutes. Then you shift to planning how you will use what you learn on your next sales call. Then you take some notes on the key ideas. You may also discuss what you've learned with a colleague. The idea is to work in small, diverse chunks. This helps keep your attention fresh and gives different neuron groups a chance to create multiple connections that support your learning process.

Or, think about learning how to play tennis. You'll spend a chunk of time just hitting the ball back and forth. Then you'll practice your serve. Then you'll watch a video showing when professionals run to the net and when they don't. This works for a better general physical workout, too. You alternate strength and endurance training. You interleave.

It may seem that moving from one method to another without completing any of the tasks at one time might slow down your learning process. But by alternating among the different pathways, you accelerate your overall progress. It also ensures recovery and rest time, which is particularly important when you're learning how to do something that involves physical muscles, making continued high performance and ongoing improvements possible.

## Link to Real-Life Situations

Eventually you will bring what you've learned into your day-to-day life. At that point, your new knowledge, skills, and attitudes will become indelibly associated with real situations. Early in your learning process, find ways to prepare your environment and the people around you for any changes you will make. This will help jump-start any habit changes you're trying to make that others may inadvertently obstruct. For example, how would a new management or problem-solving technique affect others in your work environment? It's better to enlist their interest and help early on, rather than deal with resistance later.

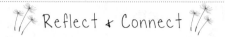

## Reflect & Connect

This is a good place to stop, do a quick review, and maybe jot down some notes. Consider using one of the note-taking formats from Tool 3. Mind-Note Formats. Or, just select a few techniques you want to use soon.

## Learn With Others

When you learn with other people you get many benefits. You translate what you're learning into your own words and look at it in new ways, which will help you create multiple associative memories. When you talk about your goals you strengthen the future-pull, and others will be drawn in to support and help you sustain focus and motivation. Being with other people also increases the amount of oxytocin (a pleasure chemical) in your body. And, research shows that working with others on a challenging project helps put you into a flow state, which is a heightened state of learning efficiency.

You can get these social learning benefits whether you are working with a team on a learning project or just giving and getting moral support from others who are not directly involved but are there for support.

In any learning situation, plan to refine your future-pull; use sleep, breaks, and spacing; interleave different activities; link with real-life situations; and learn with other people. These will help your learning last, whatever your purpose.

## How to Remember

The first of four possible learning outcomes is information you remember. It's common for adults to say, "I can't remember things," or "My memory isn't as good as it used to be." And sometimes it is hard to recall information; as you move through life, your neurons make more and more connections, so sorting through all the possibilities can be extremely challenging. However, never forget the magnificence of your brain as a memory machine. If you are discouraged about your learning journey, just step back and imagine the 90 billion neurons and 100 trillion connections that are sparking inside you right now.

Just think about how much you remember without trying. You see a child cry and wonder if she is hungry, cold, or wet—interpretations grounded in your memories. You work on a sales problem and unconsciously use your knowledge of sales pipelines to interpret where to focus—again drawing on what you already know. You recognize a friend across the road because your brain matches what you see with your memories of him. You work on an engineering problem and think about several possible causes—again, you make complex connections. Every day and every minute that you engage with the world, you're pulling information from your memory without conscious effort.

But sometimes you can't access the facts, names, concepts, or ideas that you thought you knew. What causes you to forget these things?[6] Educators and neuroscientists have some suggestions:

- You didn't forget; you simply never knew it in the first place! That is, you weren't present to learn.
- Your memory never completely stabilized. Your neurons didn't change to support the new information, perhaps because of interference from a competing and stronger idea.
- You didn't use the memory or store it for the long term. If you don't strengthen the storage and retrieval paths in your brain network, memories can "decay."
- The memory was not connected with anything important to you, so it was cleared out as junk while you were sleeping.
- It wasn't interesting enough, so your curiosity wasn't activated to a high enough level to release supporting neurochemicals like dopamine.

## Link

As you learned in chapter 1, to remember something you must be able to both store and retrieve information in your brain. This happens naturally, but you can make the process more focused and reliable.

Nobody can say what happens for certain in your learning brain, but there is agreement about a few things. You remember better when:

- An idea has vivid and multisensory brain associations.
- You stimulate a forget-then-retrieve cycle (which strengthens the pathways to and from what you want to remember).
- You use active reflection.
- You go for deeper patterns and connections.

## Make Vivid Connections

Do you know anyone who remembers everyone's name and can recite long lists of things from memory? It's easy to do if you learn how to make vivid associations. Start with a person's name—actually hear it in the first place. Remember, you have to be present to learn! Then, as a memory technique, associate it with something vivid that reminds you of their name: John Poole; see him swimming in a pool of purple water. Lisa McGinn; think of her drinking a Guinness while she holds a lease on her house. Do this while looking closely at their faces and making connections. You should also continue to do periodic review sweeps of the room, observing who is there and reminding yourself of their names and your connections. Some people even keep a small notebook. A lot of work? Yes, but you can turn it into a habit. Rewards? Definitely!

There are simple techniques for remembering lists of things, too. A very useful one is the anchor list: Use a sequence of images that you always use to help you remember (anchor) items. For example, think, "1" is a bun, "2" is a shoe, "3" is a tree, "4" is a door, "5" is a hive, "6" is sticks, "7" is heaven, "8" is a gate, "9" is a vine, "10" is a hen. To remember to go to the post office, call a friend, finish a report, or get groceries, imagine the post office full of buns, your friend wearing big old fashioned shoes, a tree with pages of your report hanging from it, a door trying to close on a bag of groceries—you get the picture. Outrageous? Yes! But it works. The brain loves associations, and it loves associations that appeal to multiple senses—especially vision.

But how do you make associations for more abstract and complex information? The same principle applies, although the "1 is a bun" technique is too simplistic for most important memory tasks. The secret is always to make connections through your other senses and modes of processing.

## Translate the Information Into Another Sensory Mode— With Emphasis on the Visual

One way to make connections is to create notes that graphically show how ideas relate to one another; images that mirror the connections you want in your brain. Some call these concept maps or mind maps, where you draw connections among ideas.[7] Develop the first draft of your map when you do the initial survey of the knowledge you want to master (see chapter 9).

Note that when you create visual connections, the influence on your memory is especially powerful because more of your brain is dedicated to processing sight than any other sense. But don't forget your other senses. Talk to yourself about what you are learning—use your own words. If there is a way to link a smell, make that association. Smells have a direct channel into your brain because they don't have to go through your thalamus and hippocampus (think about the smells that immediately remind you of home).

## Alternate From the Big Picture to Details

Do a survey that tells you a bit about the major points and structure of your learning resource. This is helpful because it allows you to periodically ask yourself, "Where do these ideas I am learning fit into the bigger picture?" Going back and forth between the outline and the details helps your brain create its own structure for filing what you are learning. You can use mind maps and other visual notes to help you do this.

## Move Around When You Learn

The impact is subtle, but working in multiple environments creates connections that may be valuable later. (For example, "I was sitting under that big tree when I learned this method.") This includes walking while you think and integrate ideas. Light exercise also keeps your oxygen levels up, which increases your ability to pay attention.

## Tell a Story About Yourself in the Future

Your brain continually makes up stories about what you experience, so use this tendency to help you learn. Be very specific about where, when, and the people around. The more concrete you make your image, the more likely you will remember when you need to retrieve the information.

## Activate Your Emotional and Creative Self

Turn what you are learning into something that will engage your more intuitive and feeling side. One way is to use metaphors. Here's an example that applies to what you are learning in this book about being a 4.0 learner:

- **If this book were an animal, what would it be?** A dolphin; it's intelligent, operating above and below the surface, sometimes playful, and an enduring species.
- **What car would this book be?** A luxury truck; it's complex, a reliable workhorse, and sleek but with a lot under the hood.
- **What country?** Any democracy that has a beautiful countryside and cities. It's a democracy because it promotes high personal power and responsibility, it's a country because it honors the emotional and automatic part of you, and it's a city because it honors the rational and conscious part of you.
- **What travel destination is it like?** Any place that combines rational city structures with the more organic world of the wilderness.

Just use your imagination and use one image to create associations that will strengthen your memory, including your feelings about what you are learning.

## Talk With Others About What You Are Learning

This helps put new information into your own words and creates a situation where others' questions can help you dive deeper into the ideas and issues. Conversations also create new associative pathways to add to the 100 trillion connections already in your connectome.

## Teach Somebody Else

There is nothing more powerful for memory consolidation than preparing to help others learn something. Why? Because in doing so, you'll discover quickly what you don't understand and develop questions and an urgency to learn. When you look for deeper patterns and associations so that you can explain the ideas in an understandable way, you prepare to make links to the real world of action. Teaching someone else, or simply imagining that you're teaching someone else, is a great way to create retrievable memories of your own.

## Test Yourself

Testing yourself before, during, and after you learn something is a great way to cement the information in your memory. Step back and think about or record what you know about a subject before you learn. Do a quick survey of the resource you are using and turn the section titles into questions. For example, this book says that 4.0 learners understand how the brain learns. You could test yourself on what you know about how your brain works before you read the chapter on your learning brain. Then, after reading the chapter, you could repeat the process. These pre- and post-tests focus your attention and consolidate your learning. They turn the process into a kind of game where curiosity and high engagement help to release neurochemicals that will assist your learning process.

### Reflect + Connect

Before you leave this section on making vivid connections, try using one of these techniques to help you remember what you are learning right now!

## Forget, So You Can Remember

There are two important sides to the memory story. First you create the memory in your brain. Then you have to be able to find it when you need it. The conventional view is that forgetting is an enemy in this process, but it can be a friend. By forgetting and then remembering, you strengthen your neural pathways for finding the information. And you also create more connections each time you remember.

When you try to remember something that you think you forgot, you put new energy into the memory. Think about it. When you search for that lost idea you probably use several memory triggers. Once you find it, all these new associations—including the connection with your current need—are now linked to that memory. This is true even if you have to go back to the learning resource to rediscover what you were looking for. When you try to remember it in the future, the memory will be stronger and there will be even more ways to find it.[8]

This is why repetition works: By repeating and reviewing important information, you strengthen mental associations while also creating new ones. You use forgetting to help you remember!

## Take Time to Reflect

If you want to reliably remember, then plan to interleave reflection with action. One reason some of these memory techniques work is that they require you to reflect—to step back in wonder and talk with yourself and others about what you are learning—in words that matter to you and your life.[9]

Admittedly, it is difficult to take time for reflection and deeper learning in today's fast-paced world, where action is highly prized and reflection looks like laziness. If you want to remember better though, you must make time for reflection. How can you do it?

- **Do a self-test before you dive in.** Ask yourself, "What do I know about the topics and situations I am about to encounter?" or "What suggestions do I think I will find in this section?" By answering the latter question, you create a useful tension between your guess about the content and what is in the section. Even if your guess is "wrong," it increases your curiosity and attention. (Don't blame me, it's your quirky brain at work!)[10] Before you started this section, I asked you to think about the learning techniques you thought you'd find here. This is a kind of pretest that can stimulate your curiosity, set up for connections between what you know and the new ideas here, and generally support your memory process.
- **Do a self-test immediately after you have processed chunks of information.** What did you discover and why is it important to you? This helps strengthen both the memory and your ability to retrieve it.
- **Practice critical reflection.** Turn new ideas over in your mind and look for deeper assumptions and connections. Connect the new information with what you agree and disagree with. Notice when your own emotional reactions and challenges to your current thinking and self-image threaten to derail deeper learning. In other words, step outside yourself and your assumptions. This additional information processing will make the information more memorable.

As one adult learning researcher points out, "You don't actually learn from experience . . . you learn from reflection on experience. You can go through life having experiences and learn nothing. Something may stick, but it's incidental learning" that may or may not be useful to you.[11]

Taking time to reflect ranks with being present to learn as the two most important practices for learning mastery. You must engage in these or your learning will not stick.

## Look for Themes and Patterns

It's common to focus on facts and ideas when you want to remember information. However, as a 4.0 learner you will look for something deeper—if you find it, you will remember much more. But, what is the "it"? Look for deeper patterns and mental models that organize the information. Again, think of the chess master who sees patterns on the board that others don't see. Think about the weather expert who can look at information about pressure, humidity, seasons, and the jet stream, and see the pattern of a just-building storm. Think about all the emotions you go through when someone close to you leaves or dies. There is a pattern to these emotions—denial, anger, bargaining, depression, and acceptance—called the grief cycle.[12] Understanding this deeper pattern helps you make sense out of (organize) the thousands of reactions you have in a loss situation.

This book offers mental models to use as you process information. The process is both rational and nonrational, deliberate and automatic; your journey can take three paths (in the moment, toward a goal, retroactive) and it draws on seven learning 4.0 practices. You'll also find new mental models related to how learning resources are structured and how you can use the learning 4.0 practices as a framework in team learning and helping others learn.

### Reflect

There are four factors of the learning landscape, seven learning 4.0 practices, and three paths to follow when you learn.

When you take time to envision and map out underlying mental models or frameworks, you set up a structure for storing more details. It is a terrific memory technique—one that is well worth your time!

## Summary of How to Remember

To retain what you learn, you need to be sure the memories are stored in your brain and that you can retrieve them when you need them. If you want to remember, it's not enough to just process the information (mine for gold). You need to take the extra steps (Figure 10-1).

### Figure 10-1. Techniques for Remembering

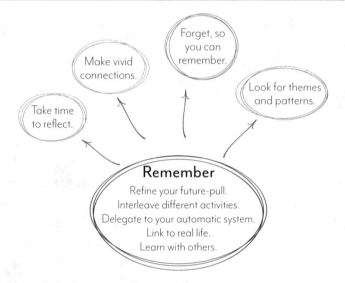

Plan a 50/50 split of your time: 50 percent taking information in and 50 percent processing it in the ways described in this section. If you don't do this, then don't blame memory problems on your age or the complexity of life. The real reason will be that you didn't take time to properly store what you've learned. You are in charge of what you learn, so take on the mantle of 4.0 learner. Wake up your prefrontal cortex and put it to work using the techniques in this section. You will significantly improve your memory by doing this.

# How to Develop Skills and Habits

Skills and habits are the second kind of learning outcome you can target. Some skills and habits are *cognitive* or *mental*: You learn a new problem analysis technique, a creative thinking method, or a way to process orders in a retail warehouse. Some are *physical*: You learn to play a sport, assemble parts, fly an airplane, or perform a type of surgery. Others are *interpersonal*: You learn new ways to give and receive feedback, handle conflict, or conduct an interview. Or you may develop *personal* skills: Manage anger, deal with anxiety, or manage your time. This section focuses on techniques that will help develop any skill or automate any habit.

## Reflect + Connect

Before you read on, do a self-test: What skill and habit change techniques do you think you will find in this section?

A key goal for developing any skill is to become so proficient that it becomes largely automatic—a new habit. However, it often takes time to become proficient in the skill. Sometimes, the new skill bumps into a stubborn habit, or it requires you to show up in the world in a different way. When you try to change, you may even uncover fears that your old habit patterns kept under wraps. For example, a person attempting to develop a new anger management skill discovers that his anger was a mask for his insecurity. Now his challenge is to do something about the insecurity!

## About Habits

You know that you have a habit if you keep doing the same things regardless of the consequences. (This applies to everything from smoking to child-rearing to leadership practices.) Your brain likes habits. They are patterns of behavior that are automatic and save energy. They don't require you to think through all the steps or even to worry about outcomes. Your habit frees your conscious attention to focus on other things.

Habits are helpful and essential, but there is a downside: They can be very resistant to change. To modify or replace them, you have to override automatic responses that are grounded in hardwired neuron connections. Then you need to reprogram the connections between the situations that trigger the habit and the new actions you want to take. This often requires a lot of conscious effort—to recognize when to do something new, to stop your automatic reaction, and then to energize yourself to do something different!

How can you develop new skills, even when it means replacing very persistent habits? Try these techniques: Be a novice for a while, use checklists and flow patterns, use perceptual learning, and support yourself through plateaus and valleys.

## Be a Novice for a While

You will develop a new skill more quickly if you are willing to be a beginner for a while. As a beginner, try some of these techniques.

### Break It Down

Break the skill or habit into parts and practice each in a low-intensity situation until you are comfortable with each part. In fact, practice beyond your comfort point. If you are learning a new way to communicate, spend several days just practicing listening and feeding back what you hear. If you are learning a new golf stroke, focus on your stance for a few games, before moving on to your backswing. Realize that you are reprogramming muscles and neuron connections. You need to help your brain see the triggering situations as signals to do something different, and then make the new practices strong enough to override the old. This is the way master musicians practice new pieces—slow and steady, one part at a time. This speeds up their ability to play the music at will.

### Follow a Script for a While

Entrench new patterns using a checklist or step-by-step approach. Even if you think you can take shortcuts, don't do it until you have mastered the steps outlined by people with more experience. There will be time to veer from the expert path later once you have mastered the basic steps. You may discover that the scripted way has benefits you would have rejected before you understood the new methods.[13]

### Watch, Work With, and Imitate an Expert

You can entrench new skills by osmosis—that is, by watching an expert perform the skill and imagining yourself executing it at the same time. This is an active observation approach that athletes use. They mentally practice, feeling their muscles move and imagining success, as they watch the movements of the best players. This visualization technique helps create the new connections and even muscle memory to support the new skill. Once you're ready, try it out—as the expert would do it—in life situations. You may want to let others know that you are trying something new.

## Get Feedback From Others

As you know, your own self-perception is not free from bias: It is easy to mix up intention and action. So, ask somebody else to tell you what they see you doing and how effective it is. If you are working on a visible skill (versus a mental skill like problem solving), ask someone to take an informal video (or create a selfie video) so you can see yourself as you swing the bat, have the feedback conversation, or give the presentation. Use the video to analyze what you see as though you are an objective observer. If yours is a mental skill, say the steps you are following out loud and get feedback from somebody who is farther along the expert road than you.

When you ask for feedback or give it to yourself, make sure you have a learning 4.0 mindset. Ask: "What is working and what am I achieving?" or "What are some parts of the skill to change or refine?" Do not say "How am I doing?" or "Give me some feedback" or any question that can be answered with one word or "yes" or "no" (for example, "Have I improved?"). These questions are too general and you will rarely get information you can use. Ask for both positive and constructive input: "What are two things that I did that worked, and what are two areas I could improve?" This will be easier to do if you treat feedback as information for learning focused on behavior and its impact, not as evaluation or a comment about you or your self-worth.

So, be a novice for a while. The idea is to master the basics and begin to feel comfortable with them in simple situations. This will help lay the foundation for more complex actions and will help you hardwire the new capability. As you become more proficient, put yourself in more challenging situations.

## Use Checklists and Flow Patterns

Sometimes it is useful to support your skills with checklists and flow patterns. Checklists contains the critical steps and practices that you must implement to be successful with a skill. They're vital for pilots, surgeons, and other professionals whose work can have catastrophic consequences if they miss specific tasks. But they can be a helpful aid for any skill that has many components. Think of it as an external memory drive that you may or may not fully download into your own long-term memory store.

A flow is a mental image of a sequence of events as they move in space and time. It is a quick way to be sure you follow skill steps and it is more resistant to mind wandering than repeatedly using a checklist. Airline pilots increasingly use flows to prepare for flight, with checklists as backups. They sweep their eyes in a standard flow from left to right (or vice versa) over their instruments, stopping at various points along the way to be sure all is well. It requires conscious attention.

You can use this flow technique to support a variety of skills. For example, think of developing your presentation skills. Imagine that you have a flow pattern that you will use whenever you give a speech. It might start with you imagining the audience. Then you imagine their needs. Next you mentally sweep through your attention-getting opening, your key points and the stories attached to them, and your closing remarks. Flows like this are ways to engage your visualization capability and your more spatial right brain.

## Use Perceptual Learning

Perceptual learning is a technique where, without instruction, guidelines, or preparation, you dive into as many situations as possible to master a skill in a short time.[14] It's a form of trial and error learning where you respond and react while receiving constant feedback about what is working and what isn't. You learn to adjust your behavior automatically based on feedback until you master increasingly difficult situations requiring the skill.

Many games use perceptual learning. As you play, you receive feedback in the form of rewards and advancement to higher levels; all the while you're learning the rules by osmosis. The fact that you can do this shows the power of your unconscious learning system. With enough practice your brain figures out rules and patterns. Perceptual learning appeals almost exclusively to your automatic system.

The only problem is that the skills you learn through perceptual learning are tacit, not explicit, which means you will have difficulty explaining the rules and patterns to yourself or others. However, perceptual learning can be a very accelerated way to develop skills. You can also add more traditional "here's how to do it" and "here is the theory" learning.

If this sounds like an odd learning technique, it isn't. You have learned most skills in your life by trial and error, with feedback. This is informal perceptual learning. The difference here is that you have a conscious goal to compress multiple, learning-rich experiences into a short period of time. It's trial and error on steroids!

## Support Yourself Through Plateaus and Valleys

As you know from your own experience, skills don't develop along a smooth and upward path. There are always snags in the road—you may improve rapidly and then stagnate or plateau. You may even seem to lose your early gains. What's happening? There are many potential causes:

- You may be focusing too much on one learning method. Learning anything requires a balance of space, sleep, and interleaving of learning methods.
- Your motivation may be waning, which will affect your neurochemicals.
- You may be distracted in ways that are not helpful for your learning.
- Your self-talk may be working against you. ("I can't master this." "This is impossible." "I won't look good if I try and fail.")
- You may have tapped into a deeper roadblock, such as an emotion or fear, that you need to name and either deal with or plow through.
- You may not be getting enough sleep, exercise, or the right diet to sustain high-energy learning.

Plateaus and valleys are often important times of consolidation, so they can contribute to developing your skill. But they are also dangerous because they usually occur before your skill is strong enough to be sustainable or before it can override and replace an old habit. This makes it easy for you to quit and go back to your old ways.

How can you manage yourself through the ups and downs and plateaus? Try these tips:

- **Get support.** Talk with a friend, colleague, or spouse about what you are trying to do and enlist the person as a cheerleader. Say what you are trying to achieve and bring your goal up in conversations when you are together. Making your learning social injects some oxytocin into the situation, puts your ego on the line, and helps you further clarify your future vision and goals.

- **Set a few small interim goals or take a break.** If you set small goals, make sure you can achieve them in the next few days. If you decide to take a break, make sure you schedule a specific time to resume your skill development work. Remember, you will get a dopamine reward for achieving a goal, so set some little steps and enjoy the small accomplishments along the way.
- **Create a "Ulysses Contract" to help motivate progress.** This is an agreement with a third party or with yourself that helps ensure you stay true to a long-term goal even when you are tempted to do something now that will override that goal. In mythology, Ulysses made his men tie him to the mast of his ship so he wouldn't be seduced by the hypnotic singing of the beautiful Sirens. Following the Sirens would keep him from achieving his bigger goal of returning home after the Trojan War. The agreement was that his crew would not untie him under any circumstances until they were out of hearing range. Think about certificates and promotions as a positive form of a Ulysses contract: When you finish a program and show competence, you receive a certificate and maybe a promotion. You can create this kind of contract with yourself, promising yourself a weekend trip or other reward you value as a proxy for your larger learning goal.

## Summary of How to Develop Skills and Habits

Skills are often difficult to develop because old habits interfere, and it takes time to master skill parts and ultimately turn them into habits. This applies to mental, physical, interpersonal, and personal skills. There may be additional complications if your ego is tied to an old way of behaving, or if your current habits cover up an emotional vulnerability. However, once you decide that a new skill or habit can help you move into the future you desire, there are steps you can take to successfully make the changes involved (Figure 10-2).

If you want to develop a skill, commit to being a novice for a while, use checklists and flows, try perceptual learning, and support yourself through the plateaus and valleys. And don't forget to use the general learning techniques listed earlier in this chapter: Create future-pull, use sleep and breaks, interleave, and get support from other people. Your ability to be a more powerful participant in your own life will be one of many rewards for this work.

## Figure 10-2. Techniques for Developing Skills and Habits

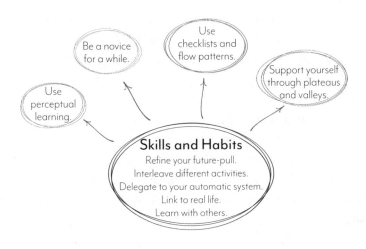

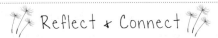

### Reflect + Connect

This may be a good time to remind yourself that this chapter focuses on four kinds of learning outcomes. You've covered the first two: remembering and new skills and habits. Consider taking a break to let the automatic function of your brain take over while you walk or do something else. When you come back, you will turn to the third learning outcome: beliefs and attitudes.

# How to Update Beliefs and Attitudes

Most people think that knowledge and skills are what learning is all about. But there is a third learning focus: your values, beliefs, and attitudes. These are your deeply and emotionally held criteria for making important decisions.[15]

Sometimes your beliefs don't serve you or your world well. Many were formed when you were young and influenced by other people, your culture, and your own immature view of the world. This book, for example, challenges the belief that as a learner you are subservient to teachers; that what experts or charismatic leaders say is always the truth; and that learning ability declines with age. Rather, it asks you to question your beliefs about your power in learning, and it challenges you to be a discerning master of your own learning process.

As a 4.0 learner, it is important to know what beliefs are guiding your choices and behavior, and you need to be willing to question them. This is what it means to be an empowered adult and constructive member in today's complex society.

Beliefs and attitudes are under-the-surface forces that shape your behavior. They can change with learning, such as when your experiences, discoveries, and the information around you proves them wrong or not appropriate in your evolving life and world. How do you acquire and refine your beliefs? This section covers four different techniques: be self-aware, recognize when beliefs are in play, do side-by-side comparisons, and load up on benefits of change.

## Be Self-Aware

Knowing your beliefs and attitudes is especially difficult because they operate as underlying, covert themes across most of your behavior. They can sometimes be overridden by external forces, such as rewards, demands from authority figures, or other situational conditions. Some of the most difficult situations in life (and tests of character) occur when your internal beliefs and values conflict with the demands of the moment. For example, you may believe it is important to treat everyone with respect, but group pressure may tempt you to exclude someone who is different.

Because beliefs and attitudes may be overridden by situational pressures, individual situations are not reliable pointers to a deeper belief. So how do you know a belief is present? One way is to notice themes and patterns in your behavior across situations. Ask yourself: "Why do I usually act this way?" "Why do I usually agree with some ideas and suggestions and not others?" "Do my emotional reactions to people or ideas tell me anything about my own beliefs?" Then you can use your answers to decide if these beliefs and attitudes are still valid.

## Recognize When Beliefs Are in Play

You can assume that when something you are learning clashes with your important beliefs, you will have decisions to make. You can ignore ideas that you don't agree with, be defensive and close down, or be curious and explore.

The obvious learning option is to explore. Watch for these signals that your values, beliefs, or attitudes are being challenged.

## You Don't Use Your Knowledge and Skills

You have the knowledge and skills to achieve a learning goal, but you don't or won't use them. Maybe you plan to change something, but then discover that although you have the ability to make the changes, you don't.

For example, you want to become a better leader. You know what it will take, and you realize that you have the communication skills a good leader needs. But you consistently fail to use your knowledge and skill. Instead, you usually act like a traditional top-down boss. Yes, it's a habit, but any habit can be replaced. What you may not have is the inner motivation to change your behaviors. As you dig deeper you realize that you value being in control, and you believe that people won't work hard unless you closely supervise them and manage rewards. This discrepancy between your stated goal and your beliefs signals that it may be time to target those beliefs for potential change.

## There's a Better Path

Sometimes your habitual actions will no longer solve the problem or there may be a better way to approach important parts of your life. For example, when you picked up this book, did you believe that learning was an important capability to improve? Perhaps not. But now you realize how critical it is to your success and personal power. Your challenge is to make that new belief strong enough to influence your learning behavior going forward.

## Discomfort With a New Perspective or Idea

When you feel tempted to dismiss new ideas or when you feel yourself becoming defensive, you may have touched a sensitive value, belief, or attitude. For example, if you find yourself saying (with emotion) things like, "I already know how to learn!" "I already am a good leader!" "These new methods for dealing with customers won't work," then you may be in belief territory. Emotional reactions are often signals that there might be a learning opportunity—that something has touched a deeper nerve. This is a good time to tune to the call. If you are going to reject the idea, at least reject it because it isn't worth learning—not because it is uncomfortable or contradicts your belief system.

When you notice these signals, step back and say to yourself: It looks like my old value, belief, or attitude of $x$ is being challenged by a new value, belief, or attitude of $y$. Then go on to do a side-by-side comparison.

## Do Side-by-Side Comparisons

It's not easy to change your beliefs and attitudes because they are usually part of an identity you've developed over time. But sometimes new information and insights require you to upgrade these important parts of you. When you think you need to reset a value, belief, or attitude, take some time to put the old view and new view side by side. What are the reasons for continuing your current belief? What are the reasons to adopt a new perspective? Figure 10-3 presents an example that focuses on beliefs about learning.

Figure 10-3. Support for Old and New Beliefs About Learning

| Old Belief | New Belief |
|---|---|
| Learning happens all the time without extra effort; it's not important to improve my approach.<br>• It is easier to expect others to take responsibility for my learning.<br>• If I continue learning as usual I won't have to learn how to be a 4.0 learner. It seems to require a lot of different thinking and skills.<br>• Things are fine as they are. | Learning is one of the most important processes in life and it will be worthwhile to master new methods.<br>• It is a more accurate reflection of reality. My actions determine most of my learning.<br>• Learning is critical for me to survive in today's changing world and at work, and I can't rely on others to do it for me.<br>• If I learn more about how to upgrade my learning I will be a better helper to others. |

Be aware that if you don't have compelling reasons for adopting a new belief about learning, you won't put the energy into learning what's in this book. For adult learners, beliefs are often a key learning target: You may think you need to develop a knowledge or skill, but the real focus, at least initially, may relate to values, beliefs, or attitudes.

## Load Up on the Benefits of Change

If you decide that you want to change a belief or attitude, load up on the benefits of making a shift. Think of yourself sitting on a seesaw. All the benefits of the old belief are heavy weights on one end that keep you from moving. You must counter those weights with benefits that are meaningful for you. Knowing and feeling the weight of these benefits will help motivate you to make new choices, take new actions, and learn relevant knowledge and skills to support the new belief.

## A Summary of How to Shift Your Beliefs

Think about the influence of your values, beliefs, and attitudes on your intentions and behavior. One new belief can affect thousands of your behaviors and may motivate changes in many skill and knowledge areas. Advertisers, educators, politicians, and religious leaders focus on values and beliefs more than individual behaviors. They know that if they can change or manipulate them, they have struck real gold. To manage your own learning, be aware of your beliefs, recognize when they are in play, do side-by-side comparisons, and load up on the benefits of change (Figure 10-4).

Figure 10-4. Techniques for Influencing Beliefs and Attitudes

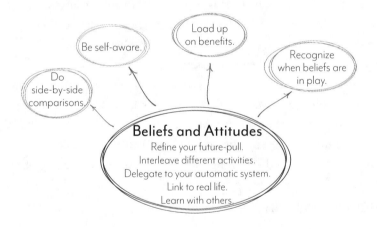

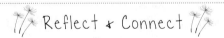

Reflect & Connect

What was most interesting and useful to you in the section on beliefs and attitudes? How aware were you of this as an important learning target?

# How to Spark Creative Insights

After reading an article or watching a video, have you ever said: "I don't remember what was in it, but it triggered several creative ideas!"? This is an example of learning that has a creative outcome. It is the fourth kind of result that your learning can achieve.

In traditional learning situations there is little room for creativity: You learn what's in the book or video or case study. Then you repeat it in a test. There are times when this is the outcome you want. In fact, in the section on how to develop skills you learned that it is helpful to be a novice and imitate an expert when you are learning a skill. But rote memorization and imitation may not be the best outcomes for a specific learning project. In today's fast changing world, your ability to create new solutions and methods is increasingly important and may often be your main learning goal.

Learning is increasingly used by 4.0 learners as a launching pad for creative ideas. When you do this, you use learning resources, not for the specific information they contain, but to trigger insights and ideas related to a problem or project. In this case, you prime your brain with your own question or problem, and then you immerse yourself in a learning resource, which may or may not be directly related to your question or problem. When ideas related to your own question or problem occur to you, write them down and then go back to the resource. By the end, you may not remember much of the specific content, but you may decide to pursue the creative ideas it sparked. Try following three steps when you want to learn for a creative outcome: Set up for creativity, use learning resources to trigger creativity, and capture your creative insights.

## Set Up for Creativity

In chapter 1, you learned that your automatic system works to solve problems and answer questions while you are sleeping or working on unrelated projects. In other words, diverting your attention from a problem can actually help solve it! You can use this amazing ability of your brain to channel your learning toward a creative outcome. Your creativity goal can exist along with other learning goals, or it may be the only learning target you have.

Note that whenever you process new information, you automatically create conditions for creative insight. It is impossible not to be creative when you are learning something new. If you are in a learning mode, your brain naturally connects new information, with what it knows and is seeking to answer. So, new memories are your own creative version of the original information. Also, whenever you retrieve a memory, you change it in some way because you're creating new connections.

You can increase your chances of a creative outcome by priming your brain with your questions and unsolved problems before you engage with the learning resource. The more "stuck" you are in your question or problem, the better. Maybe you are in a complex merger negotiation. Or, there is a difficult team issue that seems to have no solution.

The first step toward finding creative solutions is to immerse yourself in the problem or question. Turn it over in your mind. Feel the conundrum as moods, tensions, and excitements in your body. Be puzzled. Then set it aside, and get ready to turn your attention to your book, job experience, online course, learning game, or other learning resource.

## Use Learning Resources to Trigger Creativity

In this step, you let your unresolved questions incubate by immersing yourself in your resource (the course, case study, simulation, game, article, video). If your mind wanders to your problem, let it go. Don't worry about solving anything. Bring yourself back to the learning material at hand and try to get into a flow with it if you can—let your mind wander to your original questions when they occur to you. Treat your resource as a trigger to daydream about the deeper questions you are facing. You can even ask yourself, "How is my creative issue like what I'm learning in this book or video?"

When you learn for creativity, your brain makes constant associations and many won't make sense in the moment. Maybe you want to resolve a difficult interpersonal conflict with a friend. But you are about to play a game that requires magical ways to get around physical barriers. So you decide to use the game to help you find a creative solution to your conflict problem. As you play the game, random thoughts occur to you about the barriers between you and your friend, and how you might transform them. And then your automatic system retrieves past experiences that are relevant for your problem—experiences and insights that you would not have remembered if you looked for them directly. Later you turn your attention from the game to your problem with new solutions. Marie Louise von

Franz, a prominent Jungian psychologist, wrote about the power of this process: "Creative ideas [are] like keys, they help to 'unlock' hitherto unintelligible connections of facts and thus enable [people] to penetrate deeper into the mystery of life."[16]

In the process, you may or may not learn some or all lessons in the game. But that isn't your learning goal at this moment.

## Capture Creative Insights

This is the time you yell, "Eureka! I found something interesting!"

If you've primed your brain and let your thinking roam around the learning resource you are using, you may hover in or near a flow state. When this happens, the conscious part of your brain that judges and evaluates (and uses lots of energy) goes dormant. You may enter a daydreaming-like state of effortless concentration that allows moments of insight. Take advantage of this to gather all the creative thoughts that want to emerge. You don't need to act on them right away; just write them down or dictate them into a notes section on your phone and keep your creative process going.

Also, expect to have creative insights as you go about your normal day, and while you sleep. Let your automatic system take over your creative learning goal and move you toward your future vision. If you've set up your mind for creativity, you may have seemingly random strokes of insight. Think about a time when you almost gave up on finding a solution to a difficult problem, but woke up with a creative answer or thought of one while you were in the shower. This is the kind of process you have set in motion.

## Summary of How to Spark Creative Insights

As a 4.0 learner, many of your learning outcomes will be creative new insights and solutions. Sometimes your creative insights will be unplanned, but you can also make them the main goal of your learning process. To do this, set yourself up for creativity. Identify a guiding question or problem that you want to answer or resolve. Then let your mind meander and daydream while you are engaged with the new material (use learning resources as creativity triggers). Finally, capture your creative insights while you remain in a flow state where your questions and the material intermingle (Figure 10-5).

## Figure 10-5. Techniques for Sparking Creative Insights

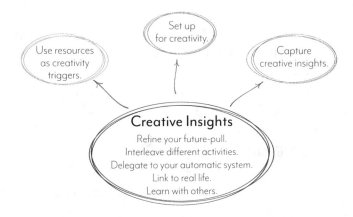

You will probably surprise yourself with many creative ideas. Some may be whimsical and irrelevant, but others may solve your problem or set you on a path to a new solution. Creativity-oriented learning is an increasingly important kind of learning outcome, requiring some new attitudes about learning resources. Depending on your goals, it's OK to use the learning material as a trigger for creativity. You may decide not to remember or use exactly what is in the learning resource you are using. But it may have stimulated new thinking you can use to answer questions and solve problems in unrelated areas of your life.

Reflect & Connect

Take a couple deep breaths, close your eyes, and tell yourself three ideas that will help your learning in the future.

## Learn to Last, in Brief

Wow. Learning has lots of tentacles. But this part of the journey is important because it's when you transform and store your learning for later use. You will get great results and enjoy the process as a 4.0 learner if you realize that there are four different learning outcomes: knowledge, skills and habits, beliefs and attitudes, and creative insights. While some learning practices apply to all four—refine your future-pull; use sleep, breaks, and spacing; interleave; learn with others—each also requires special practices of its own:

- To remember knowledge:
  - Make vivid connections.
  - Forget to remember.
  - Take time to reflect.
  - Go for deeper patterns and mental models.
- To develop skills:
  - Be a novice for a while.
  - Use checklists and flow patterns.
  - Use perceptual learning.
  - Support yourself through plateaus and valleys.
- To shift beliefs:
  - Be self-aware.
  - Recognize when beliefs are in play.
  - Do a side-by-side comparison.
  - Load up on the benefits of change.
- To spark creative insights:
  - Set up for creativity.
  - Use learning resources as creativity triggers.
  - Capture your creative insights.

By using practices like these, you create enduring memories, skills and habits, attitudes and beliefs, and creative outcomes that are ready when you need them. But having a new capability doesn't guarantee you'll use it in your daily life. What if the people and things around you are not supportive? What if events in your life trigger old habits, often without you noticing what's happening? How do you transfer learning to life?

## Link

Use the Practice 6: Learn to Last template in Tool 2 or at www.learning40.com/unstoppable to help you implement this sixth learning 4.0 practice.

As a 4.0 learner, you become a personal change agent and a kind of social engineer. The next chapter explains how to make sure your new knowledge becomes part of your life and even changes the world around you.

# 11

## Transfer to Life

Do you remember the challenge continuum from chapter 8? It showed that some learning is relatively easy to do and use, while other learning is more difficult. Some of these difficulties relate to what you are trying to learn: the knowledge, skill, beliefs, or creativity challenge involved. But other difficulties relate to using your learning in real-life situations. You have to take steps to transfer your new capabilities from learning mode to action mode. To do, this you need to:

- Recognize the transfer challenge.
- Set up for success.
- Get allies.
- Celebrate while continuing to learn.

---

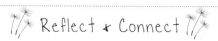 Reflect ✦ Connect

Is there a new habit or skill you would like to bring to life? Think about it as you read this chapter.

---

## Recognize the Transfer Challenge

Think about it this way. You are about to enter a situation where you want to use new learning. Your brain, your big self, and your new knowledge, skills, beliefs, and creative insights are ready for action. You also have a future vision and some intentions for what you want to do and change. So, you enter the situation (Figure 11-1).

### Figure 11-1. Intentions to Apply Learning

| You | The Situational You | The New Situation |
|---|---|---|
| · Your learning self<br>· Your big self<br>· Your new learning (knowledge, skills, values, creative insights)<br>· Future vision | · Ego identity<br>· Situation-triggered habits<br>· Future vision discount<br>· Fragile new abilities | · Physical environment<br>· People's expectations and power relationships<br>· Rules, processes, and rewards |

But the physical environment, the rules and rewards, and other people may not be ready for the changes you want to bring. In addition, despite all your plans for change, when you enter the real-life situation another part of you (let's call it the situational you) may show up and allow old habits to kick in. Suddenly that future vision and your intentions don't seem as important as just fitting in and doing what you have always done.

What happened?

You just met yourself as a part of a larger system. It's important to know how to bring your learning into this larger system—how to transfer learning to life. This involves both managing yourself and influencing the environment around you.

## The Challenge of Managing Yourself in Change

You know from chapter 2 that you bring different personas into your various life situations. That is, you perform specific roles and are known for what you do in those roles. Some of your self-esteem and ego may be attached to your situational persona and its habits. So, it may be personally threatening to make changes—especially if your new behaviors are fragile and still being refined. This is one reason to incorporate real experiences and involve others from your application environment earlier in your learning; this way you bring your environment along with you as you learn.

Another potential roadblock is the tendency of your surroundings to automatically trigger old habits. Your memory works partly because it connects actions and ideas to real-life situations. This is called episodic memory—you remember episodes of your life just as you would remember scenes in a movie. So, when you are in a real-life situation, it triggers a cascade of connections, automatically mobilizing old habits that relate to it. You may not even notice this until after you've left the scene!

In addition, when you are in a real-life situation, there are other things to focus on that are specific to the situation. Satisfaction in the moment can become so important that it overshadows future goals that conflict with it. Economists would say that in that moment you discount the future in favor of the present.

And all this happens when your new knowledge, skills, beliefs, and creative intentions are still fragile and being developed. Your development process is ongoing, after all, and doesn't happen in the tidy sequence of the seven practices presented in this book!

## The Challenge of Influencing your Environment

Your real-world environment expects some consistency in your behavior. So, if you make changes, it disturbs the habits and status quo around you. People may be surprised by your changes and intentionally or unintentionally resist them. But it's not just the people around you! You may also find that processes, rules, and rewards are not fully aligned with your new intentions. This is exacerbated when your physical environment isn't set up to support you.

Imagine this situation: In your future vision, you see yourself as a skilled leader who engages people around you. To help you move toward that vision, you learned new ways to make virtual meetings more effective. You've learned how to prepare for virtual meetings, use several meeting technologies, and get everybody involved and participating from their remote locations. You also learned ways to bring diverse views into the conversation, even when there is a mix of managers and nonmanagers in the room.

You want to try to bring the new meeting management approach into your workplace, but you realize it will present a challenge. So, before you try to use what you learned, you think about how meetings actually work in your company. You realize that like you, many of your colleagues believe virtual meetings waste a lot of time. Some team members rarely speak up, especially when people with higher authority levels are present. In addition, you realize that multitasking is the norm, the available meeting technology is unreliable, and participants rarely prepare before meetings. In other words, it will be a challenge to use what you have learned.

It's not enough to simply develop your new capabilities. You have to use them in the real world, and often the real world is not ready to support your changes. Recognizing this is the first step in transferring learning to life.

# Set Up for Success

When you bring your learning into life, many factors are involved. Take some time to figure out what you will face when you apply what you are learning or have learned. Start with a list of the forces in you and the environment that support or resist you as you transfer your learning to life. This is called a force-field analysis (Figure 11-2).

## Figure 11-2. Force-Field Analysis

**Learning Transfer Goal:**
Implement the new approach to virtual meetings I have been studying and creating.

|  | Positive Force | Negative Force |
|---|---|---|
| In me | + Vision of myself as a valued meeting leader<br>+ I am excited about this new meeting management approach | - I am anxious when I have to lead a meeting<br>- My work ethic of "do it myself" |
| In the environment | + Good team training for virtual meetings is available but expensive<br>+ Several influential team members want better meetings | - Unreliable meeting technology<br>- Some team members are reluctant to speak up<br>- Some of the team's work areas are very noisy |
| Actions to ensure transfer | To amplify positives:<br>+ Work with positive team members to refine the ideas and plan<br>+ Get brochures about the team training; encourage people to take the training<br>+ Get a few motivating quotes about being a team leader to put on my desktop | To remove or minimize negatives:<br>+ Count to 10 when I'm tempted to take on work that others should do<br>+ Talk with IT about solving our Internet bandwidth problem—show cost savings<br>+ Increase the number of times I go around the table to get input from everybody |

Make sure your list includes both the positive and negative forces, which may support you as well as make it difficult for you to succeed.[1] There are two types of forces: internal and environmental.

Internal include:

- the strength of your future vision
- the strength of the underlying values and mental models you want to bring into your world
- your confidence and expertise level in your new learning
- the strength of your old habits
- the strength of your emotions in the situation, which can be either positive or negative
- how deeply rooted your barriers or dreams are for change.

Environmental forces include:

- relationships with and expectations of the people around you
- how the system is designed to work
- your physical environment, tools, and tangible resources.

Once you understand the forces that are at work, you have to decide how to make sure your learning transfers into the real world. Plan to strengthen the positive forces. They are already working for you, so making them a bit stronger will pay many dividends. In the example in Figure 11-1, you could ask the positive team members to help set up the new meeting approach. If there are game breakers (such as the unreliable technology), decide if you need to take immediate action (such as asking IT to help solve the company's meeting technology program). It can be better to tackle the difficult issues after you have increased the strength of the positives and dealt with other less difficult issues.

Sometimes, bigger issues in your environment will make it difficult to use what you have learned. Perhaps you and the people around you are not in a direct position to fix or address them. At work, there may be problems with structure, technology, culture, processes, systems, or leadership. At home the family budget, assumptions about roles, and other aspects of life may not be working well. The community or political system around you may also need to change in some way.

It may seem that these are remote issues that you can't control. But, you are part of these environments and—if you choose to—you can find ways to rally others around you for action. If you do, what started as a personal change may extend to larger swaths of the world around you. Sometimes these kinds of change activities launch major movements (think: women's rights, racial equality, humane treatment of animals, better performance management processes in companies). But it doesn't have to be that grand. Maybe all you do is help people participate a little more in meetings or convince IT to purchase better meeting software.

The point is, if you want to bring what you've learned into your life and you're expecting some challenges, plan to boost the positive forces and reduce or try to change the negatives. Know that you are a potent force in your own environment. What you do has ripple effects throughout your world. It's up to you to bring your learning successfully to life. In fact, in these fast-changing times your learning can and sometimes should shake the world around you. So, be sure what you set in motion will have overall positive effects beyond you.

# Get Allies

One of the best ways to ensure learning transfer is to get allies. The best allies are people whose support will make it easier to succeed, or whose expectations and actions might make change difficult.

For example, in the virtual meeting example, allies would include a few people who are usually involved in those meetings and someone from IT. A person in management may also be an important ally, so it might be worthwhile to go to her and suggest a new policy, tools, or training programs focused on better virtual meetings. This creates three powerful kinds of support: an ally, support from somebody with high influence power, and support through changes in the policies, systems, and training. A triple benefit!

Some allies will have little or nothing to do with where or how you use your learning. They're simply friends, supporters, and sponsors—people who are there when you lose energy for learning and change, when you dip into a valley, have a flow or peak experience and want to celebrate, or to help you test and shape your learning practices. Be sure you take at least one of those allies along for your learning journey, especially when you are working at the difficult end of the challenge continuum.

# Celebrate While Continuing to Learn

When you take what you've learned into the real world, you're continuing your learning journey. You still create new associations in your brain, and you'll often hear new calls to learn that trigger a search for more information to support additional learning that lasts.

The point is, using is also learning. So even though you're still learning when you transfer new capabilities into the real world, it's important to recognize that you've accomplished something. One way to satisfy this need for achievement is celebrate success along the way. Your learning self needs the rewards that come from achieving goals and making progress. Make it a point to celebrate when you learn something, try it out, make an ally, influence something in your environment, or do something new rather than let an old habit take over. See these as little goals that you have accomplished.

The little bursts of neurochemicals that come with these bits of awareness will help carry you forward. One of the biggest reasons why people abandon their learning journeys is that they don't feel enough sense of progress, hopefulness, or accomplishment.

You may want to add some spice to this reward process. Make a deal with yourself that if you try something new by a specific date you will reward yourself in the future. Create a Ulysses contract; delay gratification today to create something far more important in your life in the future.

You are a powerful force in your own world, even when it seems that many forces are working against you. As a 4.0 learner, take charge of your own world. Look for support from others, but don't wait for others to make your world perfect for change. Step out of your comfort zone a bit and build in some rewards in along the way. Congratulate yourself at all parts of the journey, especially when you unleash what you've learned into your real world of work and life.

## Transfer to Life, in Brief

While you often learn for the pure joy of it—to satisfy a curiosity or explore new thinking and new worlds—you also learn to use new knowledge, skills, values, and creative insights in various situations in your life. As Benedict Carey, a science reporter for the *New York Times* put it:

> Transfer is what learning is all about, really. It's the ability to extract the essence of a skill or a formula or word problem and apply it in another context, to another problem that may not look the same, at least superficially. If you've truly mastered a skill, you carry it with you.[2]

The world around you may or may not support the changes you want to make. And you may not be fully ready to apply your new learning. But, as you discovered in this chapter, you can stack the cards to favor change when you recognize the transfer challenge, set up for success, get allies, and celebrate success while continuing to learn. In the process, you also have a chance to influence the people and things around you in ways that may make lives and work better.

 Link

Use the Practice 7: Transfer to Life template in Tool 2 or at www.learning40.com/unstoppable to help you implement this seventh learning 4.0 practice. Make a mental note to use it to help you plan how you will bring your learning into your life when you anticipate challenges from your own habits or the environment around you.

# PART 3

## Learning as Love

Learning is an act of love. It is self-love—through it you help yourself survive and thrive in this nonstop world, develop through all the stages of your life, and become all you can be as you discover and fulfill your purpose. It is love of the people around you, because being a visible learner to and with them creates a climate for taking risks and being open to change. And it is love when you are in a teaching, coaching, or mentoring role—helping others develop and learn by being a learning 4.0 role model or guiding them through the learning process.

This section brings many of the points in the book together for you in all your learning roles—as a lifelong learner (chapter 12), a learning member of a team (chapter 13), and someone who guides and assists others in their learning journey (chapter 14).

# 12

# Being a Lifelong Learner

Learning at a 4.0 level is an integral part of life in the 21st century—it's a creative and generative process that supports you in becoming all you can be. This chapter presents a picture of what lifelong learning looks and feels like. It calls you to become a more aware, curious, and competent user of the learning 4.0 practices.

Early in this book you saw how your learning journey unfolded from your time in the womb through childhood, adolescence, and into early adulthood. These were the years when much of what you learned was shaped by your caregivers and teachers. Your attitudes toward learning and your sense of power in your own learning also took form during these years. At the same time, your brain's full capabilities slowly matured, with your prefrontal cortex (your executive control center) reaching full development in your late 20s.

For some people, these first decades of development created lasting misconceptions about learning and power. For many—maybe for you—a need to please people in authority and fears of failure replaced the natural curiosity and wonder of childhood. Learning became synonymous with school, and learning skills meant "study skills" and preparing for tests. The power in learning remained with teachers, facilitators, coaches, schools—and eventually managers at work.

Learning is a lifelong process; it is a distinguishing feature of being alive. But what does it mean to be a lifelong learner in today's nonstop world and rapidly evolving information field? It certainly requires a more conscious and empowered approach than in the past, but it means more than that.

This chapter takes you further into your learning 4.0 journey. It calls on you to use your upgraded knowledge about learning to live your life more fully. To heed the words often attributed to the French philosopher and novelist Émile Zola: "If you ask me what I came to do in this world, I, an artist, will answer you: I am here to live out loud."

You, too, are called to be an artist with a life to live out loud; a life where you notice and welcome learning into your life in all its forms. It is the call to be a lifelong learner. This involves approaching life events with curiosity and wonder, traveling along all three learning paths, responding to the subtlest calls to learn, being an intelligent filter of information, feeling your emotions, and taking on your power.

# Approach Life With Curiosity and Wonder

Learning opportunities are all around you when you bring an attitude of wonder and curiosity into your life. Think of all the learning opportunities that surround you every day. Perhaps:

- You notice that there are more homeless people on the corners than usual as you walk along a city street and wonder what is changing.
- You hear politicians talking about plans for a new initiative in your community and decide to learn more about it.
- You notice a grove of oak trees and wonder how something so tall can be standing.
- You and your best friend have an argument, and unsure of your facts, you do a bit of research.
- You realize that you are not handling conflict well and want to do something about it.
- You are part of a conversation about a new business strategy and its potential implications for a team you are leading. You listen carefully and ask lots of questions.

The point to reinforce from chapter 5 is that calls to learn come from everywhere: inside, outside, from the past, from the future, or they just tickle your innate curiosity.

You can choose to ignore the calls, actively defend against them, or explore them with wonder. Any of these responses might be valid for a specific situation. Over time you may realize that you tend to react one way or another. Is something deeper influencing how you react?

Curiosity and wonder are the hallmark qualities of a lifelong learner, and they are not new to you.[1] They dominated your life when you were very small and you thought the world was endlessly fascinating. You tried everything you could until you encountered the word *no*. How you experienced that no may still be affecting your curiosity and wonder today. If you believed you needed to avoid being told *no* by not making mistakes and staying in a defined role—that the adults around you wouldn't love you if you ventured into the unknown—then your first reaction to something new may be to turn away from the learning opportunity. This defensive reaction made sense for you as a child, because your life depended on the approval of your parents or caregivers and your developing ego was at stake. But this attitude will hold you back today!

An alternative view of *no* is that adults are saying no to behavior, not to you. Parents who use *no* in this way affirm the wonder and curiosity of the child—her ego and big self—while keeping her safe and developing her ability to self-manage in increasingly complex life situations. Psychologists say that this is a *no* without the personal shame of making a mistake or failing. This constructive use of *no* sets the stage for a life full of exploration and self-confidence in the face of opportunities to explore, learn, and change.

Many adults are still dealing with negative effects of the early, more shameful no. It shows up as a need to be perfect, fear of trying something new, reluctance to ask questions, and even hesitation to show excitement, joy, or wonder.

The good news is that these rapidly changing times are an opportunity for you as an adult to either recapture or recommit to the natural wonder and curiosity you were born with. But it takes skill in addition to curiosity and wonder to navigate the increasingly complex, rich learning landscape—skill to learn on several learning paths.

## Become an Expert Traveler on All Three Learning Paths

As a lifelong learner, you know that there are three possible paths your learning can take, and 4.0 learning will help you become an expert traveler. You recognize opportunities to learn in the moment (path 1). When you are in a conversation, reading, or working, you notice potentially interesting and useful information, and—like a detective—you follow that learning thread to see where it will lead. Maybe this in-the-moment learning happened this morning when you read a newspaper article or watched a news show that piqued your interest.

See chapter 8 for details about the three paths and Tool 1. Guides for the Three Learning Paths for path-related tips.

You also recognize when you need and want to learn forward to a goal (path 2). You know to assess how difficult it will be to achieve that goal by rating it on the challenge continuum. Then you create a guiding future vision, search for resources, connect the dots into a plan, and follow through with learning practices for achieving the goal. Maybe you are working on a New Year's resolution or another bigger goal that requires you to set aside special learning time outside your normal routine.

And you also realize when there are opportunities for retroactive learning (path 3). You see finished projects, times of emotional turmoil or change, or even long periods of relative stability as potential treasure troves of insight to take into your future. You review past events through a learning lens. You think about what you intended, what happened, what you did and felt, how others were involved, and the conditions that influenced the outcomes that occurred. You turn the hidden lessons from the past into conscious insights. And if you hear additional calls to learn, you decide whether and how to respond. For example, you probably looked back recently at something you did, replayed it, and thought about how you would do it differently or what worked well to carry into the future (retroactive learning).

In other words, you launch yourself onto the three learning paths (in the moment, toward a goal, retroactive to the past) whenever it makes sense to respond to the call to learn. And, whenever you need them, you use the seven 4.0 learner practices to help you succeed.

## Respond to Subtle Calls to Learn

Almost every experience is an opportunity to learn. But some are more difficult to recognize than others. As a lifelong learner, you are more tuned in than others, so you are more likely to learn when situations like the following occur.

## Your View Is Different From Others

It's easy to miss the learning possibilities when your viewpoint is different from others, and spend time and energy thinking about what you will say and how to defend your perspective.

But, as a lifelong learner you are more likely to mentally step back and make an emotional connection with the other person by truly listening, asking questions, and checking for understanding—including why the view is important to the other person. By taking a learning approach, you know that listening and asking questions doesn't mean you agree or endorse what the other is saying. Instead, you offer your perspective as an alternative view, while also learning about other ways to think about the issues and why people believe what they do.

## Any Routine Experience

Much of what you do every day is probably routine: You act automatically, don't think much about what's happening, and see what you expect to see. Routine is important, and your brain seeks to automate as much as possible. But, as a lifelong learner, you know that sometimes routines outrun their usefulness and can even obstruct learning.

As a 4.0 learner, you take some of your routine experiences off automatic. This means that you watch what you are doing and why. You notice the results and how they affect others. You even check your physical stance and feelings as you act. You think about what you would like to change, do differently—for example, those weekly meetings, or the conversations you have with your children before or after school, your dinner rituals, how you play soccer or take a run, the magazines you have been reading for years.

## Surprise Opportunities

Many changes happen because opportunities to learn appear without warning—changes in work structure or roles, a customer cancels a big order, making a mistake that could damage an important project. As a lifelong learner, you may initially feel threatened, defensive, hope the change will go away. But, you value these as signals more than threats or irritations, and reframe your reactions as calls to learn.

## ⚘ Reflect + Connect ⚘

Have any surprise learning opportunities occurred in your life recently? Think about how you responded.

## Your Life Purpose and Need to Develop

Chapter 2 encouraged you to look at who you are and who you are becoming—your needs and life purpose. As a living, complex being, your needs and purpose are always shifting, calling you to learn, develop, grow, and change. Lifelong learners at the 4.0 level are aware of and support these inner dynamics. Like everyone, you contain many mysteries that even you cannot fathom. But, you can get better and better at monitoring what is happening in you as your life unfolds. And you can also look into yourself to discover your deeper purposes and values so that they can play a bigger role in your choices and learning.

# Become an Intelligent Filter

Every day you filter a great deal of information. You decide what to pay attention to, what is worth knowing and learning, what to ignore, and what to disbelieve.

As a lifelong learner, you are more likely to think about what you hear on the news, what you read in blogs and social media, and what marketers and politicians want to sell you. Learning 4.0 teaches you to be curious and open, but also skeptical, looking for key insights and alternative views. But you're also alert for information distortions, because you know that your brain is susceptible to manipulation (see chapters 1 and 9). You stand up for your values and beliefs, but recognize when it's time to question or replace them.

You also look deeper into things. You know that what is on the surface may just be the tip of the iceberg. You want to know the deeper causes behind people demonstrating in the streets. You wonder why a new fertilizer works, what the main ingredients are, how to apply it, and whether it is safe. When someone says "this policy leads to negative results" or gives you an example saying that it is "how things are," you ask for credible supporting evidence.

You stay curious. You go deeper before you believe what you see and hear. You ask "why?" You go for the real gold.

# Feel Your Emotions

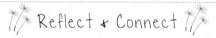

Are you more emotional or rational? What do you do when an emotion comes up? Do you feel and explore it, or try to ignore it and move on? What do you think this section will say about the role of emotions in everyday learning?

Emotions—fear, sadness, joy, anger—are inevitable in daily life. As a life-long learner, you notice your feelings and recognize when they are signals to learn: They may be telling you to develop skills to better deal with specific situations. Or you may feel excited about something and realize you want to do more of it. Or your feelings may be calls to learn from parts of you buried from childhood. Emotions often play a big role in triggering or avoiding retroactive learning. For example, while regret and the feelings attached to it are calls to learn, you may have to move through disappointment and even guilt before you can find lessons for a better future.

Many people don't notice their emotions. But you are different. As a life-long learner, with a learning 4.0 perspective, you know that emotions are an essential part of being human—that your brain's emotion center (the amygdala) colors most of its information processing, often giving positive and negative weight to new information. In fact, your amygdala will even override your more rational side when you are in threatening or stressful situations.

You know that when you try to make your emotions disappear or ignore them, they may simply lurk in your psychological underground, draining your energy and shaping your reactions. Think about how hard it is to be present to learn when you are angry, sad, or not feeling good about yourself—how depleting it is. Then think about how much energy you find when you face into the learning or change the issues the emotions relate to.

Use your emotions as an asset. Bring them into your future vision and think about what it will feel like to be in the future you want to create. Look at any strong emotions as signs that you are tapping into a deeper challenge, a major need, an archetype, or shadow issues. They are calls to learn and inevitable participants when you are learning deeply.

# Take on Your Power

The ability to learn and direct your learning is a major source of your power in life. Later stages of human evolution largely focused on our brain, which has two big purposes: to help us adapt to current conditions and to create new tools and environments for success and survival in the future. This ability to learn and direct your learning is what enables you to be an active agent in your own life and influence what's around you. This agency is the definition of power.

When you become a better learner, you increase the power in your own life. You recognize that you have one chance and perhaps 100 years to live your life to its fullest. And you see your learning attitude and abilities as key to doing this. You are active and skilled when you learn, because you continually refine the learning 4.0 practices in this book.

As a powerful player on the stage of your own life, you see learning as the force that helps you hear calls to learn (practice 1). You create and use powerful future visions to turn the calls into decision guides (practice 2). You enter the information field with confidence that you can search for and find what you need (practice 3). You connect the dots of resources and actions to form the three paths that contain your deliberate learning (practice 4). You mine for gold, avoiding fool's gold when you process information (practice 5). You know how to learn to last—remembering what you need, building skills, updating attitudes and beliefs, and using learning to stimulate creative insights (practice 6). And, you bring learning into your life, managing yourself and the conditions around you that sometimes make this difficult (practice 7). You use these practices knowing the learning landscape: your learning brain, your *self* who learns, the changing world, and the rapidly evolving information field.

This gives you power in your life and ability to harness the forces of change within and around you to increase your learning capability. There's a bonus, too. This is a power you can share with others.

# Being a Lifelong Learner, in Brief

Learning is lifelong; you can't stop it, but you can boost, focus, and expand it. So, don't hold yourself back from fully experiencing and expressing your learning potential. You know more now about that amazing brain of yours (chapter 1) and about the power of your learning self (chapter 2). You know that the world is rapidly changing (chapter 3) and that the information field is expanding (chapter 4). But you also are equipped with new learning capabilities—the seven 4.0 learner practices (chapters 5-11).

 Link

Go to www.learning40.com/unstoppable to develop a profile of yourself as a lifelong and 4.0 learner.

This knowledge positions you to become a lifelong learner—someone who is curious and capable of wonder. Someone who can switch among the three learning paths, who hears calls to learn in many life situations, and who is intelligent and discerning with information. You also feel your emotions, take on your learning power, and live life fully and courageously, holding your ground when you need to, but opening up to new ideas and ways of being when that makes sense. This is you, your *self* who learns: A lifelong learner.

# 13

## Supporting 4.0 Learning in Teams

Your attitudes and approaches to learning spill over to others when you work with them on teams and in other group settings. This chapter suggests ways to be more deliberate about how you influence learning in group situations. It also suggests ways to share the learning 4.0 mindset and skills with others.

Team learning is increasingly important in today's complex learning landscape. Social, business, family, and even many personal problems and challenges require teams to work and learn together to solve them. Innovation also depends on team learning. So, it's important to help teams create and implement a learning stance.

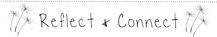
## Reflect ⚹ Connect

What teams or groups are you a part of right now? Think about them as you read this chapter.

Learning is seldom a key team focus. Usually the main purpose is performance. Teams form to accomplish something together, so the attention moves quickly to what the team will achieve, what members will contribute, and how the team will work together. There may be a slight nod to the relationship side when people share information about one another and maybe engage in a team-building activity. But the focus always shifts back to getting the work done, meeting deadlines, fixing problems, keeping things on track, and reporting progress within and outside the team.

This performance orientation often occurs in an atmosphere of unspoken agreements about power relationships, what constitutes failure and how it will be viewed, appropriate work and communication styles, and how meetings will be conducted. Learning goals are rarely mentioned. In fact, admitting to a learning goal is seen as a weakness for some people. The need to look good, to be the leader, and to be the one who knows things often drives individual behavior. The system (for example, rewards or attention from people in authority) sometimes colludes in creating this "fixed" versus "growth" mindset world.

What's lost is that an exclusive focus on performance and competition can damage performance. It can lead to risk aversion, blaming, defensive actions, distrust, and unwillingness to cooperate or share information. It can also inhibit the very synergies that team action is supposed to stimulate, such as risk taking, creative problem solving, and innovation. These synergies all depend on the team having a learning orientation and being skilled at implementing it.

It's impossible to be a high-performance team if learning is not part of the team's agenda and ethos. Learning is an important team dynamic, and there are several ways you can support and benefit from it. So plan to bring what you know about learning 4.0 to the teams you participate in, to take your colleagues to a new level of team learning. You can make this happen by launching the team on a learning trajectory, bringing a learning perspective to problems, recognizing the three learning paths, and turning the seven 4.0 learner practices into team competencies.

# Launch the Team on a Learning Trajectory

How you launch any group shapes the member's expectations and sets the stage for later relationships and actions. So be sure that learning is part of every team's self-image from the start. Use your knowledge of calls to learn (practice 1) and creating future-pull (practice 2) to help shape the team's purpose. Then create agreements about how team members will support one another's learning throughout the project.

Here is a possible scenario for a first team meeting.

Make sure that, in addition to the performance agenda, learning is part of the conversation as you discuss and document the following for the team:
- Speak a collective call to action and learning.
  - Why is this team forming?
- What is the call to action?
  - Where did it come from and what's driving it? (Remember, calls come from inside, outside, the past, the future, or just opportunity and curiosity.)
  - What is the learning call for the team as a whole?
- Create future-pull.
  - What do you want to create together?

- What are some of the learning frontiers you will venture into?
- What will success look and feel like? (Your view may change as you work and learn.)
- Together, imagine a future and describe it as vividly as you can. This is not about what the team will do, but about what you will create together. Include a conversation about the learning opportunities (breakthrough, innovation, creativity, stretch).
- GPS your now.
    - Help the team be as clear and factual as possible about what is happening right now that will change or be affected by the work you will do together.
    - This will create a tension between conditions now and the future vision and help synchronize team members' automatic systems toward a common goal.

Then, in the same meeting, help team members commit to their own and one another's learning:

- Share calls to learn. This is a vital part of creating a learning trajectory. Ask all members to tell the entire team the following:
    - What motivated competencies (knowledge and skill they have and want to use) are they bringing to the team?
    - What is calling each member to this project (from inside, outside, past, future, opportunity)?
    - What does each member hope to learn?
    - What skills or knowledge do they want to strengthen or develop?
    - What beliefs or attitudes do they want to explore?
    - Where do they hope to have creative insights?
    - How might each member help other team members to learn?
    - What support would they like from other team members?
- Encourage questions.
    - Have team members ask one another questions and explore the responses.
    - Treat this as important way for people to get to know one another as well as prepare to work with and support one another.
- Review the team's future vision and learning progress whenever you do team status checks.

How your team begins this work sets the stage for what it can achieve. So be sure to include a learning agenda as part of any team launch. This will establish a tone of stretch and mutual support that a performance focus alone cannot create.

# Bring a Learning Perspective to Problems

Think about your most profound learning experiences. They probably involve problems, roadblocks, failure, unanticipated consequences, or surprising twists of fate. But the same problems you see as learning opportunities may launch a defensive or blaming reaction from somebody else. This happens in teams, too. Power and self-esteem dynamics are always present in any group situation, so the danger of defensiveness and blaming is always there.

Even though problems and crises are rich learning opportunities, it is not easy to take an objective and exploratory view when they occur. In addition, team members inevitably have different views of any problem, bringing their own biases to understanding and shaping the solutions. Time pressures add to the difficulty of team problem solving. What starts as a group whose members are committed to exploration, learning, and mutual support can erupt into factions, actions to protect egos, or situations where the most vocal or powerful members to fix or hide problems.

When a team has a learning perspective, it sees problems, crises, and surprise opportunities as learning content to mine. The suggestions in chapter 9 are helpful here. Try to:

- **Treat the problem as a learning resource.** A problem is a unique kind of learning resource. As with other learning resources, there are specific methods you can use to analyze problems and create solutions. A learning-oriented team will step back and follow a problem-solving process together before assigning causes or deciding actions to take.

- **Be present to learn.** When problems or crises occur, it is important for your prefrontal cortex (attention control center) to move into high gear, looking through biases and distractions for the most important information. It's not a time to defend or avoid.

- **Find deep themes and patterns.** When the team takes a learning orientation it looks below the surface and beyond the boundaries of the immediate problem to see if there are more subtle causes. For example, what seemed to be a sales messaging problem may be a sign of a market shift away from the team's product.

Having a learning perspective makes it more likely that a team will quickly recognize problems and find more sustainable solutions. It unleashes the motivation and abilities of team members, rather than constraining them or diverting them into power plays.

# Recognize the Three Paths

Just as individual learning can take any of three paths—in the moment, toward a goal, or retroactively—so does team learning. Help your teams recognize and act on these path opportunities when they appear.

## Team Learning in the Moment

Teams have myriad opportunities for in-the-moment learning. There are problems to solve, plans to make, conversations with colleagues, and research activities focused on answering questions or finding alternative approaches. The challenge for any in-the-moment opportunity is often whether to recognize it and take a learning attitude or turn it into a power play. Will team members be curious, exploratory, questioning, or willing to not know for the moment. Or will these incidental situations turn into "I win, you lose" contests to show who is smartest or most knowledgeable.

When your team faces an in-the-moment learning opportunity and opts for curiosity and exploration, there is a good chance that members' oxytocin levels will increase, creating a good feeling about the team. The team may even work together in a state of flow, making them more likely to generate creative insights. Of course, this experience strengthens your team commitment and bond, something you can draw on later in more difficult times.

## Team Learning Toward a Goal

Learning toward a goal means developing a capability that you want but don't yet have, and doing it in a deliberate and planned way. For teams, there are two levels of learning toward a goal: the team level and the individual member level. Both are set in motion if your launch meeting puts your team on a learning trajectory:

- Clarify the calls to learn for the team and for individuals.
- Develop a future vision and a GPS of now that creates future-pull for the team.
- Help members to expose the learning benefits they hope for from their work on the team.

As the team unfolds its agenda, other 4.0 learning practices can come into play. A learning-oriented team will step back and search for the best resources, using scanners to help find them (practice 3). The advantage of a team is that members can divide the work. For example, some may review printed resources, while others tap into subject matter experts or look at relevant courses or apps that may relate to the team's goals and issues.

### Link

Tool 4. Scanners and How to Use Them lists some of the services, tools, and people you can go to for help to sift through all the information out there.

With the best resources in hand, the team can connect the dots (practice 4), creating a master plan and timeline for performance and learning actions. Whenever individuals or the team processes information together, the mine for gold (practice 5) and learn to last (practice 6) tips can come into play. For example, in an intense work session, a team member may suggest that the team is being held back by its own biases. Or another member may notice it's time to take a break so that members' automatic systems can have time to think about recent decisions. Another member, knowing that interleaving-related activities is good for learning, may suggest that the team shift to a new activity to boost the learning impact. Or someone may suggest a break at a high or tense point, with the plan to regroup later more refreshed and still motivated because of the Ziegarnik effect.

When you and your team are ready to implement the changes you have created, then you can turn to practice 7, transfer to life. As a 4.0 learner, you know that change initiatives often fail because people's habits or conditions in the environment interfere. You know how important it is to set up for success, get allies, and celebrate success, so you support your team in taking these additional steps.

When your team learns forward to a goal, you do it deliberately, according to a plan. However, it is the nature of learning to transform itself; as you learn you discover more about what you want to and should be learning. You and your teams need to be ready to revise or even reset your future vision, and to renegotiate it if your work is part of a larger plan. In other words, the team's learning extends beyond the completion of its work together.

## Team Learning Retroactively

Few teams look back on their experiences. In fact, it is rare to celebrate or acknowledge that a project is complete, because team members often quickly move on to the next challenges. This leaves a lot of learning on the table, however, since many of the same problems repeatedly recur. The bias for action that dominates modern life is one reason why this happens. Your brain's preference for automatic versus deliberate thought is another. This is why learning may not be as effective as it could be: Lasting learning requires a balance of deliberate reflection and action. During the reflection time, you bring hidden lessons to the surface and file them for later use. Learning requires a 50/50 split between doing and internalizing; this applies to teams, too.

There are many opportunities for a team to learn retroactively. In fact, every team project or activity is a learning resource and an opportunity for microlearning. Take a few minutes at the end of the day or activity to review what happened. Every team project deserves a review focused both on performance and learning. Look at these four areas:

- The completed project:
    - What did you intend?
    - What actually happened?
- The team's learning:
    - What worked that you will carry forward and share with others so they don't have to learn the same lessons the hard way?
    - What lessons and new insights occurred that will make future projects better and more successful?
    - How did the process of working together go?
    - What will you carry forward into future projects, and what should change?
- Individual learning:
    - How did each person develop?
    - How did members help each other learn (including specific appreciations between members)?

- Goals to extend the learning:
  - The retroactive experience can spark a call to learn forward to a new goal.

You can add a broader learning impact to your teamwork by sharing lessons learned with other teams. This will benefit you because teaching others is a good way to anchor your learning more firmly in your own brain and team culture. And, of course, there is the benefit to other groups and to the larger organization you are part of.

It takes time and effort to look back on a project, because people's energies may already be starting to move to other projects. But the effect of thoughtful review on learning is profound. You may want to hook your "what did we learn?" conversations to a celebration. One of the most powerful team learning programs I have ever been involved in always connected reviews with celebration. It was a beer company, so parties and social gatherings were part of the culture. But there is no reason why celebration during and at the end of a team's work can't be part of your or any team's process.

# Turn Learning 4.0 Practices Into Team Competencies

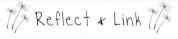

Reflect + Link

Can you list the seven 4.0 learning practices? The How to Remember section in chapter 10 suggests memory methods.

Part 2 of this book focused on the learning 4.0 practices as individual capabilities. But imagine them as team competencies—how amazing would your team experience be if you could count on your and your colleagues' ability to use the seven 4.0 practices? Think about it.

## 1. Tune In to Calls to Learn

Members of our team are aware of our own and others' learning priorities. We notice changes in our current environment and challenges that are on the horizon. We talk about opportunities to learn, whatever their source.

## 2. Create Future-Pull

Our team members have a shared vision of what we will create together. As part of that vision, we know what skills individual members bring and what each of us wants to learn while working with the team.

## 3. Search

We look for the best information to support our opinions and learning. We aren't limited to readily available information or information that agrees with our views. We use scanners to find the best resources and we divide the work to increase our effectiveness.

## 4. Connect the Dots

We organize our resources (connect the dots) to achieve our goals, by creating a master plan and timeline for performance and learning actions. However, we are also open to change as we learn.

## 5. Mine for Gold

We are competent users of information. We are curious, present to learn, and respect others' viewpoints. We watch out for fool's gold and are willing to look for deeper connections and insights.

## 6. Learn to Last

We support each other in achieving the four learning outcomes: remembered information, new skills and habits, upgraded attitudes and beliefs, creative insights. We help one another use advanced learning practices that are based on findings from brain science and psychology.

## 7. Transfer to Life

We understand that change initiatives often fail because habits or conditions in the environment interfere. We help each other transfer learning to life by supporting one another in habit changes and retooling the environment—by being allies and celebrating successes—to support new values, behaviors, and results.

One way to help turn these practices into team competencies is to introduce them when you launch the team. Then periodically check in by turning the elements of the practices into questions. For example, "Using a 1-10 scale, rate our team on each of the 4.0 learning practice statements above (1 = we are not doing this; 10 = we excel!)."

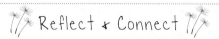

### Reflect + Connect

Consider making this book required reading for your team. You could refer to various chapters and the tools in part 4 when they are relevant to the team's work and learning. Visit www.learning40.com/unstoppable for assessments and more ways to support your teams as learning communities.

## Learning in Teams, in Brief

Team membership can be one of life's blessings or a curse. A lot depends on whether the team is a learning community or simply a vehicle for positioning and self-promotion. Having a learning orientation isn't only good for team members, though. It is also an important force for high performance: It helps create team commitment, trust, agility, and innovations, which are critical for getting good work done in today's fast-changing and complex learning landscape.

# 14

## Helping Others Learn

Every day brings chances to help others learn. A colleague asks you for help solving a problem. A child asks for help with his homework. A friend struggles with a personal problem or life stage challenge and turns to you for advice. Maybe you are in a formal leadership role, where your job is to help others develop. Unless you are a trained coach, psychologist, counselor, or educator, chances are that you have not formally developed the ability to support others' learning. So, your support for others is informal. This chapter shows you how to bring learning 4.0 practices into these important helping relationships. You will be a more valued helper while sharing the learning 4.0 framework so others can use it whenever they learn.

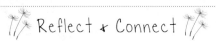

## Reflect & Connect

Who are you in a position to teach, coach, or mentor today in your family, at work, or in other relationships? Think about these people as you read this chapter.

Informal helpers are involved in 20 percent or more of all adult learning.[1] However, this well-intentioned support doesn't always make a difference, and can even interfere with learning. This happens, for example, when you talk when you should listen, act mainly as a judge (which adds to the learner's anxiety and performance stress), or even take over the process rather than helping the learner own it.

It's hard to help others learn if you aren't working to master the learning process for yourself. But thanks to the insights in this book, you now know what learning involves and are in a better position to help others learn. You know about the learning brain, the psychology of the self who is learning, the seven 4.0 learning practices, and the three common learning paths. These are the basic insights you can use both for your own learning and to help others.

Now it's time to use what you've learned in this book to help others. Think about and appreciate your role as a helper both as an act of love and as one of the best ways to develop your own learning skills. Successfully helping others involves having the right (caring) intentions, using the seven 4.0 learning practices as your helping framework, talking and listening across a variety of helping roles, and seeing helping as learning.

# Have the Right (Caring) Intentions

Helping others learn is an act of generosity and love. You share your expertise and time while showing your interest and concern for another human being. You enter with another person into that vulnerable space between knowing and not knowing—the space where a person's ego may be threatened and she will have to decide whether to close and defend or open up and learn.

In this sacred space, your intentions as a helper matter. And it is important that these intentions come from a space of caring, compassion, and love. Four intentions, which are grounded in what we know from neuroscience and psychology, are especially important from this perspective:
- Let the learner's needs and stage lead the way.
- Help increase self-management capability.
- Support a learning versus performance mindset.
- Help internalize a learning framework.

## Let the Learner's Needs and Stage Lead the Way

Have you heard the saying, "When the student is ready, the teacher appears"? Another way to think about this is that when you support others in their learning, it's about them, not you. People use their own filters when they take in information and support. It's their senses, needs, perceptions, emotions, and intentions that will determine what they ultimately learn and act on. You can influence this by manipulating rewards, punishments, and the environment to trigger new attitudes and behavior, which may seem to cause personal learning and change. But unless the person you are helping has an internal drive toward and ownership of the learning, you'll get short-term compliance at best and resentment at worst.

Certainly, there may be times when you fall back on external control, persuasion, and rewards, like when you are helping a child learn to respect, not bully others. But, as a rule, when you help adults learn, the ethical (and most effective) helping stance is to support people in the calls to learn that are coming from and through them—from their needs and life stages; their sense of past, current, and future issues; or their sense of wonder. When you think that a person is on a path that won't be in his best interests, help him see the consequences so that he can make a free and informed choice to act or not.

## Increase Self-Management Capability

Psychologists, professional coaches, counselors, and educators generally agree that a key goal in any support activity is to increase an individual's ability to self-direct and self-author. There may be times when somebody else has some control (think of a person in a highly structured degree program, or a disciplinary performance improvement plan), but these are exceptions. For most adult learning situations, the learners are and must remain responsible for their own learning process. Why? Because as you learned in chapter 2, the natural development progression of all adults is toward greater autonomy and responsibility. To take over a person's self-management role is to ask her to regress psychologically. So, a key goal when you help others learn is to increase their confidence in managing their learning in the future.

## Support a Learning Mindset

Many people are afraid to experiment, make mistakes, fail, appear to be learning, or even take time out to think versus act. Helpers often collude in creating these fears and anxieties. There may be times in the learning process when it is important to perform or even take a test—and when your role as a helper may be to evaluate and rate. But reserve this focus on perfection, performance, and evaluation for these times. When you help others, put most of your emphasis on exploration, trial and error, and alternating reflection and action. Your role is to ask questions, listen to insights, provide encouragement and support, and offer perspective on their learning process—not judge or tell them what to do.

## Help Internalize the 4.0 Learning Framework

Very few of the people you support have upgraded their learning approach to the 4.0 levels needed in today's nonstop learning world. Learning is just one of those automatic processes that most people take for granted most of the time. When they think about themselves as learners, they often feel inadequate. But in today's fast-changing world with its rapidly expanding information field, learning can't be left to chance and haphazard approaches. When you are in a helping role, you can change this. You can introduce the more conscious framework of the three learning paths and seven 4.0 practices to everyone whose learning you support. Doing this makes you a 4.0 helper—someone who helps others learn how to learn while you help.

# Use the Seven 4.0 Learning Practices as Your Helping Framework

Draw on the seven 4.0 learning practices that are at the heart of this book when you are helping others. Here's how to do it:

1. **Hear the call:** Help people notice when learning is calling them.
2. **Create future-pull:** Help people create a multisensory view of their future that will motivate action and guide deliberate goals, as well as below-conscious, automatic learning.
3. **Search:** Help people sort through the increasingly dense and varied information field. Show them how to use scanners and chose the best resources for their needs and situation.
4. **Connect the dots:** Help people select and organize their resources and plans into a learning sequence that fits their challenge and current life situation. Help them see plans as guides that may change with new opportunities and information.
5. **Mine for gold:** Talk with people about what they are learning and help them get the most out of the various learning experiences they are using. Help them recognize different points of view and find deeper patterns and frameworks.
6. **Learn to last:** Help others achieve the learning outcomes they want by using the best techniques, such as those for remembering, developing a skill or habit, updating a belief or attitude, or having creative insights.
7. **Transfer to life:** Help others manage themselves and their environment so that they can and will bring what they've learned into their day-to-day life and sustain it.

Because learning is so pervasive and you might enter somebody's learning process at any time, there is no one right formula for using these practices. In addition, the quality of your relationship with the individual, as well as his personal characteristics (for example, needs, life stage, skills and attitudes), will determine what your best kind of support will be. But if you understand how you can use the seven practices when you help others learn, you will be able to decide the best actions for situations as they come up.

## Help Them Hear the Call

You know that calls to learn come from inside people, from their immediate environment, from the future, from past experiences, and from interesting information in the moment. But often people don't hear the calls or fully explore what they mean. As an outside observer and potential helper, you can help others recognize when they are being called to learn. For example, a child may be having problems as school. You notice that there is a pattern—he consistently has trouble with math when he has to use it to solve problems—which you see as a call to learn how to think logically, and you make him aware of this. Or, imagine that you and a colleague have just heard about a strategy change in your business. You recognize that the change will require your friend to learn about a new customer segment, but she is not aware of it. You share your thinking with her, making the call to learn clear so she can think about and act on it.

## Create Future-Pull

When people internalize visions of the future, these visions can operate as goals that motivate and focus learning from the beginning to the end of a learning initiative. These visions are especially powerful for learning when the sense of the future is a multisensory one, where the learner can see, feel, and imagine a new reality. Yet, it takes committed 4.0 learners to take the time to create this powerful learning pull on their own. The process can be a lonely task that is much more enjoyable to do with somebody else. This is a natural opportunity for a helper to step in and assist the process.

As a helper, you support learners by asking them to imagine what they would like to be doing, accomplishing, seeing, and feeling at a specific time in the future. Ask where they are and who is there. Expect the vision to be a stretch and engage multiple senses. If it seems impossible, don't worry. Learning is a process with many opportunities to self-correct. Starting with a highly motivating vision can be a key to overcoming inertia and habit.

## Search

Once people have made a decision to learn, they need to find the information to make it happen. But, how do learners find what they need? Their natural tendency will be to rely on the most accessible and easiest to use information. Perhaps they'll turn to the expert in the next office, take the course a friend recommends, or open the first website or article in an Internet search. But often these are not the best resources for their needs.

You can help others sort through the information field. As a 4.0 learner, you know that scanners—people and tools to help you and others cast a wide net and narrow the learning resource options—are invaluable for finding experts, articles, books, courses, websites, and tools. There is a list of scanners in Tool 4, along with tips for how to use them. Use this list and recommend it to people you are helping.

## Connect the Dots

A person's learning may be retroactive through past experiences, forward to a goal, or in the moment. Depending on the level of challenge involved, there may be many or few, easy or difficult learning activities involved. You can play an important role in helping others gauge the difficulty of their learning agenda, and then decide and schedule the learning work they will have to do. Help them connect the dots for the best way to get to the vision that's behind their learning goals.

## Mine for Gold

The real adventure starts when people engage with a learning resource—a book, workshop, online program, experience. As a 4.0 learner, you know that different resources require different learning approaches, and you also know how important it is to be able to focus and see through biases to find the gold. So, as a helper, encourage people to use effective techniques. Ask them questions and encourage them to draw out what they need to know and make it their own. Use and refer others to the resource-specific learning tips in Tool 5. It will help you help others tailor their learning for the variety of situations they may face.

## Learn to Last

Ultimately, learning is about personal change. It happens when a person turns information into one or more of four kinds of learning: enduring knowledge, skills and habits, beliefs and attitudes, and creative insights. Show others that these four learning outcomes require different learning techniques, and use the tips in chapter 10 to suggest some options for internalizing specific learning outcomes. Give people a copy of this book and suggest they read chapter 10 so they can better manage themselves to get lasting results.

## Transfer to Life

There is a big role for you as a helper in this step. You can be an ally as well as recommend allies to support new behaviors in the real world. You can also help re-engineer the environment and give ongoing encouragement and support when someone has habits to change and new skills to hone. There are many ways you can do this, such as having weekly phone calls to check on progress, lobbying for changes in procedures and processes, creating an incentive like a dinner out after reaching a milestone, or giving periodic feedback about what you are seeing. If a big habit change is involved, be there for the long haul because it might take weeks or months to make the shift.

So, when you are in that learning support role, use the seven 4.0 learning practices as a mental framework. Don't do the work for them; part of your role is to help them become more self-directing, self-confident learners. Think about where the learner is in the process, remind yourself about your intentions, and offer the support you think will be most useful and welcome.

# Talk and Listen Across a Variety of Helping Roles

You may help others learn by taking on one or more roles. These roles vary in how much you show and tell, and how much you listen. It's tempting to think about helping as instructing, directing, telling, or teaching; for some people it even means doing some of the work for the other person. However, while some of what you do may fit into the more show and tell category, at least 50 percent of the time the situation will require the opposite. When you help adults learn, plan to do little or no show and tell and instead try to exert influence by asking questions, listening, or helping people put the what, why, and how into their own words. When you help someone reflect, you create an atmosphere of empathy and understanding. This increases trust, lowers performance and self-esteem anxiety, and makes more learning possible.

### Reflect ✦ Connect

The information in chapters 1 and 2 is a very useful backdrop for any decisions you make about helping others learn. These chapters help you understand how brains work and how personal psychology affects learning. With this knowledge, you will notice more about what others need and will be able to ask deeper questions to aid their learning process.

Reflective practices like listening, questioning, and empathizing are vital when people are hearing learning calls related to shadows, life stage transitions, and deeper or hidden needs. Take the time to help others understand what is calling them to learn and to create a vision with future-pull before encouraging any other action. Think about your relationships on a continuum where, depending on your role, the balance shifts from show and tell to listening and empathizing.

You may play one or all of the following roles with a person you are helping. However, be sure that you are always true to the four intentions: to let the learner's needs and stage lead the way, to help increase self-management capability, to support a learning versus a performance mindset, and to help internalize a learning framework (like the practices framework).

### Reflect ✦ Connect

Think about a person with whom you have a helping relationship right now. As you read on, notice which roles you are playing. Think about always having a goal to reduce the other person's dependency and to build self-management capability.

## Director

Directors tell people what to do and provide structures for doing it. In this role, you can help people move quickly through the novice stage to a point where they have skills to build on and take over their own process. But you may also create defensiveness and resistance if the learner doesn't agree to being in a temporarily dependent and novice role.

## Environment Engineer

Environment engineers provide rewards, recognition, role descriptions, and other external support for learning and behavior change. This is an important way to help if you can influence the learning and action environment. It's a way managers in formal leadership roles can help support learning and change, and encourage the successful use of new knowledge and skills in the real world. Just be sure the learner understands and accepts these actions as support rather than manipulation.

## Teacher

Teachers are sources of expert information about facts, ideas, and methods related to specific learning goals. When somebody comes to you for your subject matter expertise, you will often play this role. Be sure to help the learner mine for the gold in your teaching. Draw on specific learn to last techniques to help create the memory, skills, attitude, and creative outcomes the learner wants.

## Coach

Coaches give feedback and suggestions to help increase a person's confidence and competence in a specific area. This role involves a close personal relationship where you develop a contract to help a person achieve a specific set of goals. You will probably assist in all seven 4.0 practice areas when you coach, especially the connect the dots, learn to last, and transfer to life processes (practices 4, 6, and 7).

## Mentor

Mentors act as a listener, sounding board, witness, and cheerleader for a person's overall development. As a mentor you know the general needs, life stage, and life vision of another person. You are a supportive friend for his overall development, especially helping him recognize calls to learn and create future visions. You also encourage him through the ups and downs of the learning journey.

## Sponsor

Sponsors open doors and provide access to learning experiences and people who can provide support. As a sponsor, you may not have much personal contact with the other person. But because you have confidence in the person's intentions and abilities, you help her access your networks.

# Helping Others Learn, in Brief

When you help others, you also learn. You refine your own learning skills—the seven learning 4.0 practices presented in this book. When you share knowledge, you develop new perspectives and associations when you organize and put it into words. As a result, your own knowledge structure changes and reconsolidates. Through questions and conversation, you discover your own biases, have an incentive to review what you may have forgotten, and expand and upgrade your expertise. You also develop your communication skills, including your ability to empathize and listen. You draw on and expand what you know about the learning brain because you are looking for ways to help others learn. You also sharpen your ability to hear the deeper needs and life stage issues at work in the person you are helping; this makes you a more competent partner and friend to everybody around you. As a side effect, you will probably increase your own self-awareness.

When you help others learn, you contribute, you expand your influence, and you experience a special joy of belonging within a life context larger than you. You connect within one of humanity's biggest circles of evolution. Others played a major and multifaceted role in your earliest learning, and this has continued, directly and indirectly, throughout your life. By example and direct interactions, you can now pass your learning on to friends, family, colleagues, and people in your social networks.

## ✲ Reflect ✦ Connect ✲

How has what you read in this chapter affected your view of
yourself as a coach, guide, or mentor? How will it change your
helping practices in the future? Go to www.learning4O.com
/unstoppable for additional support for you as a helper.

You will continue in these cycles of learning and helping for the rest of
your life. As you leave this part of the book, ask yourself how well you help
others. How well do you use help from others? I hope you are drawing on,
and will continue to use, this book to support you as a wise and competent
participant, whether you are on the giving or the receiving end of the helping process.

# PART 4

---

# The Learning 4.0 Toolkit

Learning in the 21st century is a craft that requires specific knowledge, skills, and expertise—including the upgraded mental and psychological software of learning 4.0. Hopefully, your interaction with *Unstoppable You* is helping you launch this vital personal upgrade.

Part 4 provides some tools to help you throughout your learning 4.0 journey. Use them as you learn on your own, when you are learning in teams and groups, and when you teach, coach, or mentor others.

Tool 1 guides you along the three learning paths: learning in the moment, toward a goal, and retroactively. Tool 2 provides simple templates for each of the seven 4.0 learning practices. Tool 3 suggests some note-taking formats that mirror how your brain seems to manage information by assisting in associative processing and helping you store learning more successfully. Tools 4 and 5 are reference tools you can turn to for help using scanners and for tips related to specific learning situations (such as learning from reading or an app). You'll also find additional assessments, tools, and support to help you in your ongoing quest to be unstoppable through learning at www .learning40.com/unstoppable.

Your success as a 4.0 learner relies on your ability to continually update yourself in this fast-changing world around and inside you. This includes using the best tools and frameworks for your learning craft. You've come a long way from using trial and error as a child to a self-managing adult and now to an unstoppable 4.0 learner.

Congratulations for coming this far, and welcome to the next phase of this lifelong journey!

# Tool 1

# Guides for the Three Learning Paths

The suggestions in this section apply to you whether you are learning on your own, learning with others, or helping someone else learn. They expand on the descriptions of the three learning paths in chapter 8. Go to www .learning40.com/unstoppable for additional support.

## Path 1: Learn in the Moment

When something piques your interest in the moment (you hear the call to learn):

- Notice and speak the call to yourself—put your interest into your own words in the form of questions or "I wonder . . ." statements. Make your interest conscious and deliberate.
- Imagine where and when you might use this information in your future, and what it might feel like to use it (create future-pull).
- Let your curiosity be your main search tool. If you are in a conversation, ask questions. If you are reading something, follow your interests, even if it means skipping around the text. Use the best mine for gold techniques for the medium and information source (chapter 9).

- If you decide you want to remember something or if you have a creative insight, jot it down or record it in your phone. Have a notes section you can access on all your devices—a learning journal reserved specifically for in-the-moment learning. This will help you mine for gold and learn to last.

If you are learning in a team, use these suggestions to guide the group to fully learn in the moment. If you are helping someone else learn, suggest they take these steps and guide them in the process.

# Path 2: Learn Forward to a Goal

When you have a learning goal that will take time, energy, and a plan to achieve, use the seven learning 4.0 practices as a guide.

## Hear Your Call to Learn

- Where did the call to learn come from (inside, outside, future, past, or wonder in the moment)?
- What are you called to learn?

## Create Future-Pull

- Write or draw a picture of yourself as you would like to be in the future.
  - Where are you? Who are you with? What are you doing, thinking, and feeling? What's different that you are excited about?
  - Draw on as many senses as you can. Create an immersive virtual reality in your imagination.
- Remember that you are doing this to:
  - Prime your automatic, unconscious system so that you will notice learning opportunities whenever they occur.
  - Create a compelling goal that will guide your conscious learning choices and actions.

## Search for the Best Experiences and Resources

- Do a scan before you settle on the learning resources you will use.
  - Work with or use scanners.
  - Refer to Tool 4. Scanners and How to Use Them for suggestions.

- Make a list of possible learning resources and experiences to use.
  - At this point you will have a list of possible resources.
  - Use the best resources, even if they're not the ones you usually use.
  - Be ready to make some choices, at least about where to start, in the next step.

## Connect the Dots

Decide what you want do and how to connect the various parts of your learning process. See this as a tentative path that will probably change as you learn.

- Assess the difficulty level of your learning by rating it on the challenge continuum.
- Plot a learning path by identifying waypoints (actions) with some dates. Include:
  - learning resources and experiences, as well as when you plan to use and complete them
  - checkpoints for review so you can revise your vision, appreciate progress, and solve problems
  - reviews and other conversations with a coach, friend, or mentor.
- Set up for learning:
  - Set up a note-taking file to store your notes and insights. Consider using one of the note-taking formats discussed in this book.
  - Purchase courses and materials.
  - Create a learning space that will support you.
  - Remember blue and green colors and white noise support high brain functioning.
  - Identify waiting spaces (time on trains or buses) for learning activities like watching a video or reading an article.
  - Alert people who may be able to help (or interfere) and get them on board to support you.

## Mine for Gold

This is the information-processing step, when you bring information into your brain for potential later use. Try using some mining techniques:

- Tailor your approach to suit the learning resource.
  - Be sure to survey what's there before you start learning.
  - See Tool 5. Resource-Specific Learning Tips for techniques.
- Be present to learn.
  - Manage your physical energy with exercise breaks and rest stops.
  - Manage your motivation by continually asking questions and being curious, having interim goals and stopping points, and following your interests.
  - Manage and deliberately use distractions.
- Create and use mind-mirroring notes.
  - Consider using the note-taking formats in Tool 3. Note-Taking Formats.
- Spend 40-50 percent of your time processing what you are learning.
  - Think about it, craft some notes, put it into your own words, and link it to your future vision.
- Set up your immediate environment for success.
  - Remove noise or disruptions.
  - Set an intention to avoid multitasking. (Have a place to record distractions so you can deal with them later.)

## Learn to Last

There are four related but different learning outcomes: remembered knowledge, new skills and habits, shifts in beliefs and attitudes, and creative insights. Some general techniques apply to all four learning outcomes, but plan also to use methods tailored for each type of goal.

Use these techniques for all four types of learning:

- Refine your future-pull. Reconnect with and, if necessary, revise your future vision.
- Delegate to your automatic system. Use sleep, breaks, and spacing. Remember, your learning continues while you do other things. Just be sure you have internalized the information you want.

- Interleave. Alternate learning methods during a learning session to create multiple learning pathways and keep your interest and attention at high levels.
- Link to real-life situations. Make mental associations that will help anchor your memories.
- Learn with others. This both extends your learning and helps put it into your own words for better storage and retrieval.

Then, add specific techniques that are relevant for the results you want:

- To remember:
    - Make vivid connections.
    - Forget, to remember.
    - Take time to reflect.
    - Look for deeper themes and patterns.
- To develop skills and habits:
    - Be a novice for a while.
    - Use checklists and flow patterns.
    - Use perceptual learning.
    - Support yourself through plateaus and valleys.
- To update beliefs and attitudes:
    - Be self-aware.
    - Recognize when beliefs are in play.
    - Do side-by-side comparisons.
    - Load up on the benefits of change.
- For creative insights:
    - Set up for creativity.
    - Use resources to trigger creativity.
    - Capture creative insights.

## Transfer to Life

Prepare yourself and your environment to support the changes you want to make.

- Recognize the transfer challenge. Know that when you take your learning into your day-to-day environment you will probably face challenges from your own habits. And, your environment may not expect your new behaviors or innovations.

- Set up for success. Support yourself and guide changes in others' expectations and the environment around you.
- Get allies. Tell others about the changes you want to make, explain what it might mean for them, and ask for their support.
- Celebrate while continuing to learn. Learning continues when ideas, intentions, and new skills meet the real world. Find ways to support yourself through this stage of change, such as small self-rewards, checklists, or benchmarks on a calendar.

All seven steps are also relevant for team learning, and are methods you can recommend and guide when you are helping others learn.

# Path 3: Learn Retroactively

Mine the vast learning riches that may be hidden in a past experience, such as a project, event, or behavior.

1. Identify the past event or experience and decide where to go and whom to talk with (search) to review and learn from it. Consider:
   - People who sponsored, were involved in, affected by, or may have useful expertise and insights that will ensure your retroactive learning goes beneath the surface to deeper learning lessons.
   - People who received or used the output of the project or experience (customers!).
   - Documents or other information you think will be useful.

2. Have a learning versus evaluation perspective. The right mindset is critical for going deep into the lessons. To set up for success:
   - Imagine (to create future-pull) all the benefits of going back into the experience. If you are involving other people, do this together.
   - Prepare yourself and others by recognizing that going back into an experience may resurface both positive and negative feelings. Agree to seeing these as learning versus evaluation opportunities.

3. Tell the story of the experience from the perspective of an objective observer. Recognize that remembering is inevitably a creative act, so get multiple perspectives and look at multiple aspects of the project so your conclusions will be closer to reality.

Look for:

- ° Results: What outcomes did you want to produce? What direct outcomes occurred and are occurring now? Were there any secondary impacts or unintended consequences? Look at results at the end of the experience, then identify the results and ripple effects today.
- ° Actions: What happened? What did people do, and what techniques or approaches were used? What unplanned events occurred along the way, and what effect did they have? Describe the surface story of the experience—what was visible. Were there any turning points?

4. Now, go under the surface to look for deeper patterns and lessons.

- ° Tap into your brain and automatic self. Think about your unspoken feelings and thoughts before, during, or after various turning points. What was it like for you to participate in this experience? What did others say or do that affected your actions and effective participation (positively and negatively)?
- ° What subtle cues did you notice, and what did you miss that made a difference in how the experience unfolded?
- ° How would you describe the climate, environment, atmosphere, and culture surrounding this experience? What larger assumptions and biases affected what you saw, did, and felt?
- ° What did you learn about this type of experience that will help you in the future?
- ° If you were teaching others to be successful in this type of experience, what would you teach? What are the lessons learned?

5. Imagine this type of project unfolding in the future.

- ° Create a future vision of it. If you are doing this with a group, it will create a shared future-pull so that next time you are in similar situations, your lessons will come to life there.

6. If your future vision implies a new learning agenda, take the learning forward to a goal path.

Follow this retroactive learning plan whether you are looking back on a personal experience, working with a team to extract learning from a group experience, or are helping someone else pull learning from something that occurred in the past. In all three cases, conversation and sharing multiple perspectives is an enriching activity. If you are on your own looking back at a personal experience, you may want to involve somebody else as a sounding board or to ask discovery questions that help you go deeper into what happened and how you reacted.

# Templates to Guide Learning 4.0 Practices

The templates in this toolkit will help guide your use of the seven learning 4.0 practices. Use them for learning on your own, when you are learning with others, or when you are helping others learn.

# Practice 1: Hear the Call to Learn

## Why?

To make your need or interest explicit and to be sure your learning motivation is clear. If you are on a team, make sure there is agreement on what is driving the team agenda.

## How?

Ask:

- What is calling you or your team to learn?
- Where is the call to learn coming from?
- What change or development is it asking for?
- Is it connected to deeper fundamental needs, life stage challenges, shadows, values, or archetypes?

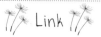 Link

For details about this practice, go to chapter 5. For downloadable worksheets, go to www.learning40.com/unstoppable.

# Practice 2: Create Future-Pull

## Why?

To create a learning direction that energizes and focuses your learning. To prime your automatic system to notice opportunities that relate to your learning direction. To set up start and end points that help you define your learning path.

## How?

One of the best ways to prime your brain to support your learning is to create a multisensory, immersive description of the future you, your team, or the person you are helping aspires to—a virtual reality future. Then create tension between now and the future by describing your current reality.

In both cases notice:

- What is the setting or situation?
- Who is there with you?
- What are you and others doing and creating?
- What are you feeling, seeing, thinking, hearing, sensing?
- What is happening?
- What is the atmosphere?

 Link

For details about this practice, go to chapter 6. For downloadable worksheets, go to www.learning40.com/unstoppable.

# Practice 3: Search

## Why?

To be sure that the information, resources, and experiences you use for learning are the best for you and your purposes.

## How?

Before you invest time, energy, and money into any learning resource, step back to scan the information field, including learning opportunities that you can access in your day-to-day life. Use scanners—people and services—to help you find what you need. This will save you time and increase the success potential of your learning.

### Choose Your Scanners

Look at the following list of scanners and pick the ones you think will help you find the best learning resources and experiences. Tool 4. Scanners and How to Use Them will help you understand what these are and how to use them.

___Citation indexes

___Course aggregators

___Crowdsourcing on social media

___Curators

___Human resources, training, and career development professionals

___Leaders in your company

___Librarians and search experts

___Mass media channels

___Job and life experience

___Periodical databases

___Personal assistant apps

___Professional associations and conferences

___Search engines

___Subject matter experts

___Your own primed brain

## Track the Possibilities

As you scan, keep a list of the learning experiences and resources you think will best help you move toward your future vision. Here are some types of learning experiences to consider:

- Articles
- Blogs and websites
- Books
- Case studies
- Coaches and mentors
- Conversations and meetings
- Courses and workshops (face-to-face or online)
- Discussions
- Experts
- Games
- Lectures and presentations
- Mobile learning
- Job and life experiences
- Periodicals or newspapers
- Podcasts
- Role plays
- Search engines (as learning resources)
- Simulations
- Social media
- Team learning and collaborative workspaces
- Video and YouTube

## Decide the Best Options

After your scan, list the specific resources and experiences you will use to help you learn. (For example, read *x* article, take *y* online class, or use *z* on-the-job project to practice.)

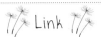 Link

For details about this practice, go to chapter 7. For downloadable worksheets, go to www.learning40.com/unstoppable.

# Practice 4: Connect the Dots

## Why?

To provide the best structure for your learning so that you stay focused on your future vision, but also remain open to new calls to learn that may arise.

## How?

Assess the difficulty of the learning challenge you face. Then plot a learning path that is robust enough to help you meet that challenge.

### Calibrate the Challenge

It's time to decide what you will do to learn. Start by rating the difficulty level of your learning project. Place an X on the challenge continuum to mark your starting point.

| 1 | 10 |
|---|---|
| Easier | More Difficult |

### Name your Path

Recognize whether your learning path is:

- **Learn in the moment.** You are in a situation that you can learn from right now, in the moment. You didn't plan for it, but you can take advantage of it.
- **Learn forward to a goal.** You want to move toward a future vision that will take extra time and effort to achieve, and you have scanned for resources. Now it's time to plot a learning course.
- **Learn retroactively.** You want to learn from an experience whose lessons you haven't yet fully mined.

### Plot Waypoints

Now it's time to plan your way forward. In your search (practice 3), you found the best learning resources and experiences for moving toward your future vision. Lay these out on a path leading toward your future vision. Think of this as a guide that you will probably modify as you learn. By drawing out your path rather than writing a list, you'll engage more of your brain to support your success.

## Equip Yourself for the Journey

Think about the learning that lies ahead as an adventure. Here is a checklist of some of the ways you can equip yourself for success:

- Add checkpoints to your journey map so you know when to pause to review, revise your vision, appreciate progress, and solve problems.
- Create a file where you will put your learning materials and notes.
- Write down or record what you already know and can do related to your future vision. See yourself on a journey from this point to the future you want to create.
- Purchase courses, apps, books, and other materials you will need to finish your journey.
- Set up a learning space that is conducive to learning and reflection.
- Put times for learning and reflection on your calendar.
- Identify waiting spaces (such as time on your commute or waiting for a spouse to shop or to pick up children) that you can fill with learning activities like watching a video or reading an article. Put these into your path plan.
- Make a list of the forces—those in you, in your environment, or from people around you—that will help or make learning difficult. Decide how to strengthen the forces for and deal with the forces against your goals.
- Think about the people who will be around you when you use your new knowledge, skills, and attitudes. Tell them about the what and why of your learning plans.
- Talk with friends and colleagues about your learning intentions and enlist their support.

Link

For details about this practice, go to chapter 8. For downloadable worksheets, go to www.learning40.com/unstoppable.

# Practice 5: Mine for Gold

## Why?

To bring useful information into your brain's short-term memory. This starts the process of neuron change and getting your entire brain ready to form new long-term capabilities.

## How?

This is the phase where you roll up your sleeves and interact with the experience, article, book, course, or coaching interaction. You bring new information and ideas into your brain and stabilize the memory traces there so they are ready to turn into lasting learning.

### Get Started

- Set up your environment for success. Remove any noise or disruptions that will compete for your attention, and surround yourself with white noise or music that will help you reduce stress levels and stay alert for learning.
- Survey each learning resource before you use it. Use the learning techniques in Tool 5 to help you mine the gold that is in the specific experience or resource.

### Mine for Gold

- Be present to learn. If you don't bring the information into your brain, there will be nothing new to store and use.
  - Manage your physical energy and motivation. Take breaks, do short exercise bursts, and talk to yourself using questions and looking for answers.
  - Manage and use distractions. Don't try to do several attention-demanding tasks at once, including listening to loud music in the background. Turn distractions into rest breaks, opportunities for your automatic system to consolidate information, or opportunities for creative thinking.
  - Go for flow by doing everything you can to ramp up your curiosity about what you are learning—lead with questions and start with the information where your interests are strongest.

- Set up mind notes that mirror what you want to store in your brain, help you process what you are learning, and link the new information to your needs and what you already know.
  - Tool 3 suggests several formats, but you can invent your own. Just make the notes visual and show connections.
- Find the real gold. You are using your learning resource because you want to learn something and you want it to help you move toward your future vision. Be selective in what you focus on. Imagine being in a conversation with the resource (the book, the person, the course designer). Ask for what you need, why something is important for you to know, or where to find what you need. Do not feel obligated to learn everything in front of you. Keep your vision, needs, and interests in mind, without being blinded by them.
- Separate real gold from fool's gold. Identify points of view and biases in yourself and your learning resource. What are your perspectives, beliefs, and attitudes related to your learning? What are the points of view, biases, and values in your information source? Keep in mind that information is power, and there are biases of some kind in everything. Notice when information—and you—is being manipulated by biasing techniques. Watch for the biasing techniques described in chapter 9:
  - just like me
  - pairing
  - simple cause and effect
  - priming
  - exposure
  - loss aversion
  - appeals to fear
  - stories over statistics
  - hindsight
  - simplification
  - narrow framing
  - ego bias.

- Look for deeper themes and patterns. What do experts see and know that nonexperts don't? Are there generalizations you can make? What is the most important information? What does a map of the content's main points and their connections look like?

 Link

For details about this practice, go to chapter 9. For downloadable worksheets, go to www.learning40.com/unstoppable.

# Practice 6: Learn to Last

## Why?

To convert what you are learning into long-term capabilities, including remembered knowledge, new skills and habits, beliefs and attitudes, and creative outcomes.

## How?

Integrate what you've learned into your brain so you get the results you want. Tailor your methods to reap new memories, skills, beliefs, attitudes, and creative insights.

### For All Learning Situations

Use the following techniques to create enduring learning:

- Strengthen the future-pull of your learning goal.
    - Take a few minutes to reconnect with your vision.
    - Be sure it is multisensory.
    - Think about it as a virtual reality and immerse yourself in it.
    - Feel what it will be like to have successfully learned.
- Use sleep, breaks, and spacing.
    - Do your most intense learning early in the morning or during your best energy period of the day.
    - Right before you go to bed, do a quick mental review of key insights from your learning.
    - Break your learning into chunks separated by exercises or other activities.
    - Use the Ziegarnik effect—interrupt learning at a high point so that when you come back you will be motivated to discover more.
- Use interleaving.
    - Alternate types of learning in defined chunks (five, 10, 15, 30 minutes).
    - Reflect, then read, then jot down some notes or give yourself a mental test.
    - You are still working on your learning project, but in different ways that reinforce each other.

- Make periodic links to your life and current knowledge.
  - Mentally anchor your learning to something important to you now.
  - Tell yourself how what you're learning connects with what you already know and do.
- Learn with others or talk with others about what you are discovering.
  - This ensures you translate your learning into your own words.
  - Others' questions will also help test your understanding and insights.
- Use what you are learning.
  - Spend 40-50 percent of your time thinking about it, crafting some notes putting what you are learning into your own words, and making links with your future vision.

## To Retain What You Want to Remember

- Make vivid connections by creating strong memory traces that have multiple connections in your brain.
  - Connect points you want to remember with each other and with other knowledge you already have.
  - Imagine yourself using the information (your visual cortex is a big part of your brain).
  - Teach and talk with others.
  - Test yourself.
- Forget, so you can remember.
  - Within the first few hours of learning something, try to remember it. Do the same thing a day or two later, and then again a week later and a month later.
  - You will have forgotten some things, but the act of forgetting and then remembering will make more connections and strengthen your retrieval pathways.
- Reflect.
  - Think about what you are learning. Focus your self-talk on it.
  - Ask yourself test questions.
  - Wonder about the point of view behind the information— what seems true, what seems untrue, and where there may be biases.

- ○ Thinking about it in a variety of ways will help you remember it.
- Find deeper themes and patterns.
  - ○ What are the main points? The main concepts and models?
  - ○ Are there generalizations or guidelines that you can transfer across situations? (For example, in music scales, the second, third, sixth, and seventh triad chord are minor chords.)
  - ○ Map or draw these out, or imagine them in some visual form.

## To Develop Skills and Habits

- Be a novice for a while. The need to be perfect is an enemy of skill development.
  - ○ Take small initial steps, mastering parts of a skill rather than the whole skill at once.
  - ○ Follow a script, imitate an expert, or get feedback to shape the small skill elements.
  - ○ It's a go slow to go fast process, where you will move toward mastery faster and won't develop bad habits to replace later.
- Use checklists and flows to identify the major steps and parts of the skill or method.
  - ○ Use a checklist to be sure you don't skip important elements, or imagine a flow sequence of activities that make up the skill or new habit.
  - ○ Create a picture in your mind where you move from one part to the next in a reliable sequence of steps.
  - ○ Make sure you visualize what is happening, rather than just using words to describe each step.
- Use perceptual learning, which is trial and error learning with a conscious learning purpose.
  - ○ Put yourself into multiple developmental situations that require the skill or habit you want to develop.
  - ○ Make it your goal to get better in each new situation, so be sure to think about what worked and what didn't, and get feedback from others.
- Support yourself through plateaus and valleys, which are inevitable when you are building new skills and habits.

- Rather than quit or be discouraged, get support from others, set and work toward smaller interim goals, and reward yourself for small improvements or even for being persistent.
- Know that your automatic system is probably at work rewiring brain connections, resting muscles, dealing with residue of old habits, and even testing the real value of doing something new.

## To Shift Beliefs and Attitudes

- Be self-aware.
  - This is difficult and seems to contradict the importance of immersing yourself in your future vision, but lift part of yourself out of the experience when you are in a learning mode.
  - Watch what you are focusing on, and pay attention to your feelings, beliefs, and emotional reactions to new ideas.
- Recognize when beliefs are in play and when you need to change a belief or attitude to move toward your future vision and learning goals.
  - Watch for these signs: You have the knowledge and skills you need, but you don't use them; you have habits that used to work but are no longer effective; you are defensive or uncomfortable with a new idea practice.
  - Ask yourself if an attitude or belief is blocking your learning.
- Do a side-by-side comparison of old and new attitudes and beliefs.
  - Make a list of all the reasons to keep the old and adopt the new.
  - Decide if you want to make a shift.
- Load up on the benefits of an attitude shift.
  - If you decide you want to shift an attitude or belief, then make a list of all the reasons not to change, and all the benefits of adopting a new attitude or belief.
  - Load up on benefits of changing until you are convinced they outweigh the reasons not to change. These kinds of shifts can be difficult and they usually affect many behaviors across many situations.

- ○ Imagine the benefits so that you create future-pull toward the changes you want to make.

## To Learn for Creative Insights

- Set up for creativity.
  - ○ Take advantage of your brain's automatic processing systems to help you find a creative answer to a question you have or a solution to a problem you face—even if it doesn't relate directly to your immediate learning activity.
  - ○ Spend some time thinking about the problem or question and tell yourself that you would like to find a creative insight.
  - ○ Then set your question or problem aside—read an article, go to a workshop, work on a project.
- Use learning resources to trigger creativity.
  - ○ While you are interacting with your learning resource, keep open to insights that might relate to your question or problem.
  - ○ Welcome the thoughts as they come; don't judge them.
  - ○ When you are learning, you are especially open to creative thoughts, so appreciate that benefit of having your brain in an exploratory state.
- Capture your creative insights.
  - ○ They may or may not be central for your larger learning goal or relate to the problem or question you want to address.
  - ○ Record them somewhere so you don't lose them.

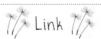

Link

For details about this practice, go to chapter 10. For downloadable worksheets, go to www.learning40.com/unstoppable.

# Template for 4.0 Practice 7: Transfer to Life

## Why?

When you want to bring learning into life, your old habits and conditions around you may keep you stuck in the status quo. You may need to take some extra steps to bring your learning to life and sustain it for the longer term.

## How?

Take these steps to ensure your learning is supported and lasts:

- Set Up for Success
  - List the forces for and against change in you and in your environment.
  - Decide how you will strengthen the positive forces and reduce some of the negatives.
  - If there are game-breakers, find ways to deal with them.
- Get Allies
  - There may be additional people who can support your change process: a colleague, manager, friend, spouse, coach.
  - Just telling others that you are making a change puts your commitment out there in public, making it more psychologically and socially binding.
  - Who will you enlist as an ally?
- Celebrate Success
  - Recognize when you have achieved something, even if it's small.
  - Build in rewards and celebrations—such as notes on your calendar that pop up every few days, rewarding yourself with something enjoyable, or setting a schedule for team members to acknowledge progress—more frequently in the early stages of your change process.
  - Appreciate every step forward and every time you fall short and learn from the experience.
  - What will you do to celebrate success along the way?

## Link

For details about this practice, go to chapter 11. For downloadable worksheets, go to www.learning40.com.

# TOOL 3

---

# Mind-Note Formats

The following are three ways to take notes that will support you as you mine for gold and learn to last. Use them to mirror the connections you want to create in your brain as you learn.

## Note Diagrams

This format helps you connect ideas that may not be organized when you initially hear, read, or experience them. The key topics may not be connected to each other. For example, the topics on the diagrams in Figure T3-1 might each refer to separate learning projects you are working on. Just create a diagonal line when you recognize a main topic, then attach related ideas where you think they belong and as they occur. Use short phrases and a few words rather than long sentences because the visual connections create a meaning environment that makes extra words unnecessary.

Figure T3-1. Example Note Diagram

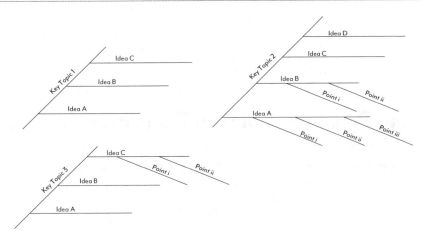

# Visual Maps

The idea of taking notes that visually show the connections among thoughts and ideas is centuries old. Visual maps—which got a boost in 1974 when Tony Buzan introduced mind maps on TV—usually look like spider diagrams. They show a network of topics and thoughts you take away from the learning resource you are using or they show the links between the ideas and your own thoughts and plans. Making a visual map is a creative and very engaging act because any topic can have multiple connections. It supports high-level information processing, helps you look for deeper patterns, and strengthens both short- and long-term memories. Just record your thoughts and connect them to show how they relate to one another.

There's a visual map of this book on page xiii, but a visual map can also look like the one in Figure T3-2. Notice that items may connect with more than one other item. The key is to make associations and find ways to organize that make sense both for the content and for your needs.

## Figure T3-2. Example Visual Map

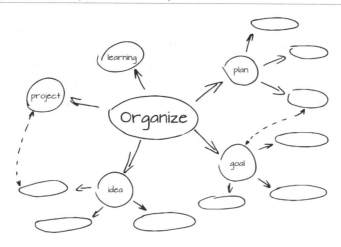

# Your Personal Learning Translator

A personal learning translator is a terrific note-taking format because it helps you pay attention and more deeply process the information and turn it into the four learning results described in chapter 10. Use the format in Figure T3-3 in any complex learning situation where there will be a lot of information.

Imagine yourself in a virtual future where you have mastered the information. Then, as you read or listen or experiment, record what you want to remember, what skills and habits you want to develop or refine, any beliefs or attitudes that you want to re-examine, and any creative insights that occur to you. This is a terrific concentration method, helping you be present to learn because you are drawing implications while you read, listen to a podcast, participate in a class, and so on. It also helps you plan how you will take your learning into your life.

## Figure T3-3. Personal Learning Translator

| The Future Vision | | | |
|---|---|---|---|
| Knowledge to Remember (facts, ideas, concepts) | Skills and Habits to Develop and Refine (physical, interpersonal, personal, intellectual skills) | Beliefs and Attitudes to Update (new ways of thinking, new priorities and values) | Creative Insights (innovative ideas) |
| | | | |
| How I Will Support Myself in Change | | How I Will Influence My Environment to Change | |
| | | | |

 Link

Go to www.learning40.com/unstoppable for a downloadable copy of the personal learning translator.

# Tool 4

# Scanners and How to Use Them

Finding the best resources for learning is one of the most difficult challenges facing 4.0 learners. Fortunately, there are a variety of scanners that can help you, and more scanning services and methods are emerging all the time. The following are some of the services, tools, and people you can go to for help to sift through the morass of information.

Does it take time to use them? Yes! But you will save time in the long run and have a better learning experience. Try them all out. Being a versatile user is what 4.0 learning is all about!

## Citation Indexes

### Examples
- Free indexes like Google Scholar
- Subscription services such as Science Citation Index, Social Science Citation Index, Arts and Humanities Citation Index, and Web of Science

### Notes and Tips for Success
These search tools can help you find the people and written material that are the most cited and referenced by experts. Resources that appear in

publications that review articles for quality rank higher—so they may be more reliable. Indexes usually focus on a subject matter area or discipline like social science, psychology, or business, so you'll need to decide if your learning need fits in a subject matter category. If your subject area is rapidly changing, you may want to limit your search to more recent years. You can specify a time range as well as topics when you search

## Crowdsource on Social Media

### Examples
- Facebook
- LinkedIn
- Twitter
- Instagram
- Social and professional networks

### Notes and Tips for Success
When you want to learn something, put out a request with your social and professional networks. Ask for suggestions on the best courses, articles, on-the-job experiences, experts, and other resources for your project. People generally like to help (partly because it releases that feel-good chemical oxytocin), so don't be afraid to let others know what you are learning and what you are looking for. You never know; you may be referred to very recent information and resources, or an emerging subject matter expert whose work is not widely known.

## Curators

### Examples
- Publishers who organize material by subject
- Subject curators in your own company
- Pinterest
- Flipboard

### Notes and Tips for Success
Museums and galleries have curators who organize their collections and ensure their authenticity. This kind of organizing is quickly expanding in

the information world to deal with the explosion of free and paid material online.

Some businesses and websites find, organize, and even summarize themes and trends for topic areas. Curators are an emerging type of scanner, so be sure to find out the curators' credentials, reach, and codes of practice before trusting what they recommend. Ask subject matter experts, publishers, professional associations, and people in your own learning and development department if there are any curators at work in your learning area.

You can also design your own curation process. Pinterest and Flipboard are popular examples where you take on a curation role—identifying your interest topics and using the service to help you collect related information.

## Leaders in Your Company or Agency

### Notes and Tips for Success

If you work for a business or agency, turn to people in leadership roles as scanners. Share your future vision with them and get advice about the knowledge and skills you should consider developing. Ask them to recommend on-the-job experiences, learning resources, and people who can help you learn. This will also build your network and help you begin to enlist these leaders as allies for learning.

## Learning Professionals in Your Organization

### Examples

- Human resources
- Training department
- Career or talent development department

### Notes and Tips for Success

Whether your company is big or small, there are probably people who know where to find learning resources for general and specific skills and knowledge building. Give them a call to discuss your future vision and ask for their help in finding courses, on-the-job opportunities and special assignments, and other learning support. You may even discover in-company programs, financial assistance, or policies related to time off for learning.

By talking with these in-house people, you will continue to strengthen your support network. They will discover more about you, your interests, and your energy to learn. By talking with them you may be able to set a longer-term networking process in motion that will affect your future opportunities!

## Librarians, Library Guides, and Information Scientists

### Notes and Tips for Success

The new library is not what it used to be. Librarians were always trained in information research, but today this means being able to find any kind of information that is out there. These search experts know how to shape search questions and to find a wide array of resources. They can also help you determine whether the resources you find are credible.

University or company libraries are often worth checking out, and they usually have a search service online. Check out the "library" section of any university's website; scroll around the resources related to your learning topics and goals. Many university libraries provide resource guides for key fields which are updated regularly. University of Queensland in Australia has a wonderful library guide, which you can access at guides.library.uq.edu.au.

## Online Course Aggregators

### Examples
- Onlinecollegecourses.com
- Udemy.com
- Coursera.org
- Udacity.com
- KhanAcademy.org
- Lynda.com
- SkillSoft.com

### Notes and Tips for Success

There are thousands of courses and workshops out there. It's impossible for you to know about all of them, but there are ways to zero in on the resources that are more likely to help you. Online course aggregators are a great search tool. Some help you find online courses and refer you to the sites that contain them. These can act as a form of one-stop shopping, because major universities and educational institutions often list their online and other courses with them. Other aggregators offer a broad range of free and fee-based courses organized by topic.

Don't just take the first workshop or course that comes along, unless it is required or provided by your employer. It's worth a few minutes of searching using these online aggregators. And, scrolling through the programs that are available will probably help refine your view of what you need.

## Periodical Data Bases

### Examples
- Newspapers.com
- Wikipedia: List of Academic Data Bases and Search Engines
- Scholar.google.com

### Notes and Tips for Success

Periodicals are publications that come out on a regular basis. They vary in how scholarly they are, how rigorous their trustworthiness rules are, and whether they are free or subscription-based.

Refereed journals are the most scholarly because the articles in them go through a peer review and have to meet other criteria for validity and reliability. Next are newspapers and magazines written by journalists who are trained to operate according to a professional code of objectivity. Finally, there are popular magazines that may or may not contain information you can trust.

The number of periodicals available is staggering, but periodical databases can help you search for what you need. Take a few minutes to find a database that will lead you to useful resources; look at how writers are talking about what you want to learn and find an article or two that you could use in your next learning steps.

## Personal Assistant Apps

### Examples
- Siri
- Cortana
- Viv
- Alexa

### Notes and Tips for Success

Personal assistant apps help you find information. Questions and clear vocal commands are key for success in this rapidly growing scanner category. Be alert for specialist assistants and software that will help you curate or find quality information in the increasingly dense information world.

## Professional Associations and Conferences

### Notes and Tips for Success

If there is a professional association or conference that deals with some of the issues related to your future vision, check it out. Find a conference agenda, do a quick overview of the topics covered, see who is speaking about your interest areas, and look for what is trending. Use what you learn to help refine your vision and search.

Take a look at the association's list of leaders and board members. Have any of them written useful books or articles, or posted a video or webinar related to your learning quest? Maybe there is an expert you want to talk to. The people who lead the association or its special interest groups may be able to help you refine your goals or find learning resources and experiences.

Becoming a member of any ongoing profession or interest area will allow you to keep your scanning process going.

## Search Engines

### Examples
- Google
- Yahoo
- Bing

### Notes and Tips for Success

Everybody uses search engines to answer spur-of-the-moment questions. But what about using them to help you define and find resources for your learning project?

To be successful, you need to understand how search engines are organized so you're not duped by their advertising bias (they put paid listings first!). Also, the search terms you use matter and should be specific to what you are looking for. It's possible to learn a lot by scanning search engines—

asking questions, reading top-line information, asking more questions, and continuing to follow where they lead you. Hopscotching through search engines can give you an amazing overview of your learning area, helping you shape your thinking and even your future vision before you commit to going beyond the headlines.

When you search, be specific and use the most important words first. Search engines use Boolean logic: words like *and, or, not* help you expand or refine your search. So, shape your search using precise terms and phrases with Boolean logic:

- Use *and* or + to narrow your search.
  - For example, searching *learning* and *adult* means the entry must have both words, but not necessarily together or in sequence.
  - The search engine assumes *and* when several words are together.
- Use *or* for either this or that.
- Use *not* to narrow the search.
  - For example, leadership universities not books.
- If combining *and* with *or,* put the *or* terms in parentheses.
  - For example, learning and (adults or seniors or college students).
- Use quotation marks if you want to specify exact phrases.
  - For example, "formal learning."
- Avoid punctuation and words like *a* or *the* unless it is important to the search.
  - For example, the name of an article or book, "the learner's guide."
- Don't capitalize.
- Use the basic word rather than plural or past tense.
- Watch what comes up on autocomplete (the words below your search box) as you're typing. It may contain idea threads you want to follow.
- Use the tilde sign (~) if you will accept similar words or synonyms.
  - For example, searching for ~learning brings up education as well as learning.

## Subject Matter Experts

### Notes and Tips for Success

If you know people who have contacts and expertise in your learning area, get in touch with them. Ask them specific questions, such as, "What major knowledge, skills, and values or beliefs are key to success?" and "Who are the leading thinkers?" Talk about your future vision and get advice about resources, experiences, and experts to incorporate into you learning journey. Ask for advice on how to proceed. This also helps expand your network, creating potential allies for learning, as well as ongoing relationships and support.

## Video and TV Services and Channels

### Examples

- TV or cable channels
- Internet streaming services
- YouTube

### Notes and Tips for Success

There may be TV, cable, or Internet streaming channels or video services related to your interest areas. Services like Netflix and Amazon Prime also have search capabilities you can use to find potential video material. And YouTube has a great search function for finding channels and individual videos.

By searching these services, you will see what is trending and how people rate the videos. However, you need to be aware that popularity is only one factor, and it may not be the best search criterion for your needs.

## Your Primed Brain

### Notes and Tips for Success

Your brain is a fantastic search engine for scanning your immediate world. Once you have a future vision, your brain will be on alert to automatically notice opportunities, resources, and experiences related to it. The key is to have a future vision and enough curiosity to put your brain on alert!

# Tool 5

---

# Resource-Specific Learning Tips

As a 4.0 learner, you can learn from any resource. You understand the benefits, pitfalls, and deeper structures of each learning resource you use. And you know what techniques work best for each. This tool will help you learn better from many learning resources. Refer to it whenever you are in a learning situation and want to be as efficient and effective as possible.

## Journal Articles or Professional Publications

### What 4.0 Learners Know
Benefits:
- Read at your own speed and in your own order and depth.
- You can stop to reflect, associate, and take notes.

Be aware:
- It's easy to be passive and lose attention.
- Information you need may be buried.

Structure you can expect:
- Key information will be in the abstract, beginning, and ending (results, conclusions, discussion, areas for further research).
- The first few sentences in each section usually tell you the section's main points.

## What 4.0 Learners Do

- Find out about the author's credentials and affiliations. Be sure she has expertise you can rely on, and make you're reading as close to a conversation with a real person as you can.
- Survey by reading the abstract or summary at the beginning, the introductory paragraph, the last paragraphs, and section headers plus their first sentences. Stop and tell yourself what the article is about and why it may be important. Note if it is a study, a literature review, or a theory article. Clarify what you want.
- Read the results, discussion, and conclusion sections early. Stop, get up, and create a remembering framework by telling yourself what the main points are. You could create a visual map to help you integrate your thinking as you learn.
- You don't have to read everything—read what you need or want to read. (Just taking the three previous steps is often enough!) Imagine you are having a conversation with the author, and go where your questions lead you. You don't have to read from beginning to end!
- If it's a long article, stop at a high-interest point to take a short break. Or set a timer to read in 15-30 minute chunks and then stop and walk around or change your environment.

## News Articles

### What 4.0 Learners Know

Benefits:

- Contain current information
- Written by trained journalists, so there should be some objectivity or known bias.
- Structured to be read and skimmed quickly

Be aware:

- The information usually focuses on events rather than analysis.

Structure you can expect:

- Key information—who, what, when, where, why, and how—appears in the first paragraph or two.
- More detailed information follows in order of importance (most to least).

### What 4.0 Learners Do

- Read the first paragraph to discover key information, then decide whether to read further.
- Stop reading when you have enough information.
- Remember that news articles are structured for quick skimming.

## Blogs

### What 4.0 Learners Know

Benefits:

- Information is usually brief, but sometimes you can click "read on" to learn more.
- Blog posts are dated and usually listed from most to least recent.
- If the blog or website author is an expert, it usually reflects his most recent thinking.

Be aware:

- Blogs are opinion pieces, not objective articles.
- Anyone can publish a blog. Be sure to find out the author's background and credibility.
- If it is an ongoing feature on a website, the information may be biased toward selling you something.

Structure you can expect:

- Blogs are usually short and reflect the thought process of the author.

### What 4.0 Learners Do

- Check out the blogger's background and other works to determine his credibility and potential points of view and biases.
- If there are section headers, do a quick overview to anchor your understanding of what is in the blog.
- If there are statements of fact or statistics, keep the overall bias of the blog in mind. Check for citations and make a mental note of the credibility of the source.

# Nonfiction Books

## What 4.0 Learners Know

Benefits:

- The author has taken time to assemble thoughts and information on a topic.
- Information in professionally published books has been edited and reviewed in some way to ensure readability and quality.
- You can be flexible, skim, skip, read, or scan.

Be aware:

- Many people feel guilty if they skip sections or chapters or don't read a book from front to back.
- Self-published books may be poorly written, or the content may not have had editorial or other review.

Structure you can expect:

- Copyright date and author information give some idea about the author's expertise in the area and the currency of the information.
- Introduction, overview chapter, and table of contents tell you how the author wants you to see and use the book.
- The summary and conclusions generally give a succinct review of key messages and points.
- The index shows the amount of emphasis on topics and where to find information on specific topics.
- The bibliography tells you something about the scope and possible bias of knowledge that is behind the book. It shows how recent some information may be and may contain additional resources for your learning.

## What 4.0 Learners Do

- Do a quick overview before you read—see what it contains and how the chapters look. (Are there section headers, summaries, or graphics?)
- Check out the author's background and qualifications. Add a level of extra scrutiny if the book is self-published.
- Study the table of contents and summarize the content in your own words.

- Read the overview, summary chapters, or any parts that provide the big picture. Notice the author's point of view, value system, and biases.
- Create a mental framework for yourself. Tell yourself what will be valuable for you and make a quick plan for how you will read or use the book. Decide whether you are taking any notes. Doing this makes it more likely you will remember what you read. It's worth it!
- Read the book as though you are in a two-way conversation with the author: Will you start at the beginning and let her start the conversation and lead the way? Or will you start someplace else to answer your important questions?
- Go to the index, find the terms that most interest you, and read from the index by only reading the pages for the topics that interest you (this is an amazing and highly focused technique).
- Follow your curiosity, not worrying whether you are reading everything. It can be an advantage to not have all the background: You may say to yourself, "I wonder what this term means. I see it was introduced in a previous chapter. I think I will go there next."
- Periodically recap and link what you are reading with your future vision or something important to you.

## Case Studies

### What 4.0 Learners Know

Benefits:
- They're a safe way to apply new concepts and practice problem solving in a low-risk situation that is rich with potential learning points experts have helped organize.
- If you read them with others, the opportunity to talk about ideas and approaches is a good way to learn to last.

Be aware:
- The lessons may not be clearly relevant to your own situation and needs.
- Debriefing—where key lessons are discussed—is often not done well or omitted.

Structure you can expect:

- The beginning introduces key players, their interests, the problem situation, and case challenge.
- May include historical information for background that will influence how you should respond.
- You may have to interpret charts and data sheets that contain financial or other information.
- They may also contain potential solutions to analyze.
- There should be a debriefing where you can test your observations and solutions and compare them with more experienced conclusions.

## What 4.0 Learners Do

- Review the case to see what it contains, paying special attention to the introductory material and the last paragraphs, or wherever the questions you must answer are found.
- Tell yourself why you are going to use this case study: What do you intend to learn and use, and how does it fit your future vision and anticipated future situations?
- Thoroughly read the case, looking for clues and keeping the history in mind. Understand the key issues that are at the heart of the case before trying to solve any problems it presents.
- Do a SWOT analysis: What are the strengths, weaknesses, opportunities, and threats that are affecting the case?
- Use any analytical models or checklists that apply to understanding the case or opportunities. Using a model will help ensure that you don't miss important options and ideas.
- Debrief what you have learned: What do you want to remember? Are there any skills you want to develop? Were you exposed to any new values or beliefs? Did you have any creative ideas? Draw out deeper themes, patterns, and best solutions; don't just experience the case at a superficial level. If you don't mine for the gold it is just experience, not learning.

# Formal Coaches and Mentors in Supportive Relationships[1]

## What 4.0 Learners Know

Coaches support you in implementing a specific short-term or long-term development agenda. Although they offer their knowledge, they don't provide technical advice or direction. Their main value is the support they provide for your immediate or transformational change.

Mentors provide different support (such as technical expertise or deep knowledge of the industry or your organization) that relates to your general development and success rather than specific short- or long-term goals. Their main value is the content support and access they provide.

Benefits:

- Coaches help you learn how to set goals, create learning agendas, and manage personal change.
- Coaches help you dive deeper into your big self to connect your learning with deeper self-insights, needs, and purpose. A goal is to grow personally in the process.
- Mentoring relationships offer expert wisdom and guidance in the subject area of your future vision or help making connections or career moves.
- Both provide personal support and encouragement to pursue your future vision.

Be aware:

- Your relationships with coaches and mentors are personal, requiring mutual respect, trust, and commitment. Don't work with anyone you don't trust.
- Although you are learning from and being supported by the coach or mentor, you are a partner in every conversation and make the final decisions about what to do and accept. Don't slip into dependency.
- The more you know about yourself, the better partner you will be with a coach or mentor.

Structure you can expect:

- Coaching relationships are contractual; you both agree to roles, actions, and timeframes. They generally follow these stages: Meet and contract. Discover and clarify your future vision. Discover more about your big self. Identify and connect the dots. Work together and then end the relationship as mutually agreed in the contract.

- A mentoring relationship is usually less formal. You have a person to contact when you need advice, direction, or connections.

## What 4.0 Learners Do

- Coaches and mentors will help you refine your calls to learn, future vision, and other learning 4.0 practices. Start with some self-knowledge of your strengths and weaknesses. Have an idea about what you want and need before searching for support. Go to www.learning40.com/unstoppable for self-analysis tools that will help you do this.
- Choose your coach or mentor carefully. Know what to expect and check their credentials and references. Many coaches are certified by a credentialing organization.
- Have an exploratory meeting where you share your initial view of your needs, and the coach or mentor presents himself, describes his credentials and background, and explains how he works.
- Agree about the scope of the relationship and put it in writing if you can. See this as a contract where you commit to making it work.
- Have regular conversations focused on your learning plans and progress. Be sure to be an active participant; go deep into conversations; and be open to surprise and new understanding of yourself and your options.
- Recognize when it's time to end the formal coaching or mentoring relationship. Mark the ending with appreciation and recognition of the role both of you played. Don't let the relationship slowly fade away.

# Face-to-Face Courses and Workshops

## What 4.0 Learners Know
Benefits:

- Someone has designed a learning experience for you by selecting information, materials, and methods.

- You can have real-time interactions with a subject matter expert, including asking questions and requesting additional learning suggestions.
- You can have a variety of learning-related conversations with fellow participants (to help you mine for gold, learn to last, and plan for transfer to life).

Be aware:

- You have participated in face-to-face courses all your life, so it may be difficult to take a fresh look and have primary control over your learning process.
- It's easy to see courses as events in time or as something to attend, like a performance, rather than part of your learning journey.

Structure you can expect:

- They are preceded by an agenda, overview, and possibly pre-work.
- They start with an introduction to help you get acquainted with other participants and share your personal agenda.
- They may include a variety of learning resources and experiences, post-course activities and recommendations, and tests or other proof of learning.

## What 4.0 Learners Do

- Realize that you will be in an experience that somebody else structured. Commit to making the most of this time away from your daily routine.
- What you do to prepare will have a huge impact on your learning results. So, set up for a powerful learning experience:
  - Review course materials and pre-work to set up a mental framework for your learning.
  - Notice what learning resources and experiences will be part of the workshop and review this tool's learning tips for them.
  - Refine your future vision related to how you want your life and work to be affected.
  - Imagine coming back after the workshop. Whose help would make transfer to life easier?
  - Think about your upcoming experience at two levels: What immediate skills and habits will you develop or change? Are

there deeper or incidental personal or life goals that
these skills will help you achieve?
- ○ Set up your note-taking method.
- ○ Plan how to get physical exercise while you're in
the workshop.
- Do everything possible to connect the dots, mine for gold, and
learn to last. Consider using one or more of the learning 4.0
practice templates (Tool 2).
- Watch for points of view and bias. Ask what alternative methods
and points of view exist.
- Use your learning 4.0 knowledge to help others learn! Ask: How
do you think this course will help you in your life? How will you
use this on the job (future-pull)? What will help and interfere with
using your learning? What will you do about it (transfer to life)?
Doing this will also help you have other insights and action ideas.
- After the workshop or course, take steps to transfer to life so you
pull your learning through to action.

## Online, Self-Paced Courses and Workshops[2]

### What 4.0 Learners Know
Benefits:
- Learn on your own time and in your own best learning space.
- Chunk your learning and possibly go back to repeat sections.
- They often include mixed media, which aids your learning process.

Be aware:
- Many online courses have not been designed by professional
development or learning specialists, so mining for gold and
learning to last may be challenging.

Structure you can expect:
- There may be a menu of topics and time estimates for
completing them.
- Tests or assessments may have standards for passing or
receiving certificates.
- There may be time limits for completion and strict standards
that affect your learning sequence and process.

## What 4.0 Learners Do

- Survey the course before you start:
  - ○ Pay attention to intended learning outcomes.
  - ○ See the topic menu and time estimates for segments.
  - ○ Is there visual support (visuals makes material more memorable) or just text?
  - ○ Will you be able to stop when you want or repeat sections?
  - ○ Note the length—if you don't have time to do the course, don't take it now.
  - ○ Download relevant apps and be sure you know what web addresses and phone numbers to use.
- Will others be participating in the course? How will your learning affect theirs? Commit to being an active learning partner. Reach out to one or two other participants for more in-depth partnering to learn.
- Future-pull is an essential practice to help you stay motivated. Create a mental image of yourself as a master of the content and connect with your personal call to learn.
- Plan your time and block it on your calendar. Remember the importance of breaks and spacing.
- Set up your learning space, technology, materials, and note-taking format on your computer. Consider setting up a split screen so you can take notes as ideas occur to you, or draw visual notes on a tablet or note paper.
- If possible, interleave the course with alternate learning activities.
- If there are tests that give feedback on your incorrect responses, consider intentionally picking the wrong answers to get the additional information that shows up. (This is a form of trial and error learning; we often learn more from mistakes than correct responses.)

# Online, Synchronous Courses and Workshops

## What 4.0 Learners Know

Benefits:

- Learning at the same time as others can help keep you going.

- You can share ideas, ask questions, and talk about application while you are learning.
- You benefit from the diversity of participants and what they bring to the discussions and projects.

Be aware:

- Commitment levels of others may vary.
- It is easy to try to multitask unless there is also a real-time video connection.
- Technology can (and probably will) be problematic. You'll need time and patience to get online and deal with interference, dropped calls, or frozen screens.

Structure you can expect:

- A menu of topics and segments.
- Interaction opportunities such as chat, breakout rooms, and polling.
- Visual elements, such as charts, graphs, and models.

## What 4.0 Learners Do

- Survey the course and prepare in the same way as for self-paced e-learning.
- Be active—use the chat function, ask questions, contribute, and try out ideas.
- Set up a split screen so you can take notes as ideas occur to you, or draw visual notes on a tablet or note paper.
- If possible, connect with another participant to have more in-depth, application-oriented conversations offline.
- Agree to check in on a schedule of your choice with one or two other participants to talk about the transfer to life process, discuss issues, and get emotional or other support.

## Discussions

### What 4.0 Learners Know

Benefits:

- The interactions with others are interactive and engaging, and stimulate oxytocin and other neurochemicals that may help you feel good as you participate.

- It is easy to move into a flow state of concentration if the topic is interesting.
- You put your ideas into your own words and hear them expressed in other ways, which helps create more memory associations.
- You can clarify your values, attitudes, and beliefs because conversations often bring out differences in these.

Be aware:

- Discussions require listening and group interaction skills. The pace of conversation may be slow, so it's tempting to let your mind wander unless you use mine for gold and learn to last methods.
- Group norms may discourage real issue discussion.
- Your ego may get in the way of learning if your self-esteem is threatened.
- Different viewpoints may be threatening, causing emotional reactions that make it difficult for you to listen.
- If you are the more powerful person, you may (intentionally or unintentionally) dominate. If you are less powerful, you may withhold your ideas.
- Without some structure, discussions can be disorganized and easily move off topic.

Structure you can expect:

- Dependent on the structure that you and others bring to them.

## What 4.0 Learners Do

- Have a dual goal of both sharing and learning.
- Be aware of similarities and differences in biases, points of view, attitudes, beliefs, and values. Lay them on the table as you do facts.
- Recognize that the purpose of a learning discussion is idea exploration, not agreement.
- Summarize periodically to check your perception. Restate others' viewpoints and look for the vulnerable side of your own view and beliefs.
- Check into your own curiosity if your interest is waning and find a question you care about to throw into the mix.
- Keep active and engaged by playing a variety of task-related and people-centered roles.

- Do a quick group recap after the discussion to build more mental associations and further clarify what you learned and how you might use it.

## Current Experience

- In the moment learning
- Developmental or stretch assignments
- Learning on-the-job
- Working on something with friends, fellow professionals, your family, people with similar interests

### What 4.0 Learners Know

Benefits

- Your life is a series of experiences. Each is a potential opportunity to learn.
- Experiences are already multisensory, so your brain can make multiple associations, making memory easier.
- Your brain has a special ability to remember experiences (episodic memory).
- Experiences are rich in calls to learn.

Be aware:

- Most of what you do in daily experience is run by habits or immediate rewards and consequences. So, what you learn may not be the best or deepest learning.
- Experience is messy and not naturally organized for learning. You have to consciously extract the best learning from it.
- When you deliberately learn from experience, you openly examine problems and failures. The culture around you may make it difficult to expose and explore problems.
- While you can plan some learning proactively, many lessons from experience are only obvious after the fact, and they may be lessons you did not intend to learn.
- It takes conscious energy to direct your attention to deeper learning from experience, especially if you are contradicting habits or requirements from yourself or others.

Structure you can expect:

- Because much of what you learn is governed by your automatic system, you risk missing learning points.
- Your experiences are often shaped by entrenched habit patterns and by feelings and assumptions that may or may not be the best for the situation.
- Sometimes what you do is structured by others.
- If you want to pull deeper learning from experience, you need to focus conscious attention and use mine for gold methods.

## What 4.0 Learners Do

- As a 4.0 learner, remind yourself to be alert for opportunities to learn—to hear the call.
- When you hear the call to learn, speak the call to yourself.
- Take a minute or two to imagine where and when you might use this information and what it might feel like to use it (create future-pull).
- Take one of two approaches—or combine them:
  - Watch your learning (reflect) while you are learning. Talk to yourself about what you want to learn and what you are learning. Notice any habits or biases that are operating for you in the situation.
  - Get into a flow state where you are only focusing on the experience. Then reflect.
- Let your curiosity be your main search tool. If you are in a conversation, ask questions. If you are reading something, follow your interests even if it means skipping around the text.
- Set up a key learning file or have a notebook that is easy to access. Keep notes of what you are learning about yourself, the environment, the type of problem or project you meet along the way, and the insights that relate to your goal.
- Make your learning social. Talk with others about what they see and what you are learning and then get feedback by asking questions, such as, "What did I do that seemed to work? What didn't work as well?"

- When possible, celebrate success; close activities, projects, and assignments by showing appreciation to others and talking about lessons learned.

## Past Experiences

### What 4.0 Learners Know
Benefits:

- Past experiences are part of your life story. Look at that story to see what you learned.
- Transform regrets and disappointments or second-guessing into something positive for the future.
- Increase the learning value of the experience by retrieving information to help shape new connections that strengthen and refine memory.

Be aware:

- You may have strong emotions related to the experience, which will affect your post-experience learning process.
- Every time you call up a memory, you change it. So, the memory you have will never be the experience as it was.

Structure you can expect:

- Experiences exist in time, so one way to look at their structure is from beginning to end in a time flow. Anything else will be a structure you provide.

### What 4.0 Learners Do

- This is one of the three learning paths (learning retroactively) presented in this book. See Tool 1 for more ideas.
- Identify where you will search for the learning contained in the experience and who will be involved in the learning process itself.
- Prepare to have the right mindset for learning versus evaluation. Imagine the benefits of going back into the experience, and acknowledge potential emotional land mines.
- Tell the story of the experience from the perspective of an objective observer: What were the results? What were the actions, events, and methods used?

- Go deeper: What were the feelings, turning points, subtle cues that were noticed or missed, or other factors like culture, assumptions, biases, environment that played a role?
- What lessons will you bring into the future?
- Create a new future vision. If it implies additional learning, use learning 4.0 practices to move forward to a new goal.

## Experts

### What 4.0 Learners Know

Benefits:

- Subject matter experts have networks, broad knowledge of their areas, stories from experience, and an intuitive sense of future issues and opportunities.
- From experience and study, they know the deeper patterns and key success factors for their areas.
- They can help you find learning resources or provide the information and tips you need.

Be aware:

- Many experts have developed expertise they can't describe, so what they tell you are key success factors may not be what makes them experts.
- It is easy to be intimidated by experts or feel uncomfortable, which interferes with your ability to have a conversation about your interests and needs.
- Many experts do not understand learning or learning 4.0, so they may say or do things that are not helpful to you as a learner.

Structure you can expect:

- Expertise takes the form of knowledge, skills, mental models, checklists, analytical tools, and frameworks. Experts are able to see patterns in messy situations or that novices don't see; they have perspectives, including views of cause and effect over time, that help them distinguish critical from irrelevant information and events.
- Explicit expertise is when the expert can tell you what it is.
- Tacit expertise is when the expert is unaware of what she is doing or seeing because the expertise has become automatic.

## What 4.0 Learners Do

- Know what you want from the subject matter expert. Is it broad or narrow?
- Share your future vision and ask for feedback and ideas to expand or shift it. Ask for the expert's future vision, too!
- Questions and curiosity are key. You want to be in dialogue, not be the recipient of a lecture. Use the following kinds of questions to help you get more than surface information:
  - Ask about key knowledge areas and how the expert keeps up-to-date on them.
  - Ask what the most important skills (mental, interpersonal, personal, physical) are.
  - Ask if there are different points of view, approaches, or philosophies, and how they differ.
  - Ask what the main mental models, concepts, and mental checklists are that the expert uses to see deeper patterns and know what to do in important situations.
- Assume that there are many areas of tacit expertise and try to discover them by asking the expert to describe several common and difficult situations where her expertise was needed. Ask about failures as well as successes.

## Games[3]

## What 4.0 Learners Know

Benefits:

- Games are engaging and it is easy to motivate yourself through them.
- There is extrinsic support and rewards to help you keep learning.
- Games may use artificial intelligence or virtual reality, which provide a rich learning simulation in a safe environment.
- Well-designed games will notice and help you quickly correct errors, allowing you to shorten your learning time with an accelerated and feedback-rich experience.

Be aware:

- Winning may become more important than learning the game's lessons.

- The game may not be well designed to achieve the stated purpose.
- The difference between the game world and the real world may be too great for learning transfer to easily occur.

Structure you can expect:

- Early rounds are usually set up to help you learn how to play. As you build skills, the game may progress in difficulty.
- Game rules often are set up to mirror real-world context or constraints. If there are time constraints in the real world, the game rules might constrain time as well.
- Game elements may be similar to a real-world job context or task. Knowing how similar may help you evaluate the purpose and value of the elements.
- Fun within a learning game is often less about entertainment and more about mental engagement. It is not necessarily fun in the same way as a commercial game might be.

## What 4.0 Learners Do

- Know the game's goals and intended lessons learned.
- Prime yourself with knowledge of your own real-world and learning goal. This will make it easier for your brain to link to the game's lessons.
- Game rules, tutorials, and helpful hints enhance your learning experience and speed time to proficiency in a game. Skipping them only increases your mental challenge while you are playing the game.
- As you experience a learning game, notice what it is helping you learn and how it is trying to help you. Is it illustrating a concept or situation? Offering you practice and repetition so you can learn information you need to know from memory? Or letting you practice a skill or use judgment?
- Games help you to learn by playing and making mistakes. Notice what you're learning as you explore the game's environment and figure things out through trial and error. Make mistakes intentionally to see what happens.
- Pay attention to feedback. You can try something and see an almost immediate effect, which enables you to adjust your behavior

accordingly. The feedback you get can give you cues on how to improve.

- Feel free to fail and try different things. Turn off your evaluative mindset and experiment.
- Reflect on the experience. Translate the game's lessons into insights for your real world.

## Lectures, Presentations, and Speeches[4]

### What 4.0 Learners Know

Benefits:

- Get an overview on a topic in a short time if the presenter is an expert and current in the area.
- Gain current ideas and insights that may not yet be in print or other formats.

Be aware:

- Spoken information occurs at a slower pace than your reading and thinking speed, so it is easy to be passive, lose attention, or multitask.
- The talk may not be well organized or directly relate to your learning goal.

Structure you can expect:

- If it is a well-organized talk, there will be:
  - an introduction to get your interest
  - an overview of the key points
  - a presentation of key points and supporting material
  - a summary and review.

### What 4.0 Learners Do

- Have an initial, clear intention to learn from the presentation. Develop a quick future vision of yourself knowing more about the topic and using it in a real situation.
- Set up for success. Turn off your phone and text messages and sit near the front to minimize distractions.
- Listen for an overview of the key points and jot them down to set a listening structure in your mind.

- Use notes in a graphic way to zero in on main ideas and key terms, keep yourself interested and active, and organize your thoughts.
- Notice biasing techniques.
- Listen for the deeper insights, such as the speaker's values and beliefs and his views of trends and issues.
- Think of questions whether you ask them or not (formulating your questions is a good brain-engagement technique; asking questions enhances assertiveness and speaking skills).
- Draw on the speaker's scanner expertise by asking about the best resources in the field.
- Mentally recap key points and discuss them with somebody after the presentation.

## Podcasts[5]

### What 4.0 Learners Know

Benefits:

- You can listen on a personal device anywhere if you have downloaded it or there is wireless access.
- If it is a recording, you can stop at any time to process information.
- Imagine podcasts playing into your "theater of the mind," where you connect what you are hearing with what's in your long-term memory.

Be aware:

- It is difficult to learn by just listening—spoken information is often slower than your brain processes, and there may be a lot of visual and mental competition.
- Podcasts are not the best sources if what you are learning is complex and detailed or requires a demonstration.
- It is difficult or impossible to skip across information you don't need.
- If the podcast is live, you will not be able to stop, rewind, and reflect. You will have to do mental review and make associations as you listen.

Structure you can expect:

- Podcasts are typically structured by episodes. Some might be a single interview with someone or a focus on a single story or piece of learning.
- Some podcasts have a news show format, with multiple topics related to a general theme.
- Podcast episodes generally do not have any internal navigation. But there may be "show notes" that summarize what is discussed, key points worth calling out, or links to other resources and information.
- Podcasts, especially those created for public distribution, include information about the podcast creator (background, expertise, experience with subject) and any guests that appear (background, expertise, experience with subject). These often link to other resources.

## What 4.0 Learners Do

- If possible, download podcasts so you have more flexibility when you are listening and learning.
- Set your attention: Why are you listening to this podcast? What might it relate to in your life?
- Survey any overview material so you know what the podcast contains. Know the overall structure and length, as well as the background and expertise of the people providing information.
- Before playing the podcast, adjust things like computer volume, or set up headphones. Close your door; turn off notifications, email, and other potential distractions; or make other adjustments to minimize distractions (remember, multitasking slows and interferes with learning).
- Stop the podcast periodically to put your learning into your own words. Imagine yourself using the knowledge and skills in your own life situations. (Practice the 50/50 rule: 50 percent taking information in and 50 percent processing it.)
- If you can't complete the podcast in one sitting, consider stopping at interesting points so that you will be motivated to come back.
- If you are in a place where you can be hands-free, jot down notes using the personal learning translator or other note-taking format

(Tool 3) and include the time in the podcast that the idea, thought, or question occurred. This will create an index of key points and questions that are synced with the podcast, and gives you an excellent reference if you want to go back for a review.

- If the podcast has a lot of content that is not completely new, check to see if there is variable speed playback, which will allow you to listen at a faster speed (probably no faster than 1.5x speed). The faster playback is also a great way to do a quick refresher, even with more complex content.

## Role Plays

### What 4.0 Learners Know

Benefits

- Examine issues, situations, and actions from other perspectives by trying on various role play personalities.
- Test new ideas, learning, actions, feelings, and reactions in an experimental, low-risk setting.
- Simulate what happens in real situations and feel what it is like to use specific techniques and skills.
- Receive feedback that can help you further refine new behaviors.
- Have an opportunity to observe and give feedback to others, making it more likely you will be able to self-manage your own behavior in similar situations in the future.
- Some role plays include videotaped opportunities to see what happened from an observer's vantage point.

Be aware:

- Many people have stage fright, believing they have to perform like professional actors.
- It may be tempting to overact and lose the opportunity to see what it is like to try out and learn from using new skills, behaviors, and styles.

Structure you can expect:

- An introduction to the role play, including the general situation and characters involved.
- Specific instructions for each role that only the person playing the role knows.

- An allotment of time to play the role, usually with an observer or in a videotaped situation with an opportunity to replay examples or the video.
- A feedback session following the exercise (with or without video playback). Usually you can talk about what you did and what you think your impact was. Then, the other party and observers will talk about what they saw happening.

## What 4.0 Learners Do

- When the role play is introduced, pay close attention to the situation, characters, and intended learning opportunities.
- Lobby to be in a role that will optimize your learning and stretch you! Try to get out of your comfort zone!
- Take time to understand your assigned role, motivation, and the background to the role-play situation.
- Before you go into the exercise, think about the skills, methods, knowledge, and values you want to use while you are in character. This is play and a chance to try something new. If it will help you be more experimental, tell your role-play partners that you are going to try or even exaggerate doing something new.
- Keep alert while you are playing the role. If you feel yourself slipping into old patterns, take a deep breath, regroup, and get back on the learning path.
- In the feedback stage, ask open-ended questions about what others saw and heard you do and say while you were in the role. Explore, don't defend. If feedback-givers slip into an evaluation role, ask for specific examples and remind them that this is an experimental situation where examples of actions and their impact are more valuable to you than performance ratings or evaluative comments.
- When you are in the observer role, be as objective about what you are seeing as possible. Say, "When this happened, you said $x$ and you did $y$. This seemed to cause $z$." Be descriptive, not evaluative.
- Be supportive to others; encourage them to try things out.

# Virtual, Computer-Based, or Video-Based Simulation

## What 4.0 Learners Know

Benefits:

- It is motivating and engaging.
- Safely apply theories and methods in a near-real, often complex but time-compressed situation, and to experience how events may evolve over time.
- Test how processes and systems will work before they go live.
- If it is a group simulation, you can explore alternate views and ideas on the topic and make decisions as a group.
- Discover best practices or explore potential outcomes of scenarios and actions where the best practices are unknown.
- Experiment and innovate in a safe environment.

Be aware:

- The purpose is to learn how to interpret and deal with complex situations alone or in a group-decision setting, not just to enjoy the simulation or win if it is competitive.
- It may be difficult for some to fully participate and try solutions out if participants are from the same organization but differ in rank.

Structure you can expect:

- Introduction to the setting, roles, and background.
- Learn background for your specific role.
- Participate in the simulation.
- Debrief the exercise.

## What 4.0 Learners Do

- Use your future vision skills before you begin. Understand the purpose of the simulation and then imagine what it will feel like to be successful in similar situations. Create a powerful future-pull that is meaningful to you.
- In the simulation:
  - If it is a group experience, use the simulation as an opportunity to build relationships and networks, as well as to experiment with strategies and tactics.

- ○ If you are in a group where you have a higher or lower rank than others, be aware that the power difference may affect behavior. If you have a higher rank in real life, make it a point to listen to others and encourage different points of view. If you have a lower rank, take courageous steps to offer your views with directness and respect.
  - ○ Look for deeper patterns and lessons in what is happening, either while you are in the simulation or in short reflection stops along the way.
  - ○ Go for creative solutions and scenarios. This is a simulation, so don't be constrained by traditional ways of thinking. Try out new concepts and practices.
- Debriefing is critical. It serves two purposes: to extract learning from the experience and to develop mental models for future situations. Look at what happened and the results, but also at the effect of external and organization factors.
- When debriefing actions and impacts, focus on what happened and what the longer-term consequences may be.

## Social Media

### What 4.0 Learners Know
Benefits:

- Tapping social networks is a fast way to search for learning resources.
- Being part of networks keeps you continually informed about interests and shifting trends.
- When you need to find resources or want other learning help, you can easily tap into your networks and significantly expand your reach.
- You can find people with similar interests whom you may want to work with on a learning project.

Be aware:

- People in your networks may not be able to help if your learning need is outside the scope of their interests and connections.
- Be careful about what you share. Information you put into social networks will be there for others to find.

- It is easy to only associate with people who have similar views. Reality can get easily distorted and defined by a narrow view and shared biases.

Structure you can expect:

- People generally cluster in interest, professional, or social groups.
- Some groups are open and others require you to request membership or show some other qualification related to joining.
- Some groups are curated and have active leadership and coordination.

## What 4.0 Learners Do

- Keep your social networks current. From time to time, scan the Internet to find networks related to your interests.
- When joining a social network, see what groups and interest areas are available. Spend time to set up your interests and security screens.
- Step back and scroll through the blogs and commentaries on the sites you are monitoring. Look for deeper patterns of thinking and emerging issues and topics. Think of your communities as a microcosm of a larger group.
- Remain aware of other social groups and perspectives. Watch for biases in your groups. Ask, "Are there other valid ways of thinking about this?"
- When you turn to social networks to help you search for learning resource ideas, be as clear as you can about what you are looking for.
- Always thank people for helping, and if you can, let them know if you took their advice.
- Contribute your ideas, helpful comments, and responses to others' requests. Make sure your contributions to group tone and climate are positive.

## Team Learning

## What 4.0 Learners Know

- Learning is a deeply social process.
- Even when you learn alone, you draw on insights and frameworks developed by others.

### What 4.0 Learners Do

- See chapter 13, "Supporting 4.0 Learning in Teams," for more information.

## Video and YouTube[6]

### What 4.0 Learners Know

Benefits:

- Visuals and moving images are generally easy to pay attention to.
- You remember more of what you see in a video than what you only hear.
- It is best for subjects that can be better understood if you see them in action than subjects that are more conceptual.
- May provide a vicarious experience—you feel as though you are having the experience yourself.

Be aware:

- Video is a "cool" medium, so you can easily slip into default mode where you get lost in the visuals and story, turn off your conscious thought, and miss the learning.
- The production and learning quality of videos varies widely because anyone with a video camera can produce them. It is up to you to find worthwhile videos for your purpose.

Structure you can expect:

- There are four common types of learning videos: sequence videos, talking head videos, screen capture videos, and animated videos.
- There may be a built-in menu (table of contents). Or you may have a list of times when specific actions occur.
- Many educational and learning videos follow this structure:
  - Opening: Usually a set up shot with overview information or something to grab your attention.
  - Content presentation, possibly in sections.
  - A close with a call to action like an invitation to learn more, watch another video, take a quiz, sign up for a service, like the video, or share the video.

A special note about YouTube:

- YouTube videos may be organized into channels. Within the channel, the owner can organize videos into playlists or let the videos stand alone.
- You can provide your own structure by curating content and creating your own playlists from others' video content.
- You can also subscribe to others' channels so that you are notified when they post new content.
- YouTube recommends related videos based on the content just watched. However, this content may or may not be relevant. Just because it's recommended, doesn't mean it will match your need.

## What 4.0 Learners Do

- Survey the video description, information about the video creator, how it is organized, and its length. Is there a menu that will allow you to skip around to meet your needs and interests?
- Know why you plan to use the video—how it will fit into your learning process and what you hope and expect to learn.
- Before playing the video, adjust things like volume or set up headphones. Close your door, turn off notifications and email, and make other adjustments to minimize distractions.
- Make sure you have the appropriate amount of time to view the video.
- Pause the video at times to think, review, or research related information. You may risk not returning to the video, but doing this will help you stay alert and create learning that lasts. If you pause at a high point, you will be more motivated to return to see what happens next.
- Have a notepad, sticky notes, or document open when you start watching the video. Jot down notes and include the time in the video that the idea, thought, or question occurred. This will create an index of key points and questions that are synced with the video, which gives you an excellent reference if you want to go back for a review.

- If there is a lot of content that is not completely new, check for variable speed playback and watch at a faster speed.
- Imagine yourself in the video scenes. Who would you be? What would you do? How are your situations similar and different? Treat this as a vicarious experience.
- Consider doing a screen capture of a memorable visual that you can use to trigger your memory later.
- Identify people you want to follow on YouTube, create your own playlists, and request alerts when new content is added.

# Appreciation

As the world and learning requirements change rapidly around us, we find ourselves in the early stages of figuring out the new learning paradigm. Hopefully, *Unstoppable You: Adopt the New Learning 4.0 Mindset and Change Your Life* will contribute to and stimulate conversations about this evolving world. I mention conversations now because they played a role as this book unfolded. I've explored ideas and the learning framework with many people. Some talked with me about the general idea and concepts. Others reviewed parts of the book as they developed and gave comments from a learner or executive perspective. Still others examined parts from a technical and scientific perspective, providing insights from neuroscience, psychology, and talent development. Several Millennials and people from other generations gave feedback. I consulted other seasoned learning and development professionals, and 50 talent development leaders responded to an ATD-sponsored international survey on learning-related issues. Their ideas all helped make this a better book.

Some individuals went a step further by reviewing the book. For this I want to recognize Jacqueline Burandt, Ira Chaleff, Annette Clayton, Lauren Cozza, Joe Doyle, Constance Filling, Suzanne Frawley, Ann Herrmann, Rachel Hutchinson, Kaye Illetschko, Martin Illetschko, Bruce Jacobs, Kimo Kippen, Sandi Maxey, Magdalena Mook, Ken Nowack, Julie O'Mara, Daniel Radecki, Richard Rossi, Deb Santagata, Martha Soehren, Sharon Wingron, Jytte Vikkelsoe, and Robert Yeo.

Thanks also go to Cammy Bean, Sharon Boller, Randy Emelo, Jonathan Halls, Dawn J. Mahoney, Magdalena Mook, and Matt Pierce for their contributions regarding learning strategies for several resources in Tool 5: Resource-Specific Learning Tips.

For support in what has been a deeply transformational personal process for me, I want to publicly thank Jim Howe for providing a great writing space in Vermont, and for your unwavering optimism and encouragement throughout the process; Walt McFarland, for your support and for generously providing access to your networks; and Richard Rossi, for always-astute reminders to stay connected to people's problems and interests. I also appreciate my sister, Kaye Illetschko, for saying, "I wish I'd known these things earlier," and my late sister, Rita Moldenhauer, a role model lifelong learner who transcended the limitations of Down syndrome and taught me a lot about a special kind of joy that comes from learning.

The folks at ATD have been a stalwart link between my desire to shift paradigms and the more practical needs of book publishing and marketing. I want to thank Pat Galagan, Ann Parker, Clara von Ins, Timothy Ito, and Tony Bingham for your sponsorship within ATD and your confidence in me and this topic; Kathryn Stafford and Melissa Jones, my ATD editors; Iris and Fran, my ATD designers; and the marketing team that is bringing this book to individuals, leaders, and organizations who can benefit from it.

There are hundreds of other people who have influenced this book. Many I never met in person, or only brushed past briefly as fellow speakers and participants in conferences, meetings, corporate workshops, and university programs where we have explored topics like artificial and augmented intelligence, psychology, philosophy, neuroscience, cognitive science, learning and adult education theory and practice, training and adult development, meditation, and mysticism. In many cases I have read and learned from their books, articles, and videos. Those most directly relevant to *Unstoppable You* are cited in the references.

Then there are the many lessons and insights I have gained from clients in business and government, academic leaders, and people whose learning I have supported since I began teaching at the University of Minnesota, then moved to corporate America, and finally in South Africa and other countries, including the United States. These diverse experiences with people and organizations facing learning and change challenges help keep my ideas and suggestions anchored in real-world problems. There is nothing like experience to round the sharp edges of theory and creative ideas so they can be useful in the real world.

# Notes

## You: A Lifelong Learner

1. D. Eagleman, *Incognito: The Secret Lives of the Brain* (New York: Pantheon, 2011).

## 1 Your Learning Brain

1. Plato, "The Allegory of the Cave," *The Republic,* Book VII.
2. D. Eagleman, *The Brain: The Story of You* (New York: Pantheon), 793.
3. According to Jerry W. Rudy, in *The Neurobiology of Learning and Memory* (2014), there are five overlapping stages in how a neuron changes: An impulse comes to a neuron and destabilizes its current structure. Then after about 15 minutes, calcium comes in and works with other chemicals to temporarily rebuild and reorganize things (at this point what you are learning is in your short-term memory). In some cases, the change continues, with more calcium coming in. New proteins are generated and the modified neuron content begins to stabilize. If the stimulation is strong enough, the memory consolidates and is tagged for retrieval (i.e., it becomes a long-term memory). Some neurons become very stable and resist change even when you want to change (i.e., they support enduring habits).
4. Sebastian Seung introduced the term *connectome* in a 2010 TED Talk, and then published the concept in a 2013 book, *Connectome: How the Brain's Wiring Makes Us Who We Are.*
5. The word *hippocampus* comes from the Greek *hippo* meaning "horse" and *kampos* meaning "sea monster."
6. C. Koch, "Neuronal Superhub May Generate Consciousness," *Scientific American,* November 2014.
7. J. J. Ratey and M.D. Spark. *The Revolutionary New Science of Exercise and the Brain* (New York: Little Brown, 2008).
8. Psychologists and economists are very interested in dual process views of

human mental functioning. What this book calls *automatic* and *conscious processing*, others, like psychologist Keith Stanovich and Richard West, call *System 1* and *System 2* or *Type 1* and *Type 2* processes. Daniel Kahneman, a psychologist who won the Nobel Prize in economics, talks about our ability to think fast (*automatic*) and slow (*conscious*).

9. This quite apt description of how your brain works on automatic appears in Eagleman, *Incognito*.

10. Various arguments for longer sleep appear in T. Doyle and T. Zakrajsek, *The New Science of Learning: How to Learn in Harmony With Your Brain*. (Sterling, VA: Stylus Publishing, 2013).

## 2 Your Self Who Learns

1. In the early part of the 20th century, psychoanalysts like Sigmund Freud and Carl Jung brought a new awareness of the human inner world into the relatively new field of psychology. We now know much more about the internal forces, drives, needs, and factors that influence human behavior and learning.

2. C.G. Jung and M.L. Von Franz, *Man and His Symbols* (New York: Laurel, 1964).

3. Joseph Campbell introduced the concept of the hero's journey in his book, *The Hero With a Thousand Faces*. It presents the stages we go through when we learn something: There is a *call to adventure* that the hero must accept. The hero then moves into the *unknown*, where she experiences challenges, dangers, and uncertainties. Various helpers come along to offer support (which may be accepted). There are various trials and hurdles that the hero must deal with to earn personal growth. Ultimately, the hero changes and grows in some way. The final challenge is to bring the new insights back into the world. This general adventure pattern informs many of the practices in learning 4.0.

4. Many psychologists believe Campbell's description of the hero's journey has more masculine than feminine overtones because it is generally drawn from epic adventures about someone who was born into power (e.g., Odysseus was born to be a king) and then conquers external challenges to prove he is worthy of his birthright. Psychologists like Maureen Murdock (1990) and Clarissa Pinkola-Estes (2003) present an alternative view that draws from fairy tales, myths, and traditional stories. This alternative view of the heroine's journey focuses more on internal journeys—growth that happens when a person is shut off from the outside world (e.g., in a tower, in a long sleep, or while being held back by wicked stepsisters). Both perspectives are useful when you think about your own learning journey.

5. The concept of archetypes was introduced by Carl Jung to help describe psychological instincts that are part of the human evolutionary heritage.

6. Abraham Maslow's hierarchy of needs is one of the most enduring theories in psychology. While he originally identified five levels of need, he

later determined that there was a higher, more spiritual, contribution-oriented need beyond self-actualization. He defined it as service to others, to a cause, or to an ideal, and called it "self-transcendence." When you read about Kegan's work in this chapter, note that his highest level of consciousness is similar.

7. E. Erikson, *Identity and the Life Cycle* (London: Norton, 1964).

8. R. Kegan, *The Evolving Self: Problem and Process in Human Development* (Cambridge: Harvard University Press, 1982).

9. To learn more about fixed and growth mindset, see C. Dweck, *Mindset: The New Psychology of Success*. For the first writing on external and internal locus of control, see J.B. Rotter, "Generalized Expectancies for Internal Versus External Control of Reinforcement," *Psychological Monographs: General & Applied* 80(1): 1-28.

## 3 The Fast-Changing World

1. R. Kurzweil, "The Law of Accelerating Returns," *Kurzweil Accelerating Intelligence*, March 7, 2001.

2. Kurzweil, "The Law of Accelerating Returns," 2001.

## 4 The Information Field

1. B.J. Fogg of Stanford, quoted in Ian Leslie, "The Scientists Who Make Apps Addictive," *The Economist*, October-November 2016, 67-71.

## 5 Hear the Call to Learn

1. Learn more about the role of your shadow in chapter 2.

2. Strengthen your learning fitness at www.learning40.com/unstoppable.

3. Self-talk is a major force in our lives. It helps shape thinking, self-confidence, and sense of power. It can be a major asset in learning when it focuses on shaping goals, recalling information, and more. Robert Kegan and Lisa Laskow Leahy's book *How We Talk Can Change the Way We Work: Seven Languages for Transformation* suggests ways to talk to yourself and to others. These are relevant to 4.0 thinking and learning.

## 6 Create Future-Pull

1. R. Fritz, *Your Life as Art* (Newfane, VT: Newfane Press, 2003), 1. Fritz is a musician and filmmaker who has worked extensively with behavioral scientists and artists. He writes about the impact of the creative tension between a goal and reality, which he calls "structural imprinting."

2. Technically, virtual reality depends on computers, headsets, and other technology to create a multisensory simulation you experience as "real." But you have the power to use your brain's imaging powers (imagination) to do the same thing. When you create your own virtual reality projection, you actively

program yourself to move in the direction you desire. It's a very powerful self-management and learning method.

3. R. Fritz, *The Path of Least Resistance: Principles for Creating What You Want to Create.* (New York: Ballantine Books, 1989).

4. S.R. Covey, *The 7 Habits of Highly Effective People: Powerful Lessons in Personal Change* (New York: Simon & Schuster, 1989).

5. Read more about the power of future-pull in Fritz, Canfield, and Mackey—all listed in the references.

6. Chapter 1 describes your automatic system in more detail.

## 7 Search

1. C.S. Dweck, *Mindset: The New Psychology of Success* (New York: Ballantine, 2006).

## 8 Connect the Dots

1. N. Kaya and H. Epps, "Relationship Between Color and Emotion: A Study of College Students," *College Student Journal* 38(3), 2004.

2. F. Moss, L.M. Ward, and W.G. Sannita, "Stochastic Resonance and Sensory Information Processing: A Tutorial and Review of Application," *Clinical Neurophysiology,* 115(2), 2004, 267-281.

## 9 Mine for Gold

1. Moss, Ward, and Sannita, "Stochastic Resonance and Sensory Information Processing," 267-281.

2. J.J. Ratey, *Spark: The Revolutionary New Science of Exercise and the Brain* (New York: Little Brown, 2008).

3. B. Ziegarnik, "On Finished and Unfinished Tasks," in W.D. Ellis (ed.), *A Sourcebook of Gestalt Psychology* (New York: Humanities Press, 1967).

4. J. Medina, *Brain Rules: 12 Principles for Surviving and Thriving at Work, Home, and School,* 2nd ed. (Seattle: Pear Press, 2014), 103-124.

5. S. Kotler, *The Rise of Superman: Decoding the Science of Ultimate Human Performance* (New York: Houghton Mifflin, 2014).

6. M. J. Bresciani-Ludvik, ed., *The Neuroscience of Learning and Development: Enhancing Creativity, Compassion, Critical Thinking, and Peace in Higher Education* (Sterling, VA: Stylus Publishing, 2016), 187.

7. For more information, I recommend taking a quick look at the discussion on the Johns Hopkins Sheridan Libraries website of how to evaluate information, http://guides.library.jhu.edu/evaluatinginformation.

8. The movie *Sully* was directed and produced by Clint Eastwood (Warner Brothers, 2016).

9. R.R. West, R.J. Meserve, and K.E. Stanovich, "Cognitive Sophistication Does Not Attenuate Bias Blind Spots," *Journal of Personality and Social Psychology* 103(3), 2012: 506-519.

## 10 Learn to Last

1. Eagleman, *Incognito.*
2. I. Wilhelm et al., "Sleep Selectively Enhances Memory Expected to Be of Future Relevance," *Journal of Neuroscience* 31(5), 2011: 1563-1569.
3. Ziegarnik, "On Finished and Unfinished Tasks."
4. N.J. Cepeda, E. Vul, and D. Rohrer, "Spacing Effects in Learning: A Temporal Ridgeline of Optimal Retention," *Psychological Science,* 11, 2008: 1095-1102. H.P. Bahrick et al., "Maintenance of Foreign Language Vocabulary and the Spacing Effect," *Psychological Science* 4(5), 1993: 316-321.
5. S. Pan, "The Interleaving Effect: Mixing It Up Boosts Learning," *Scientific American,* August 4, 2015.
6. Rudy, *The Neurobiology of Learning and Memory,* 237.
7. J.D. Novak and A.J. Canas, "The Theory Underlying Concept Maps and How to Construct and Use Them," Technical Report IHMC CmapTools (2006-01, Rev. 2008-01, Institute for Human and Machine Cognition, Pensacola Florida). T. Buzan, *Mind Map Handbook: The Ultimate Thinking Tool* (New York: HarperCollins), 2004.
8. H. Roediger III and J.D. Karpicke, "The Power of Testing Memory: Basic Research and Implications for Educational Practice," *Perspectives on Psychological Science* 1(181), 2006.
9. J. Mezirow, F*ostering Critical Reflection in Adulthood* (San Francisco: Jossey-Bass, 1990).
10. Roediger's astounding research into the "testing" effect points out the power of a pretest where you guess key points before you learn, even when you have no preknowledge. Then test yourself afterward. The memory impact is significant! H. Roediger and J.D. Karpicke, "The Power of Testing Memory."
11. K. Taylor and C. Marienau, *Facilitating Learning With the Adult Brain in Mind* (San Francisco: Jossey-Bass, 2016), 217.
12. E. Kubler-Ross, *On Death and Dying* (London: Macmillan, 1974).
13. D. Schon, *The Reflective Practitioner: How Professionals Think in Action* (New York: Basic Books, 1983).
14. P.J. Kellman and C.M. Massey, "Perceptual Learning, Cognition, and Expertise," *Psychology of Learning and Motivation* 58, 2013: 117-165.
15. *Values, beliefs, attitudes,* and *intentions* are all terms that operate as personal decision criteria and perception filters. I use beliefs or attitudes for short. An excellent and respected source of research and ideas about this important affective area is M. Fishbein and I. Ajzen, *Belief, Attitude, Intention and Behavior: An Introduction to Theory and Research* (Boston: Addison-Wesley, 1975).
16. M.L. von Franz, "The Process of Individuation," in C.G. Jung, ed., *Man and His Symbols* (New York: Laurel, 1964).

## 11 Transfer to Life

1. Kurt Lewin, an early leader in the arena of human systems change, introduced the idea of force-field analysis in 1943. It remains one of the best ways to think about and plan to influence the many factors that affect whether or not you will use what you have learned.
2. Sinah Goode, quoted in B. Carey, *How We Learn: The Surprising Truth About When, Where, and Why It Happens* (New York: Random House, 2014), 154-155.

## 12 Being a Lifelong 4.0 Learner

1. Ian Leslie's book *Curious: The Desire to Know and Why Your Future Depends on It* (New York: Basic Books, 2014) is a great exploration of this vital topic.

## 14 Helping Others Learn

1. A. Tough, *The Adult's Learning Projects: A Fresh Approach to Theory and Practice in Adult Learning* (Ontario: Ontario Institute for Studies in Education, 1971).

## Tool 5 Resource-Specific Learning Tips

1. Thank you to Magdalena Mook, executive director and CEO, International Coach Federation, and Randy Emelo, founder and chief strategist, River, and author of *Modern Mentoring* (ATD Press, 2015), for their contributions to this section.
2. Thank you to Cammy Bean, author of *The Accidental Instructional Designer: Learning Design for the Digital Age* (ASTD Press, 2013), for her contributions to this section.
3. Thank you to Sharon Boller, co-author of *Play to Learn: Everything You Need to Know About Designing Effective Learning Games* (ATD Press, 2017), for her contributions to this section.
4. Thank you to Dawn Mahoney, Learning in the White Space (www.dawn-jmahoney.com), for her insights about learning in lectures and presentations.
5. Thank you to Matt Pierce, instructional designer and media producer, TechSmith Corporation, and Jonathan Halls, author of *Rapid Video Development for Trainers* (ASTD Press, 2012) and *Rapid Media Development for Trainers* (ATD Press, 2017), for their insights about how to learn from podcasts.
6. Thank you to Matt Pierce, instructional designer and media producer, TechSmith Corporation, and Jonathan Halls, author of *Rapid Video Development for Trainers* (ASTD Press, 2012) and *Rapid Media Development for Trainers* (ATD Press, 2017), for their insights about how to learn from videos and YouTube.

# References

Ackermann, S., F. Hartmann, A. Papassotiropoulos, D.J. de Quervain, and B. Rasch. 2013. "Associations Between Basal Cortisol Levels and Memory Retrieval in Healthy Young Individuals." *Journal of Cognitive Neuroscience* 25(11): 1896-1907.

Aihara, T., K. Kitajo, D. Nozaki, and Y. Yamamoto. 2010. "How Does Stochasti Resonance Work Within the Human Brain? Psychophysics of Internal and External Noise." *Chemical Physics* 375(2-3): 616-624.

Arbinger Institute. 2016. *The Outward Mindset: Seeing Beyond Ourselves.* San Francisco: Berrett-Koehler.

Aschwanden, C. 2015. "My Own Worst Enemy: Why We Act Against Our Better Judgment." *Discover Magazine,* October. http://discovermagazine .com/2015/nov/12-my-own-worst-enemy.

Bahrick, H.P., L.E. Bahrick, A.S. Bahrick, and P.E. Bahrick. 1993. "Maintenance of Foreign Language Vocabulary and the Spacing Effect." *Psychological Science* 4(5): 316-321.

Benson-Armer, R., A. Gast, and N. van Dam. 2016. "Learning at the Speed of Business." *McKinsey Quarterly,* May.

Bloom, F.E., M.F. Beal, and D.J. Kupfer, eds. 2003. *The DNA Guide to Brain Health.* New York: Dana Press.

Bresciani-Ludvik, M.J., ed. 2016. *The Neuroscience of Learning and Development: Enhancing Creativitiy, Compassion, Critical Thinking, and Peace in Higher Education.* Sterling, VA: Stylus Publishing.

Buzan, T. 2004. *Mind Map Handbook: The Ultimate Thinking Tool.* New York: HarperCollins.

Campbell, J. 1972. *The Hero With a Thousand Faces.* Princeton: Princeton University Press.

Canfield, J., and D.D. Watkins. 2007. *Jack Canfield's Key to Living the Law of Attraction: A Simple Guide to Creating the Life of Your Dreams.* Dearfield Beach, FL: Health Communications.

Carey, B. 2014. *How We Learn: The Surprising Truth About When, Where, and Why It Happens.* New York: Random House.

Cepeda, N.J., E. Vul, and D. Rohrer. 2008. "Spacing Effects in Learning: A Temporal Ridgeline of Optimal Retention." *Psychological Science* 11: 1095-1102.

Connolly, C., M. Ruderman, and J.B. Leslie. 2014. "Sleep Well, Lead Well: How Better Sleep Can Improve Leadership, Boost Productivity, and Spark Innovation." Whitepaper. Center for Creative Leadership.

Covey, S.R. 2004. *The 7 Habits of Highly Effective People: Powerful Lessons in Personal Change.* New York: Simon & Schuster.

Crick, F.C., and C. Koch. 2005. "What Is the Function of the Claustrum?" *Philosophical Transactions of the Royal Society B* 360(1458): 1271-1279.

Csikszentmihalyi, M. 2008. *Flow: The Psychology of Optimal Experience.* New York: Harper Collins.

———. 2014. *Flow and the Foundations of Positive Psychology: The Collected Works of Mihaly Csikszentmihalyi.* Dordrecht: Springer.

Doyle, T., and T. Zakraisek. 2013. *The New Science of Learning: How to Learn in Harmony With Your Brain.* Sterling, VA: Stylus Publishing.

Dweck, C.S. 2006. *Mindset: The New Psychology of Success.* New York: Ballantine Books.

Eagleman, D. 2011. *Incognito: The Secret Lives of the Brain.* New York: Vintage.

———. 2015. *The Brain: The Story of You.* New York: Pantheon Books.

Economist. 2015. "The Hard Problem: What Is Consciousness." *Economist,* September 12.

———. 2016. "Special Report Artificial Intelligence: The Return of the Machinery Question." *Economist,* June 25.

Erikson, E. 1994. *Identity and the Life Cycle.* London: Norton.

Evans, J.S.B.T., and K.E. Stanovich. 2013. "Dual-Process Theories of Higher Cognition: Advancing the Debate." *Perspectives on Psychological Science* 8(3): 223-241.

Fishbein, M., and I. Ajzen. 1975. *Belief, Attitude, Intention and Behavior: An Introduction to Theory and Research.* Boston: Addison-Wesley.

Fogg, B.J. 2003. *Persuasive Technology: Using Computers to Change What We Think and Do.* San Francisco: Morgan Kaufmann Publishers.

Friedman, T.L. 2007. *The World Is Flat : A Brief History of the Twenty-First Century.* New York: Picador.

Fritz, R. 1989. *The Path of Least Resistance: Principles for Creating What You Want to Create.* New York: Ballantine Books.

———. 2003. *Your Life as Art.* Newfane, VT: Newfane Press.

Glenn, J. 2016. "2050 Global Work/Technology Scenarios." The Millennium Project, Washington, D.C.

Goleman, D. 2005. *Emotional Intelligence.* New York: Bantam.

———. 2006. *Social Intelligence: The Revolutionary New Science of Human Relationships.* New York: Bantam.

Graziano, M.S. 2013. *Consciousness and the Social Brain.* New York: Oxford University Press.

Hall, M.J. 2014. *Designing Worklearn Networks: Making Magic Happen With Your Profession.* Lake Placid, NY: Aviva Publishing.

Hasenstaub, A., S. Otte, E. Callaway, and T. Sejnowski. 2010. "Metabolic Cost as a Unifying Principle Governing Neuronal Biophysics." *Proceedings of the National Academy of Science* 107(27): 12,329-12,334. DOI: 10.1073/pnas .0914886107.

Jaworski, J. 1996. *Synchronicity: The Inner Path of Leadership.* San Francisco: Berrett-Koehler.

Jung, C. 1981. "The Archetypes and the Collective Unconscious." In *The Collected Works of C.G. Jung,* vol. 9, pt. 1.

Kahneman, D. 2013. *Thinking, Fast and Slow.* New York: Farrar, Straus & Giroux.

Kaya, N., and H.H. Epps. 2004. "Relationship Between Color and Emotion: A Study of College Students." *College Student Journal* 38(3): 396.

Kayes, A., D. Christopher, and D. Kolb. 2005. "Experiential Learning in Teams." *Simulation & Gaming* 36(10): 1-25.

Kegan, R. 1982. *The Evolving Self: Problem and Process in Human Development.* Boston: Harvard University Press.

———. 1994. *In Over Our Heads: The Mental Demands of Modern Life,* 4th ed. Boston: Harvard University Press.

Kegan, R., and L.L. Lahey. 2002. *How the Way We Talk Can Change the Way We Work: Seven Languages for Transformation.* New York: Jossey-Bass.

Kellman, P.J., and C.M. Massey. 2013. "Perceptual Learning, Cognition, and Expertise." *Psychology of Learning and Motivation,* 117-165.

Khan, H.I. 1998. *The Music of Life: The Inner Nature and Effects of Sound.* Medford, OR: Omega Publications.

Koch, C. 2014. "Neuronal Superhub May Generate Consciousness." *Scientific American,* November 1. www.scientificamerican.com/article/neuronal -superhub-might-generate-consciousness.

Kotler, S. 2014. *The Rise of Superman: Decoding the Science of Ultimate Human Performance.* New York: Houghten Mifflin.

Kubler-Ross, E. 1974. *On Death and Dying.* London: Macmillan.

Kula, R.I. 2006. *Yearnings: Embracing the Sacred Messiness of Life.* New York: Hyperion.

Kurzweil, R. 2001. "The Law of Accelerating Returns." *Kurzweil Accelerating Intelligence,* March 7. www.kurzweilai.net/the-law-of-accelerating-returns.

Lakoff, G., and M. Johnson. 1999. *Philosophy in the Flesh: The Embodied Mind and Its Challenge to Western Thought.* New York: Basic Books.

Leslie, I. 2015. *Curious: The Desire to Know and Why Your Future Depends on It.* New York: Basic Books.

———. 2016. "The Scientists Who Make Apps Addictive." *Economist,* October/November, 67-71.

Lewin, K. 1997. "Defining the Field at a Given Time." *Psychological Review* 50(3): 292-310. Republished in *Resolving Social Conflicts & Field Theory in Social Science.* Washington, D.C.: American Psychological Association, 1997.

Lombardo, M.M., and R.W. Eichinger, 2004. *Career Architect Development Planner,* 4th ed. Los Angeles: Lominger International.

Mackey, C. 2015. *Synchronicity: Empower Your Life With the Gift of Coincidence.* London: Watkins Publishing.

Marsick, V.J., and Watkins, K.E. 1990. *Informal and Incidental Learning in the Workplace.* New York: Routledge.

Maslow, A.H. 1967. "A Theory of Metamotivation." *Journal of Humanistic Psychology* 7: 93–127.

———. 1969. "The Farther Reaches of Human Nature." *Journal of Transpersonal Psychology* 1(1): 1-9.

McIntosh, M. 2016. "Neurobiology and Evolution: Why Your Brain Won't Let You Make Rational Decisions." LinkedIn Pulse, June 24.

McLagan, P. 2002. *Change Is Everybody's Business.* San Francisco: Berrett-Koehler.

———. 2013. *The Shadow Side of Power: Lessons for Leaders.* Washington, D.C.: Changing World Press.

McLagan, P.A., and P. Krembs. 1995. *On the Level: Performance Communication That Works,* 3rd ed. San Francisco: Berrett-Koehler.

McLagan, P., and C. Nel. 1995. *The Age of Participation: New Governance for the Workplace and the World.* San Francisco: Berrett-Koehler.

Medina, J. 2009. *Brain Rules, 12 Principles for Surviving and Thriving at Work, Home, and School,* 2nd ed. Seattle: Pear Press.

Mezirow, J. 1990. *Fostering Critical Reflection in Adulthood.* San Francisco: Jossey-Bass.

————. 1991. *Transformative Dimensions of Adult Learning.* San Francisco: Jossey-Bass.

Moss, F., L.M. Ward, and W.G. Sannita. 2004. "Stochastic Resonance and Sensory Information Processing: A Tutorial and Review of Application." *Clinical Neurophysiology* 115(2): 267-281.

Munoz, L.M.P. 2013. "Stress Hormone Hinders Memory Recall." *Cognitive Neural Science Society,* July 24. www.cogneurosociety.org/cortisol_memory.

Murdock, M. 1990. *The Heroine's Journey: Woman's Quest for Wholeness.* Boulder, CO: Shambhala Publications.

Novak, J.D., and A.J. Canas. 2008. "The Theory Underlying Concept Maps and How to Construct and Use Them." Technical Report IHMC CmapTools. Institute for Human and Machine Cognition.

O'Neil, J., and V. Marsick. 2007. *Understanding Action Learning.* New York: AMACOM.

Pan, S. 2015. "The Interleaving Effect: Mixing It Up Boosts Learning." *Scientific American,* August.

Peale, N.V. 1980. *The Power of Positive Thinking.* New York: Fireside.

Pinkola-Estes, C. 2003. *Women Who Run With the Wolves: Myths and Stories of the Wild Woman Archetype.* New York: Ballentine Books.

Plato. 280 BCE. "The Allegory of the Cave." In *The Republic, Book VII.*

Pope, S. 2011. "When It Comes to Checklists, Go With the Flow." *Flying,* July 13. www.flyingmag.com/technique/tip-week/when-it-comes-checklists -go-flow.

Ratey, J.J. 2008. *Spark: The Revolutionary New Science of Exercise and the Brain.* New York: Little, Brown.

Robinson, D., and J. Robinson. 2015. *Performance Consulting: A Strategic Process to Improve, Measure, and Sustain Organizational Results,* 3rd ed. San Francisco: Barrett-Koehler.

Roediger, H.L. III, and J.D. Karpicke. 2006. "The Power of Testing Memory: Basic Research and Implications for Educational Practice." *Perspectives on Psychological Science* 1:181.

Ross, H.J. 2014. *Everyday Bias: Identifying and Navigating Unconscious Judgments in Our Daily Lives.* Lanham, MD: Rowman & Littlefield.

Rotter, J.B. 1966. "Generalized Expectancies for Internal Versus External Control of Reinforcement." *Psychological Monographs: General & Applied* 80(1): 1-28.

Rudy, J.W. 2014. *The Neurobiology of Learning and Memory,* 2nd ed. Sunderland, MA: Sinauer Associates.

Schon, D. 1983. *The Reflective Practitioner: How Professionals Think in Action.* New York: Basic Books.

Seung, S. 2013. *Connectome: How the Brain's Wiring Makes Us Who We Are.* New York: Mariner.

Siegal, L.L., and M.J. Kahana. 2014. "A Retrieved Context Account of Spacing and Repetition Effects in Free Recall." *Journal of Experimental Psychology: Learning, Memory, and Cognition* 40(3): 755-764.

Smart, A. 2016. "Is Noise the Key to Artificial General Intelligence?" Psychology Today.com, June 9. www.psychologytoday.com/blog/machine-psychology /201606/is-noise-the-key-artificial-general-intelligence.

Stanovich, K.E., and R.F. West. 2000. "Individual Difference in Reasoning: Implications for the Rationality Debate?" *Behavioural and Brain Sciences* 23: 645-726.

Taylor, K., and C. Marienau. 2016. *Facilitating Learning With the Adult Brain in Mind.* San Francisco: Jossey-Bass.

Tough, A. 1971. *The Adults Learning Projects: A Fresh Approach to Theory and Practice in Adult Learning.* Ontario: Ontario Institute for Studies in Education.

Tsien, J.Z. 2007. "The Memory." *Scientific American,* July, 52-59.

———. 2015. "A Postulate on the Brain's Basic Wiring Logic." *Trends in Neurosciences* 38(11): 669-671.

Von Franz, M.L. 1964. "The Process of Individuation." In *Man and His Symbols.* Edited by C.G. Jung, New York: Laurel.

Vygotsky, L.S. 1978. *Mind in Society: The Development of Higher Psychological Processes.* Cambridge, MA: Harvard University Press.

West, R.R., R.J. Meserve, and K.E. Stanovich. 2012. "Cognitive Sophistication Does Not Attenuate the Bias Blind Spot." *Journal of Personality and Social Psychology* 103(3): 506-519.

Wilhelm, I., S. Diekelmann, I. Molzow, A. Ayoub, M. Mölle, and J. Born. 2011. "Sleep Selectively Enhances Memory Expected to Be of Future Relevance." *Journal of Neuroscience* 31(5): 1563-1569.

Wilson, C. 2011. "Neuroandragogy: Making the Case for a Link With Andragogy and Brain Based Learning." Midwest Research to Practice Conference in Adult, Continuing, Community and Extension Education, Lindenwood University, St. Charles, MO, September 21-23.

Zander, R.S., and B. Zander. 2000. *The Art of Possibility: Transforming Professional and Personal Life.* London: Penguin.

Zeigarnik, B. "On Finished and Unfinished Tasks." In *A Sourcebook of Gestalt Psychology.* Edited by W.D. Ellis, New York: Humanities Press.

Zimmer, C. 2011. "100 Trillion Connections: New Efforts Probe and Map the Brain's Detailed Architecture." *Scientific American,* January 1.

# About the Author

 I have always loved learning and been curious about how to learn better and make learning meaningful.

I began doing my own research on learning as an undergrad. Because of my interests in psychology, business, and learning, I negotiated an unconventional master's program incorporating special research and interdisciplinary study at the University of Minnesota, leading to an advanced degree in adult education.

I took what I had learned about learning to others, while continuing a rigorous personal learning and research agenda that has never stopped. In one of my first attempts to bring this new approach to others, I designed a study skills program for the University of Minnesota's General College. Many of my students were veterans returning to civilian life and starting a university education. Initially, I thought they needed to update their skills, but I soon discovered their main needs were more personal—related to self-esteem and other issues. It was at this moment I truly began to appreciate the importance of a total-person focus in learning. Eventually, I launched the program Reading and Information Handling Systems. Work with my first client, 3M Company, led to referrals to other major corporations in Minnesota, then other parts of the United States and globally. It launched many years of intense work with GE, NASA, and other organizations that were focused on learning, learning design, and creating a learning organization.

As time moved on, my focus expanded to include the broader arena of organizational learning and change. I worked with businesses and agencies to create learner-centered programs that incorporated short modules on how to self-manage learning within courses and workshops. As it became clear that my life's purpose was to support personal and business transformation, I became increasingly committed to understanding and promoting adult and organizational learning in all its forms. I began a company, McLagan International, to help advance that cause.

While my learning and development company grew, the field of business learning and development was also growing. I became very active in the expanding human resource development field, directing two internationally known competency studies to help define it, and taking on leadership roles in the American Society for Training & Development (now the Association for Talent Development) and the Instructional Systems Association.

Meanwhile, I wrote or co-authored several books to share my insights, research, and experience, including *Getting Results Through Learning, Helping Others Learn: Designing Programs for Adults, On the Level: Performance Communication That Works, The Age of Participation: New Governance for the Workplace and the World, Change Is Everybody's Business,* and *The Shadow Side of Power: Lessons for Leaders.*

As the pace and challenge of change globally accelerated, my work shifted to large-scale change initiatives that required developing people and reshaping organizations. While continuing my work in the United States, I moved to South Africa in the early 1990s, helping several major businesses and state entities launch major human resource development and change management initiatives.

Throughout my journey, it has become increasingly clear to me that the environment for learning is changing radically and exponentially, not incrementally. Learning skills, confidence, and mindsets are not keeping up with today's challenges, smart tools, and neuroscience and psychology research. It is a problem that education, training, and development professionals cannot solve on their own despite vast improvements in learning programs and technologies. It is increasingly clear that we all need to move beyond the learning capabilities we were born with (1.0), the learning skills we developed in school (2.0), and the capabilities we upgraded when we left school for a more self-managing role (3.0). Thus the idea of 4.0 learning, the approach to learning in *Unstoppable You,* began to take form.

# Index

In this index, the following abbreviations are used: *f* for figure, *n* for note, and *t* for table.